# From bin Laden to acebook

**10 Days of Abduction, 10 Years of Terrorism**

International Edition

MARIA A. RESSA

# from
# bin Laden
# to
# acebook

## 10 Days of Abduction, 10 Years of Terrorism

International Edition

Imperial College Press

ICP

*Published by*

Imperial College Press
57 Shelton Street
Covent Garden
London WC2H 9HE

*Distributed by*

World Scientific Publishing Co. Pte. Ltd.
5 Toh Tuck Link, Singapore 596224
*USA office:* 27 Warren Street, Suite 401-402, Hackensack, NJ 07601
*UK office:* 57 Shelton Street, Covent Garden, London WC2H 9HE

**Library of Congress Cataloging-in-Publication Data**
Ressa, Maria.
   From Bin Laden to facebook : 10 days of abduction, 10 years of terrorism / by Maria A Ressa.
   pages cm
   Includes bibliographical references.
   ISBN 978-1-908979-53-7 (hardcover : alk. paper) -- ISBN 1-908979-53-4 (hardcover : alk.
   paper) -- ISBN 978-1-908979-54-4 (pbk. : alk. paper) -- ISBN 1-908979-54-2 (pbk. : alk. paper)
   1. Terrorism and mass media--Philippines. 2. Social networks--Philippines. 3. Abu Sayyaf
   (Organization)  I. Title.
   HM741.R474 2013
   302.3--dc23

                         2012048835

**British Library Cataloguing-in-Publication Data**
A catalogue record for this book is available from the British Library.

In-house Editor: Monica Lesmana

Typeset by Stallion Press
Email: enquiries@stallionpress.com

Printed in Singapore.

# About the Book

The two most wanted terrorists in Southeast Asia — a Malaysian and a Singaporean — are on the run in the Philippines, but they manage to keep their friends and family updated on Facebook. Filipinos connect with al-Qaeda-linked groups in Somalia and Yemen. The black flag — embedded in al-Qaeda lore — pops up on websites and Facebook pages from around the world, including the Philippines, Indonesia, the Middle East, Afghanistan, Australia, and North Africa. The black flag is believed to herald an apocalypse that brings Islam's triumph. These are a few of the signs that define terrorism's new battleground: the Internet and social media.

In this groundbreaking work of investigative journalism, Maria Ressa traces the spread of terrorism from the training camps of Afghanistan to Southeast Asia and the Philippines. Through research done at the International Center for Political Violence & Terrorism Research in Singapore and sociograms created by the CORE Lab at the Naval Postgraduate School, the book examines the social networks which spread the virulent ideology that powered terrorist attacks in the past 10 years.

Many of the stories here have never been told before, including details about the 10 days during which Ressa led the crisis team in the Ces Drilon kidnapping case by the Abu Sayyaf in 2008. The book forms the powerful narrative that glues together the social networks — both physical and virtual — which spread the jihadi virus from bin Laden to Facebook.

# About the Author

Author in Basilan, Philippines, March 16, 2011. Photograph by Beth Frondoso

**M**aria A. **Ressa** is the CEO and Executive Editor of Rappler, a social news network which uses a hearts-and-minds approach to news through a patented mood navigator.

Ms. Ressa has been a journalist in Asia for more than 25 years, most of them as CNN's bureau chief in Manila (1987–1995) and Jakarta (1995–2005). She was CNN's lead investigative reporter focusing on terrorism in Southeast Asia, and wrote *Seeds of Terror: An Eyewitness Account of Al-Qaeda's Newest Center of Operations in Southeast Asia* in 2003.

In 1987, she was one of the founders of independent production company, Probe. In 2005, she took the helm of ABS-CBN News and Current Affairs, for six years determining strategic direction and managing more than

1,000 journalists for the largest multi-platform news operation in the Philippines. Her work aimed to redefine journalism by combining traditional broadcast, new media and mobile phone technology for social change.

She taught courses in Politics and the Press in Southeast Asia for her alma mater, Princeton University, and in broadcast journalism for the University of the Philippines. *FROM BIN LADEN TO FACEBOOK: 10 Days of Abduction, 10 Years of Terrorism* is part of her work as Author-in-Residence and Senior Fellow at the International Center for Political Violence & Terrorism Research at S. Rajaratnam School of International Studies (RSIS) in Singapore. She is also the Southeast Asia Visiting Scholar at CORE Lab at the Naval Postgraduate School in Monterey, California.

# Acknowledgments

Most of this book was written while I was Author-in-Residence and senior fellow at the International Centre for Political Violence and Terrorism Research (ICPVTR) in Singapore. Thank you to RSIS Dean Barry Desker and ICPVTR's management and staff. A special thank you to ICPVTR founder and the author of *Inside Al-Qaeda*, Rohan Gunaratna, for giving me the resources and the academic freedom to flesh out early ideas of how terrorism and emotions spread through large groups of people. Analyst Diane Junio, along with HDB neighbors Yey Junio, Loi Ramos, Ava Avila, and Jet Olfato, made sure I had company, food to eat, and movies to watch.

The year 2011 was a time of transition after six turbulent but fulfilling years as head of ABS-CBN's News and Current Affairs division. Thank you to Gabby Lopez for trusting my judgment and respecting my decisions not just during the hostage crisis but in the extensive organizational revamp and the years I led the division. In accumulating the bricks and mortar of events for this book, I had help from reporters Ces Drilon, Jay Ruiz, and Maan Macapagal. My assistants Gina Jaculo and Anne Yosuico organized, filed, and transcribed, always working beyond their job descriptions. Libby Pascual is an amazing Human Resources Manager, and I thank her for her insights into not just ABS-CBN but the people we managed as well. Thank you to Mario Santos for his legal guidance, to Ana Espiritu for helping me allocate money to turn ideas into reality, and to Cheryl Favila and Chi Almario for trusting me enough to jump at a crucial moment and become key leaders of the news team.

I was thrilled to discover Core Lab's work at the Naval Postgraduate School and to work with former JSOTF-P Commander Col. Greg Wilson, Dr. Sean Everton, Dr. Nancy Roberts, Robert Schroeder, and Daniel Cunningham.

The sociograms here were mapped by Daniel LeRoy, Daniel Cunningham, and Seth Gray, with inputs from Greg Wilson and Sean Everton. CORE stands for Common Operational Research Environment, and my appointment as its Southeast Asia Visiting Scholar allowed me to work "in research and advanced analytical methods to illuminate the dark networks of Southeast Asia."

In each country, there were numerous people who gave generously of their time and insights. To the Oreña family — Lourdes Espiritu Oreña, Joyce Oreña, Ces' sons Ory, Miko, Gian, and Andre — and Communications Secretary Ricky Carandang, thank you for your trust. Thank you to former Philippine President Gloria Macapagal-Arroyo, former Cabinet Secretaries Ronaldo Puno Jr., Ric Saludo, and Eduardo Ermita, Mai Jimenez, Len Bautista-Horn, former Armed Forces Chief Hermogenes Esperon Jr., former Armed Forces Chief Gen. Eduardo Oban Jr., former WesMinCom Chief Lt. Gen. Raymundo Ferrer, Lt. Col. Randy Cabangbang, GPH CCCH Secretariat Maj. Carlos Sol, Chief Supt. Jaime Caringal, Col. Alexander Macario, Gen. Romy Tanalgo, Lt. Col. Benedict Arevalo; former JSOTF-P Commanders Col. David Maxwell, Col. Bill Coultrop, Capt. Robert Gusentine, U.S. Special Forces Maj. Adam Kimmich, Capt. Ed Lescher, Capt. Stacy Lyon, Maj. Tyler Wilson, Lt. Marc Calero; Philippine Government Peace Panel Head Marvic Leonen, MILF Peace Panel Head Mohagher Iqbal, Cotabato reporter Ferdie Cabrera, my ex-CNN and former Probe Producer Judith Torres, Singapore's President Tony Tan, former Deputy Prime Minister Wong Kan Seng, Permanent Secretary Benny Lim, and Minister of Home Affairs' Director of Community Engagement Ong-Chew Peck Wan, Indonesia's President Susilo Bambang Yudhoyono, Foreign Minister Marty Natalegawa, Indonesian Ambassador to the United States Dino Djalal, Anti-Terrorism Council Head (BNPT) Insp. Gen. (ret.) Ansyaad Mbai, Brig. Gen. Tito Karnavian, Dewi Fortuna Anwar, Malaysia's former Prime Minister Mahathir Mohamad and former Defense Minister and now Prime Minister Najib Tun Razak.

Thank you to Imperial College Press and World Scientific, for taking an unorthodox book mixing different disciplines, to Christopher Yaw for his patience and Monica Lesmana her hard work, perseverance and methodical approach keeping us on track in the final days. Thank you to Joey Hofileña and Mario Bautista, who looked over the manuscript with legal eyes, and to Canadian Broadcasting Company's (CBC) Adrienne Arsenault for generously sharing her transcripts and insights. It helps to look at old problems with new eyes.

My gratitude and love to my family — my parents Peter and Hermelina, my sisters Mary Jane, Michelle, and Nicole, and my brother Peter Ames — for bearing with my long absences and news addiction.

Many of the principles of social network theory laid out in this book form the foundation of the company I now head, Rappler. Each day we evolve these ideas and use social networks for social good. Thank you to my Rappler family, all anal at the core: Business Head Lala Rimando, Activist Voltaire Tupaz; my co-geeks with vision — Gemma Bagayaua-Mendoza and Josh Villanueva; and some of our twenty-somethings who help us redefine every minute and give me great hope for the future: Analette Abesamis, Bea Cupin, Paterno Esmaquel II, Patricia Evangelista, Michelle Fernandez, Carmela Fonbuena, Natashya Gutierrez, Ayee Macaraig, Purple Romero, KD Suarez, and Katherine Visconti. Thank you, Domeng Magora, for keeping my crazy hours for more than a decade, and Taffy Santiago, who has helped streamline my life since 1987. Her organizational skills have helped clean out cobwebs, set up safe houses, and charter evacuation flights, only some of her many unorthodox tasks through our days with CNN, ABS-CBN, and Rappler.

Manny Ayala, Raymund Miranda, Nix Nolledo, and Marilen Tantamco round out our merry band of journalists with the workings of our new platform, the Internet. Marites Vitug honed in on the justice system and gave us a strong push to help define exactly what reforming that means to our country today. Cheche Lazaro has been a partner through more than two decades of battles. Chay Hofileña's unwavering support of media ethics and doing the right thing bridged both ABS-CBN and Rappler. Beth Frondoso remains a constant force — the photographer of the book and my sounding board about the Philippines, political systems, rebel groups, and media organizations. Thank you to Glenda M. Gloria, whose knowledge of the workings of the Philippine Armed Forces is unparalleled, for her guidance and hard work as we transitioned from leading a news group of more than a thousand people to our little start-up with big dreams.

Finally, let me end by thanking these men and women, each of whom is a hero in his or her own way: Frank and Grace Oreña, Sen. Loren Legarda, Senior Supt. Winnie Quidato, and of course, at the center, Ces Oreña-Drilon, Jimmy Encarnacion, and Angelo Valderrama. They made me look at the terrorism I have reported for so long and reminded me it's about the life and death of people we love. I hope never to live through anything like this again.

# Contents

# Cast of Characters

## *Al-Qaeda*

**Osama bin Laden:** The creator and leader of al-Qaeda's global terror network.

**Khalid Shaikh Mohammed (KSM):** Al-Qaeda's military chief until his capture in March 2003. Secretly indicted for the 1993 World Trade Center bombing, he admitted he was the mastermind of the 9/11 attacks, a plot his cell hatched in the Philippines in 1994.

**Ramzi Yousef:** The mastermind of the 1993 bombing of the World Trade Center, he fled to the Philippines and began training members of the Abu Sayyaf. Working with his uncle, Khalid Shaikh Mohammed, he set up the first al-Qaeda cell in Southeast Asia in the Philippines. Their most ambitious plot involved simultaneous mid-air explosions, foiled by authorities in an operation that unearthed other plots, including the blueprint for 9/11. Yousef was arrested in 1995 and is serving a life sentence in a U.S. prison.

**Wali Khan Amin Shah:** An Afghan war veteran who fought with Osama bin Laden, he arrived in the Philippines in 1993 and trained members of the Abu Sayyaf. He was arrested in 1995 and convicted in a New York court.

**Abdul Hakim Murad:** Ramzi Yousef's high school classmate, he was the first commercial pilot recruited by al-Qaeda for a suicide mission. He was arrested in Manila in 1995 and is now serving a life sentence in a U.S. prison.

**Mohammed Jamal Khalifa:** Osama bin Laden's brother-in-law, he came to the Philippines in 1988 to create a financial network that spread an extremist version of Islam and to support terrorist cells. He seemed to have been the first to try to unite the different Muslim groups. Much of the financial infrastructure he created still exists today.

**Omar al-Faruq:** A Kuwaiti of Iraqi descent, he fought in the Afghan war and was sent to Southeast Asia as "al-Qaeda's most senior operative based in Indonesia and the Philippines." He told authorities he set up training camps inside the MILF's Camp Abubakar and was the liaison between "the Arabs" and MILF chief Hashim Salamat. Involved in other plots in the region, he was arrested and sent to a U.S. prison in Iraq. He was killed in 2006, about a year after he escaped from prison.

**Abu Abdulrahman Qasamollah:** An Afghan war veteran from Saudi Arabia, he funneled money to the Abu Sayyaf and, in at least one instance, directly to Radullan Sahiron. He was part of the financial network set up by Mohammed Jamal Khalifa.

**Al-Sughayir (Mohammed Saleh Sughayer):** A "known financier of al-Qaeda and Jemaah Islamiyah," he funded money through charities and set up Safinatun Najah, "a front to fund the Abu Sayyaf."

## *Jemaah Islamiyah (JI)*

**Abu Bakar Ba'asyir:** The emir and spiritual leader of Jemaah Islamiyah. In 2008, he formed Jemaah Ansharut Tauhid, the latest evolution of the Darul Islam network involved in terrorist attacks.

**Abdullah Sungkar:** Cofounder, along with Ba'asyir, of Jemaah Islamiyah. He offered the group's services to Osama bin Laden. He died of natural causes in 1999.

**Hambali (Riduan bin Isamuddin):** The operations chief and second-in-command of Jemaah Islamiyah, he planned and executed numerous terrorist attacks across Southeast Asia. He began working with KSM as early as 1994 and was simultaneously a member of al-Qaeda.

**Azahari Husin:** The most skilled bomb-maker of Jemaah Islamiyah. Trained in Afghanistan and the southern Philippines, he designed JI's largest and most lethal bombs for Bali in 2002 and 2005, the Marriott Hotel in 2003, and the Australian Embassy in Jakarta in 2004. He was killed by Indonesian police in November 2005.

**Noordin Top:** Azahari's deputy and protégé in bomb-making. He helped design the Marriott bomb in 2003, the Australian Embassy bomb in 2004, and the Bali bomb in 2005. He developed multiple plots and bombs in 2009, including the twin bombings of the Ritz-Carlton Hotel and the Marriott Hotel. He was killed by Indonesian police in 2009.

**Dulmatin:** JI's third-generation bomb-maker, a skilled leader who helped build the Bali 2002 bombs, then fled to the southern Philippines from 2003 until 2007. When he returned to Indonesia, he regenerated the Darul Islam network and helped create the Aceh training camp that was discovered by authorities in 2010. Dulmatin was killed by Indonesian police in March 2010.

**Umar Patek:** The brother-in-law of Dulmatin, Patek is a skilled explosives-maker who helped train members of the Abu Sayyaf and the MILF. An Afghan war veteran, he was arrested in 2011 in Abbottabad, Pakistan, the same town where Osama bin Laden was killed by U.S. operatives four months earlier. He is now in an Indonesian prison.

**Marwan (Zulkifli bin Abdul Hir):** Malaysian head of Kumpulan Mujahideen Malaysia, he became JI's most senior leader in the Philippines. Trained as an engineer in the U.S., he carries a US$5-million reward on his head and is one of the most-wanted terrorists in Southeast Asia. Marwan and Muawiyah were the targets of the first U.S. smart-bomb attack in the Philippines in 2012.

**Muawiyah (Mohammed Abdullah Ali):** A Singaporean sympathizer of the MILF, Muawiyah came to the Philippines and joined the JI leaders who first found sanctuary with the MILF, then transferred to Jolo with the Abu Sayyaf in 2005. He participated in the 2009 kidnapping of three members of the International Red Cross and is a key Singaporean target.

**Fathur Rohman al-Ghozi:** An Indonesian veteran of the Afghan war who helped set up the JI camp inside MILF territory, Camp Hudaibyah. He was a key figure in the bombing of the Filipino ambassador's house in Jakarta in 2000 as well as the Rizal Day bombings in the Philippines. He united JI plots in Singapore, Indonesia, and the Philippines. He was captured and held in a prison in the Philippines until he escaped and was killed.

**Nasir Abas:** Afghan war veteran who headed JI's Mantiqi 3, which covers the Philippines and parts of Indonesia. He set up the JI training camps inside the MILF territory in the early 1990s.

**Hashim Abas:** Nasir's brother, he was the JI leader in Singapore who planned the truck-bombing attacks against embassies and other targets. His voice narrated a surveillance tape found in an al-Qaeda hideout in Afghanistan.

**Abdullah Sunata:** The head of Kompak, a group allied with JI, he helped bring Indonesians like Dulmatin and Umar Patek to the Philippines in 2003. Sunata played a key role in maintaining links between JI, the MILF, and the Abu Sayyaf. He was arrested in June 2005 and is now in an Indonesian prison.

**Zulkifli (Ahmad Faisal bin Imam Sarijan):** An alumnus of JI feeder school Pondok Ngruki in Solo, he was the JI leader in the Philippines from 2000 until his arrest in 2003. He played a key role in bringing together the Abu Sayyaf and the MILF. He is in prison in the Philippines.

**Bahar (Hari Kuncoro):** Dulmatin's brother-in-law, he and his wife fled to Mindanao with Dulmatin in 2003.

**Ridwan:** Originally a Kompak activist, he joined JI and became Dulmatin's bodyguard when he fled to Mindanao with Dulmatin in 2003.

## *Abu Sayyaf*

**Abdurajak Janjalani:** Founder and leader of the Abu Sayyaf, he formed the extremist group by pulling together former members of the Moro National Liberation Front. He was killed in a firefight with police in December 1998.

**Khadaffy Abubakar Janjalani:** Abdurajak's brother, he took over as the leader of the Abu Sayyaf from 1998 until 2006.

**Radullan Sahiron:** A former member of the Moro National Liberation Front, he was a founding member of the Abu Sayyaf and is now its most senior leader. He engineered the kidnapping of Ces Drilon, Jimmy Encarnacion, and Angelo Valderrama in 2008.

**Wahab Akbar:** One of the Abu Sayyaf's founders, he later joined government and served three terms as governor of Basilan. He was elected to the House of Representatives and was killed in a bomb attack outside its buildings in November 2007.

**"Mohammed":** One of the founding members of the Abu Sayyaf who has direct knowledge of its plots and attacks since it began, as well as its financial network. One of the protégés of bin Laden's brother-in-law, Mohammed Jamal Khalifa, he has since turned double agent and helped the police during the kidnapping of the ABS-CBN team in 2008.

**Abu Sabaya (Aldam Tilao):** An engineering student and police trainee who lived in Saudi Arabia for several years, Abu Sabaya joined the MNLF, then later became a key leader of the Abu Sayyaf. The U.S. put a US$5-million reward on his head for the kidnapping of American missionaries Martin and Gracia Burnham. He was killed in 2002.

**Commander Robot (Ghalib Andang):** A former houseboy of Sulu's Governor Sakur Tan, he joined the Abu Sayyaf in 1995 and became one of its most colorful leaders. He was the face demanding ransom during its most notorious kidnappings. He was captured and killed in the Bicutan prison operations in 2005.

**Doc Abu (Ahmad Jumdail Gumbahali):** One of the key leaders of the Abu Sayyaf in 2008, he sheltered JI leaders Marwan and Muawiyah in his camp in Jolo. The first U.S. smart-bomb attack in the Philippines targeted the three of them and successfully killed Doc Abu, his son, and other Abu Sayyaf members in February, 2012.

**Isnilon Hapilon:** One of four Abu Sayyaf leaders indicted in the United States for their role in the 2000 kidnappings of Filipinos and Americans, he is the only one alive and carries a US$5-million reward on his head.

**Yassir Igasan:** One of two Abu Sayyaf leaders in Jolo whom the military thought succeeded Khadaffy Janjalani, he is seen as more of an ideologue. Intelligence reports show he doesn't command a lot of troops, but that he studied Islamic jurisprudence in Syria.

**Edwin Angeles:** One of the founding members of the Abu Sayyaf who also acted as a government informant. He rose through the ranks and became Janjalani's deputy until he was assassinated by "Mohammed" in 1999.

**Albader Parad:** A senior leader of the Abu Sayyaf who was behind a series of kidnappings, including that of three workers of the International Committee of the Red Cross in 2009. A cousin of Sulu Vice Governor Lady Ann Sahidulla, he was killed by Filipino forces in February 2010.

**Commander Putol (Sulaiman Pattah):** The leader of the Abu Sayyaf group which kidnapped and held Ces Drilon, Jimmy Encarnacion, and Angelo Valderrama. Since he is one-armed, he carries the same pseudonym as Radullan Sahiron, the man for whom he works. In the book, the name Commander Putol refers to Sulaiman Pattah.

**Borhan Mundus:** Mohammed's classmate in Darul Imam Shafie, he worked for Mohammed Jamal Khalifa after graduation and became part of the financial network which funneled money from Saudi Arabia to the Abu Sayyaf.

**Gulam Mundus:** A brother of Borhan and Khair Mundus, he is the leader of Markazzos Shabab, which intelligence sources say is a front organization funneling money to the MILF.

**Khair Mundus:** One of the Abu Sayyaf's key leaders, he was arrested in May 2004 but escaped from prison and now leads the Abu Sayyaf group in Basilan.

**Yacob Basug:** A former member of the Abu Sayyaf who joined the MILF, he collaborated with "Mohammed" on a bombing to divert military attention away from the Lamitan siege, the only time the military cornered the top leaders of the Abu Sayyaf.

**Mohammed Said:** The father of one of the kidnappers of Ces Drilon, Jimmy Encarnacion, and Angelo Valderrama, he was one of the first members of the Abu Sayyaf. He was involved in kidnappings and later helped shelter Marwan and Muawiyah after the first U.S. smart-bomb attack in the Philippines.

**Sali Said:** A key member of the Abu Sayyaf that kidnapped the ABS-CBN team, he was assigned to guard Jimmy Encarnacion. He was the first, along with Kimar, to actually pick up Ces, Jimmy, and Angel and kidnap them.

**Kimar:** The nephew of Radullan Sahiron, he joined Sali Said in kidnapping Ces, Jimmy, and Angel from their vehicle. He was a key member of the team which held the three for ransom for 10 days.

## *Rajah Solaiman Movement (RSM)*

**Ahmad Santos:** Founder and leader of the Rajah Solaiman Movement (RSM) until his arrest in October 2005. Born Catholic, he converted to Islam and entered the financial network created by Mohammed Jamal Khalifa. He also married one of the Dongon sisters, a family whose women married top Abu Sayyaf leaders. A former broadcaster, he was allegedly in-charge of the Abu Sayyaf's media arm when he was arrested. He worked closely with JI leaders Umar Patek and Muawiyah.

**Dawud Santos:** The brother of Ahmad Santos, he also converted to Islam and traveled with his brother to the MILF camps in the late 1990s. When their house was raided and explosives were discovered, Dawud was arrested. ABS-CBN anchor Julius Babao reported his story and was accused by former President Gloria Macapagal Arroyo of helping a terrorist.

**Khalil Pareja (Abu Jihad Khalil):** After Santos was arrested, Pareja, whose sister is married to Santos, took his place as the leader of RSM. He uploaded one of the first YouTube videos linking Filipino groups to a global jihad and is a case study of how Facebook and social media transform online moves to offline actions in the real world. When he was arrested by Filipino authorities in March 2012, he was preparing to join the jihad in Yemen.

## Moro National Liberation Front (MNLF)

**Nur Misuari:** A student activist and university professor, he was the leader of the MNLF, the largest Muslim separatist group in the Philippines. It signed a peace agreement with the Philippine government in Jakarta in 1996 and has since splintered into different factions.

**Abdurahman Jamasali:** A nephew of Misuari, he was the MNLF Vice Chairman and key backroom negotiator. He was a local government under-secretary and was one of the negotiators during the 2000 Sipadan kidnappings. He helped broker a possible surrender of Radullan Sahiron and Doc Abu in 2007 and was killed on October 19, 2007.

**Habier Malik:** An MNLF commander who held the commandant of the Philippine Marine Corps and 20 others hostage for two days in February 2007. He was later considered a rogue MNLF leader, and the government offered a ₱1 million reward for his capture.

**Mameng Biyaw:** A former member of the MNLF, but now seemingly working with the Abu Sayyaf. He was arrested by the military in connection with the ABS-CBN kidnapping but was released soon after. He is a relative of Radullan Sahiron.

## Moro Islamic Liberation Front (MILF)

**Hashim Salamat (Salamat Hashim):** A true ideologue, he was part of the MNLF until he formed a breakaway group which was first based in Cairo, Egypt, then Lahore, Pakistan, until it was formally established as the Moro Islamic Liberation Front (MILF) in 1984. As the MILF's founder and driving force, his international contacts paved the way for its involvement in the Afghan war and a global jihad. He died after suffering a heart attack on August 5, 2003.

**Ebrahim al-Haj Murad (Al-Haj Murad Ebrahim):** After the death of MILF founder Hashim Salamat, Al-Haj Murad took over as the group's chairman. A civil engineer by training, he is viewed as more moderate than his predecessor. He continues to deny an institutional link between the MILF and JI although he doesn't discount personal ones which may have given JI members sanctuary in MILF camps.

**Mohagher Iqbal:** The chief negotiator for the MILF, he joined it in 1972 and has been involved in peace negotiations for more than 14 years. Now one of the group's leading ideologues, he became chairman of the MILF's committee on information in the early 1980s.

**Muklis Yunos:** An Afghan war veteran, Muklis met key JI leaders in Camp Saddah in Afghanistan, including those who carried out the 2002 Bali bombings. The leader of the MILF-SOG (Special Operations Group), Muklis worked with Fathur Roman al-Ghozi on the Rizal Day bombings in December, 2000. He was captured in a bizarre intelligence sting operation in May 2003.

**Umra Cato:** An MILF leader who sheltered members and leaders of Jemaah Islamiyah, he broke away from the MILF in 2011 to form the Bangsamoro Islamic Freedom Fighters (BIFF).

# Prelude — 10 Days, 10 Years

My cellphone ringer is loud and insistent. It's early Monday morning, June 9, 2008. I had been the head of the news group of ABS-CBN, the Philippines' largest media conglomerate, for three years. I'm used to calls at all hours, but nothing prepared me for what happened next — when I stopped being a journalist and became an actor in national affairs. Through the haze of sleep, I punch the button.

"Hello?" I rasp.

"Maria?" says the voice on the other end of the line.

"Ces, is that you?" I ask. Ces Drilon is one of our network anchors. Petite and energetic, she is a tireless reporter with nearly 25 years experience under her belt. I stumble to the bathroom, trying to clear the cobwebs from my head. I'm disoriented and trying to figure out why night-owl Ces sounds wide awake.

"Maria, this is all my fault. You're on speakerphone. We've been kidnapped, and they want money." Behind her voice, I hear several people speaking loudly. I clear my throat, feeling a cold chill that fills me with fear.

"Who's with you, Ces? Are you okay?" Despite my panic, I control my voice. Adrenaline pumps through my body. I think this can't be happening.

"I'm okay, Maria. Jimmy and Angel are okay." Our cameraman, Jimmy Encarnacion — a fantastic, artistic shooter, and his assistant, Angelo Valderrama, are with her. She stops to listen to a voice behind her.

"*Mag-Tagalog ka*! (Speak Tagalog!)" says the man brusquely.

"Who's with you? Who are they?" I ask. She translates into Tagalog and asks her kidnappers: "*Sino daw kayo*? (Who are you?)"

"*Sabihin mo* — *Lost Command*. (Say we are the Lost Command.)" a voice responds. The voices get muffled, like a hand had been placed over

1

Ces Drilon walking with armed men in Jolo, Sulu, June, 2008.
Screengrab from clandestine video shot by Jimmy Encarnacion.

the phone. I feel strangely dead inside. It was either that or panic completely. The Lost Command is a euphemism: they were either being held by the Abu Sayyaf or criminals who would soon bring them to the larger terrorist groups for safe-keeping. With the voices still in the background, I hear Ces again.

"Maria, I'm very sorry. Am I fired? You can fire me when this is over."

"What?! Are you crazy?" This is typical Ces — quick to act, quick to admit when she's wrong, always focused on work. I marvel that even in this situation she is thinking about her job.

"Do you know where you are?" I ask. The voices get louder. I imagine armed men around her. In my mind, I picture them surrounding her because they are loud and disorganized — voices speaking over each other in a dialect I couldn't understand.

"Tell them not to hurt you. We can talk about this. Don't worry. We'll get through this," I say, trying to reassure her. I try to remember all the past kidnapping cases I'd reported, mentally ticking best practices, trying to break down the different phases of our response. I run to my desk, get my note-book and start making a list of what we would need to do immediately. The beginning hours are crucial in a kidnapping in the southern Philippines. In the past, the kidnappers themselves are sometimes ambushed by larger, better-armed groups who want a cut of the ransom. Or the group brings the kidnap victims to the larger armed groups for "safe-keeping" in exchange for a cut of the ransom. Either way, the more time passes, the more armed men are involved. So the faster we move, the greater the chances we can get them out before other armed groups are alerted.

"*Sabi nila, 'huwag tawagan ang military o gobyerno.* (They said, 'don't call the military or government),'" Ces says. "*Tatawagan ka ulit.* (We'll call you again.)"

The line is dead.

That began one of the most challenging 10 days of my life. In more than 25 years as a journalist, I've been on the front-lines in wars, riots, protests, and bombings around the world. I thought I had seen it all: caught in the crossfire between the military and protestors in different countries; death threats from rebel groups, right-wing supporters and not-so-veiled threats while tracking al-Qaeda's networks in South and Southeast Asia. I've had to evacuate my team numerous times from conflict areas, but I had never been in a situation like this. Nothing compares to this. I felt incredibly powerless, buffeted by conditions beyond my control, and yet determining the actions that might either save or kill my friends and colleagues.

I was no longer just reporting the actions of other people; I was leading our crisis team towards the single goal of getting our people home safely. I relied on past experience — decades working with security and intelligence officials across Southeast Asia. I was there when the Abu Sayyaf carried out its first attacks as well as at nearly every major kidnapping in the southern Philippines. I met with negotiators from the Philippines and the commando-style foreigners multinational companies brought in for the Wakaoji kidnapping in the early days. Living in Mindanao for periods of time, juxtaposed against more than a decade's reporting from Indonesia gave my CNN team unique experience.

During the early days when communications between different countries' intelligence agencies about Islamist threats didn't really exist, our reporting helped piece together the extent of al-Qaeda's influence in Southeast Asia — anticipating the discovery of Jemaah Islamiyah, its arm in Southeast Asia, after the 9/11 attacks.

Three kidnap-for-ransom cases captured international attention and cemented this practice as a flourishing business for the Abu Sayyaf in its strongholds in Basilan and Jolo. In 2000, the Abu Sayyaf made one of its first political demands after it kidnapped more than 50 people — mostly teachers and students — from two elementary schools in Basilan. In exchange for the hostages, it asked the United States to release three terrorists held in U.S. prisons, including Egyptian Sheikh Omar Abdul Rahman, the blind cleric, and the Abu Sayyaf's former trainer, Ramzi Yousef (the man who bombed the World Trade Center in 1993 and the nephew of the architect of 9/11).

A little more than a month later, the Abu Sayyaf group from Jolo kidnapped 21 people from seven countries. All would later be released for ransom. Finally, there was the kidnapping of U.S. missionaries Martin and Gracia Burnham in 2001. They were held captive by the Abu Sayyaf for 376 days — one year and eleven days. On the day Gracia was rescued, her husband, Martin, was killed.

I remember their faces and their ordeals. In the beginning, I didn't understand why the government and its agents repeatedly violated its own no-ransom policy even while publicly denying they did. Off-the-record, they would tell me they had no choice. You spend a lot of time waiting when you're reporting one of these hostage situations, and one of the ways I passed the time was to think about what I would do if I were in charge of the negotiations. Except I never thought I would actually have to do it one day.

I know the mistakes made and the tactics that worked. I also know the Philippines and the weaknesses of its institutions. The rivalry between the police and the military means they don't share information well, and when they do, context is often sacrificed and vested interests take over. National government officials work through local politicians who have their own agendas. Many — both local and national figures — have been accused of taking a cut of past ransom payments. In many parts of Mindanao, law and order is weak; governance is weak; corruption is rampant. Often, power is in the hands of men with guns. In short, it's as close to anarchy as you get in a functioning democracy.

There's another unavoidable reality: the entire community benefits from a kidnap-for-ransom case. It's a cottage industry — with the kidnappers sharing the spoils with their relatives and friends, helping in the end to fuel the local economy. That's part of the reason people turn a blind eye, and why so many kidnap victims go home safely. It is a cycle that will not stop unless fundamental problems are addressed.

After Ces' phone call, I knew we had a choice: we could solve the problem by going top-down — contact President Gloria Macapagal-Arroyo and her cabinet officials and wait for them to organize crisis teams (which could take days, leaving us at the mercy of an unwieldy and political bureaucracy); or go bottom-up — start from the grass-roots, identify the people on-the-ground whom we can trust to act immediately. I watched many nations try to get their citizens out through a top-down approach and knew its shortcomings all too well. There would be delays, people in charge who may not understand the situation, and conflicting interests. Inevitably, national officials would work through local proxies — so why not do it ourselves?

We chose to go bottom-up: identifying contacts and sources we could work with in the police, military and local government. Moving fast depended on trust. That was an advantage for us: I trusted not just my team, but the men who acted as bridges to these agencies. We coordinated with the national government, but we set the strategic direction and identified the tactical responses.

This is a story of how a journalist — supported by key officers of the Philippine National Police and the Armed Forces of the Philippines — led negotiations against the Abu Sayyaf. These are the decisions I made and the reasons behind them. I couldn't sleep much in those 10 days — afraid a wrong decision would doom my friends, struggling to maintain a pragmatic hope for the families engulfed in national politics — all too aware of the uneasy dynamics between media, government and the public we serve.

About six months after this kidnapping, three members of the International Committee of the Red Cross (ICRC) were kidnapped by members of the Abu Sayyaf from the center of Sulu's capital. Unfamiliar with the political and security landscape in the Philippines, they chose a top-down approach and dealt primarily with officials in Manila. Frustrated and desperate, their officers met with me several times to ask how we were able to resolve our crisis in days while theirs stretched on for months. Seeing through their eyes validated the route we took. We ruffled feathers of top officials in Manila, but we did what was best for our people. That is also part of the reason I'm writing this book. No guidebooks exist for what we've gone through. While there's no formula that fits every kidnapping, our story presents some lessons. This is my attempt to help those who may be unlucky enough to face a similar situation.

Leading the crisis team gave me invaluable knowledge to further analyze the terror networks I've spent much of my professional life documenting.

My first book, *Seeds of Terror: An Eyewitness Account of Al-Qaeda's Newest Center of Operations in Southeast Asia*, chronicled the incredible violence I lived through for a decade beginning in the late 80's as CNN's lead reporter in the region. *Seeds of Terror* pinpoints the reason why: many of the attacks and conflicts were fuelled or instigated by al-Qaeda and its regional arm, Jemaah Islamiyah. It shows how the ideology, transplanted from Osama bin Laden's training camps in Afghanistan, took root in our region and affected our societies.

September 11, 2011 marked the 10th anniversary of the 9/11 attacks. Four months earlier, U.S. President Barack Obama sent navy seals in a covert operation and killed Osama bin Laden. I couldn't help but juxtapose our 10 days of hell with bin Laden's 10 year reign of terror. October 12, 2012 was the 10th anniversary of the Bali bombings, Southeast Asia's 9/11. *10 days, 10 years*. That was how this book's title began because I wanted to take counterterrorism ideas and frame them in a narrative that show their real world implications. This is how bin Laden affected my world.

2011 was the year I discovered technology that allows researchers to map extensive social networks and what flows through them. I began to look at the evolution of terror networks, particularly after bin Laden's death and tried to understand how terrorism spreads. Despite the prevalence of suicide bombers in other parts of the world, no Southeast Asian suicide bomber existed — until the Bali bombings in 2002. It was an ideology — and technique — that spread to our region. How did that happen and why? Can we map it? The maps included in the book were done by the Naval Postgraduate School's CORE lab in the United States. CORE stands for Common Operational Research Environment. CORE lab does the most advanced applications I could find that bridge academic analysis and counterterrorism operations.

The framework of analysis in this book uses this exciting new discipline that surfaced in the past decade to fuse my passions in media and terrorism: the study of social networks, which merges personal psychology, group dynamics and sociology to look at how emotions and complex behavior spread through societies. Here I draw on the ground-breaking — and sometimes controversial — work of Harvard professors Nicholas Christakis and James Fowler (who later moved to University of Southern California). They focused on "a human superorganism" — social networks of large groups of people and how being part of particular networks influences individual behavior. Using new technology, we can map these networks, giving us

God's eye-view. We have long known the pull of terrorism works best among family and friends, but social network theory provides a new language and perspective that may help us anticipate future developments in the propagation of terrorism, particularly as the Internet and new technology further transform our lives.

I study terrorism because I'm fascinated by what motivates people, particularly moderate Southeast Asians, to become terrorists. Why do they kill innocent civilians? Why would they want to kill themselves? In the past, analysts tried to answer these questions by studying individuals, but social network theory says groups exert their own power over individuals, and larger groups can make people behave differently from the way they would if they were alone. Under this paradigm, terrorists are ordinary people who are molded by their networks. I looked at the application of these theories to the networks created by al-Qaeda and Jemaah Islamiyah. I even applied lessons I learned from running the news organization of ABS-CBN, the Philippines' largest media conglomerate.

As the head of a news network in charge of a convergence strategy, I studied social networks for our election campaigns. Using conclusions from the papers of Christakis and Fowler, I learned to seed our campaigns with emotions — spreading hope and empowerment beyond the physical world to the virtual world through social media networks. Through focus-group discussions and surveys, we documented its spread and impact on our society. What I find fascinating is that many of those lessons apply in studying the spread of terrorism.

Strangely, while going back over these trying days and studying it in the context of violent crimes and terrorism, I find the best of human nature juxtaposed against its brutality — the courage and extraordinary teamwork of Ces Drilon, Jimmy Encarnacion and Angelo Valderrama; the bold initiatives of the Philippine National Police's acting head of intelligence, Winnie Quidato, who — often improvising — went undercover and always did what was needed above and beyond our expectations; Police Anti-Crime Emergency Response (PACER) negotiator Wed Iglesia, who — although he normally avoids journalists — merged with our crisis team and guided us through each excruciating phone call; and, Frank and Grace Orena, Ces' brother and sister, who — despite their fears — handled the phone calls for the families and our network with equanimity.

In the succeeding pages, you'll meet many more men and women who played crucial roles like former broadcast journalist turned legislator, Senator

Loren Legarda, who stepped in at a dark point in the negotiations, and then Department of Interior and Local Government Secretary Ronaldo Puno. Former President Gloria Macapagal-Arroyo asked her cabinet to give our efforts their full support despite her condemnation of Ces' original intent to interview Abu Sayyaf leader Radullan Sahiron.

You'll also meet key members of the Abu Sayyaf, who highlight the ties that bind. One of its founders, a man I introduce as Mohammed, fleshes out the group's history, its close ties to bin Laden's brother-in-law, and the reasons why young, idealistic men like him joined the violence. He and I have met several times in the past few years, particularly because he travelled to Jolo to help us resolve our crisis. Sali Said was one of the first two who actually kidnapped — physically picked up — the ABS-CBN team. His father was trained by al-Qaeda operatives and sheltered key leaders of Jemaah Islamiyah. Through their lives, I hope you'll see social network theory in action.

A quick note on style: Through out the book, I use first names when writing about colleagues like Ces, Jimmy and Angelo; I use last names when referring to everyone else, including government officials, except in the case of Sulu vice governor Lady Ann Sahidula. Everyone just called her Lady Ann, and I decided to keep that. There are many different spellings of "Radullan", the first name of Sahiron, the most senior member of the Abu Sayyaf and the man who orchestrated the kidnapping of our team. I use the spelling chosen by the United Nations.

Life — and decisions made by officials — look much easier from the outside, largely because the complexity of what happens behind the scenes is hidden. This is another reason why I'm writing this now. It's an attempt to take assumptions and add context — from someone who's seen the way things really work. The Filipino public — and journalists — tend to demonize what they don't know or understand. Everyone wants a quick fix, but the problems which give rise to terrorist groups are complex and find their roots in the basic problems of governance. I learned that even when you're calling the shots, circumstances beyond your control can make you powerless.

In the succeeding pages, you'll see that groups aren't monolithic: the names are placeholders — labels — for quickly shifting social networks harnessed by particular leaders for their own purposes. While the government calls them terrorists, to some people they're freedom fighters against a corrupt and unjust system. This is another reason why using social network theory is interesting: it provides not just an analysis but also a solution — a way to stop the jihadi virus from spreading. Beyond the military's kinetic action points, this is a battle for hearts and minds against a virulent ideology. The way to win that battle is by understanding how ideas and emotions spread through social networks and counteracting them.

I started out wanting to unravel ideas and trends in an academic study, but the journey to write this book turned strangely personal. In trying to understand the underlying struggle beneath news events, I began to understand people and what motivates us. The core motivation in bin Laden's terrorism is simple and universal: we want to be with people like us, people who share our views. Except bin Laden turned this into a violent embrace of fundamentalism and tribe which spread to our region. Indonesian Abu Bakar Ba'asyir echoed Osama bin Laden when he said: "Between us and them, there will forever be a river of hatred." Tribe, combined with poverty, explains the situation in the southern Philippines. It's a thin line between humiliation and fury, which easily turns into violence.

Finally, there were many instances when I was writing when I grew deeply frustrated at the "terrorism" problem in the Philippines. It's not ideological — which, in many ways, makes it easier to address: unaddressed grievances against its Muslim "Moro" population; endemic corruption; a power structure harnessed by an elite that gives little back to the people. What do we need to do? Build institutions. Give the people jobs. Create a meritocracy. Create a justice system that works. These are the same goals as building a nation. If we focus on that, the roots of terrorism and rampant crime will be addressed. Easy to write. Hard to implement.

The only way to understand the problem is to see it in isolation and in context. This book looks at concentric circles — a global war against the jihadi virus which spread from the training camps in Afghanistan. Inside that largest circle is Southeast Asia, where the jihadi virus spread and co-opted Jemaah Islamiyah. At the innermost core is the Philippines — the training ground, a complex brew you can't understand unless you see how Indonesia, Singapore and Malaysia affect it and how events in that innermost core affect the outermost circle.

I write this with great hope — that if we see the problems clearly — we can take the right steps forward, address core issues and stop the jihadi virus from spreading. If we understand how it spreads, we can deconstruct it and use the same social networks — both in the physical and virtual worlds — to fight it.

# Kidnapped

**1**

---

She was beginning to feel she had made a terrible mistake. It was Sunday, June 8, 2008, and they had been walking for most of the day in torrid heat. Now hours after sunset, there seemed no end in sight, and they were no closer to the promised interview with Abu Sayyaf leader, Radullan Sahiron. Surrounded by heavily armed men, they were trudging through lush vegetation in a remote island in the southern Philippines.

45-year-old Ces Drilon spent much of the past two decades reporting on Muslim insurgencies and rebellions located on the big southern island of Mindanao and the Sulu island chain southwest of Mindanao. This is the area where most of the 5% Muslim minority live in the largest Catholic nation in Asia. The Abu Sayyaf, the most extreme and violent among the Muslim groups, operates in the islands of Basilan, Jolo and Tawi-Tawi. Ces and her two cameramen, Jimmy Encarnacion, and Angelo Valderrama were somewhere on the island of Jolo, 648 square miles of rugged mountains and jungle with a population of 620,000.

Ces nearly slipped when a rock dislodged beneath the foliage under her foot. She caught herself and kept her eyes on the man in front of her. He was wearing military camouflage from head to foot, except for the gray baseball cap over his long hair tied back in a ponytail. He had his machine gun slung around the back of his neck, his hands on each end of the gun, ready to swing into action if needed. He carried a red bag over his right shoulder, and that was what Ces focused on as she tried to keep pace.

Some of the foliage they waded through was as high as her shoulder and when she wasn't careful, it would swing and hit her as she stepped in his wake. The blades were sharp, and although at times she was unaware of it, their fast walking pace left cuts on her face. She could hear insects buzzing around her as she awkwardly adjusted the blue veil she wore around her

Jolo, Sulu. March 16, 2011 Photo by Beth Frondoso.

head. She wore it as a sign of respect for her Muslim hosts, but her clothes were wet. They clung to her skin, making her uncomfortable. And the dirt had mixed with the rain, leaving mud on her jeans and shoes. The slight drizzle turned into a downpour and forced the group to quickly seek shelter under an abandoned stilt house. Their armed escorts began to set up hammocks using the legs of the elevated wooden structure, laying down blue tarpaulin-like heavy duty plastic on the ground so they could rest. The men set their guns aside and began to pray.

Ces had taken risks before, but this was different. She was disobeying direct orders to be here. She felt she was right in trusting her source, but now it was turning into a desperate hope. She was beginning to doubt her judgment and was starting to second-guess herself. Her cameraman, 39-year-old Jimmy Encarnacion, was beginning to worry as well, but he didn't want to scare his assistant, 32-year-old Angelo Valderrama. What they didn't know was that all of them felt the same way, but no one spoke — all hoping their fears were wrong. They settled together in one corner — sore, soaked, tired and afraid. If all had gone according to plan, they should have been back in their hostel by now. Instead, they were somewhere in the middle of Indanan, Sulu on Jolo — an island many called the "Wild, Wild West" because it's largely ruled by men with guns. The more men and the more guns, the stronger you are.

Ces knew her office would be worried, but she had no way of contacting them. Their armed escorts had taken away their equipment, bags and cellphones. They were picked up in the morning by her contact, Mindanao State University Professor Octavio Dinampo, and the man he referred to as their "safe conduct pass," Mameng Biyaw, a former member of the Moro National Liberation Front (MNLF), once the Philippines' largest Muslim separatist group until it signed a peace agreement with the government in 1996.

Many members of the Abu Sayyaf were former members of the MNLF, like Radullan Sahiron, who with the group's founder, Abdurajak Janjalani, splintered from the MNLF to form the extremist Abu Sayyaf, which combined *Salafi* Wahabbist ideology with a separatist agenda. Janjalani was killed in a firefight with the Philippine police in December 1998.[1] His brother, Khadaffy Abubakar Janjalani, succeeded him as the group's leader until his death in a clash with the military in 2006.[2] Most assumed Sahiron, allegedly the most ideologically-driven among the remaining senior leaders inherited the mantle of leadership. Mameng Biyaw, their "safe conduct pass," is Sahiron's relative, and that meant his presence with their group protected them from harm. At least that's what Dinampo claimed.

Except Biyaw had left them hours earlier. In one of their stops, two of the heavily-armed men wearing combat fatigues signaled Biyaw to step to the side. Ces remembered seeing them going away from the group then realizing that when the men returned, Biyaw wasn't with them. She turned to Dinampo.

"What happened to Mameng?" Ces asked.

"He probably went ahead to meet with Radulan and to make sure everything is okay for our arrival," whispered Dinampo.

Jimmy and Angel noticed Biyaw's absence during the long afternoon walk. Ces told them what Dinampo said, but that only added to their uneasiness about their situation. Now sitting in the dark, Ces couldn't help herself. Shortly after the men finished their prayers, she stood up and walked to the armed man with long hair who seemed to be in-charge. Jimmy and Angel could hear parts of their conversation while Dinampo moved closer.

"Is this where we'll do the interview?" asked Ces.

"Not yet," he answered. "We have to wait for our commander here."

"Can I have my cellphone so I can call the office? They'll be worried."

---

[1] Rewards for Justice Program, U.S. State Department. See http://www.rewardsforjustice.net/index.cfm?page=sahiron&language=english
[2] Ibid.

The man turned to his companions and spoke to them softly before responding.

"No, I don't think so. Only the Commander can make that decision," he said. "We'll have to wait for him."

"What about my bag? Can I have my bag so I can fix myself?"

He took a second to think about it then gestured behind him, and the bag appeared. He handed it to Ces, who took it and opened it. Immediately, she knew something was wrong. All her money was missing.

"My money's gone. Why is my money gone?" Ces asked.

"Don't worry. We'll return it when you go back."

"This isn't what you told me would happen. Maybe we shouldn't do the interview anymore."

Dinampo stepped in.

"No, Ces, Radullan will come," Dinampo reassured her. "He promised to do the interview."

Around that time, a group of young boys came with food and water. The men gathered around the food and brought plates for their "guests." The food, in succeeding meals, wouldn't change much. Sometimes it would be a pack of noodles the four would have to share. Sometimes it was a portion of rice with a can of sardines. Whatever it was, it nearly always wasn't enough. After eating, they settled down. The men encouraged them to get some rest, and because they were so tired, they tried. When Jimmy turned to look, Ces was curled up on one of the blue plastic bags. Her eyes were closed, but she couldn't sleep. Jimmy found a spot near her, gesturing to Angel to stay on her other side. This was the way it would be — both of them protecting their reporter, wary of her beauty in the jungle and its effect on their kidnappers. They treated her with such respect it created an invisible shield against the armed men. At least that's what they hoped.

\* \* \*

Shortly after midnight, a flurry of activity woke them up. Another group of armed men, led by the Commander, arrived. Dinampo, who was whispering with some of the men, looked up then made his way to Ces.

"This is our worst case scenario," he said. "That isn't Radullan so that means we'll still have to go to him."

When Ces heard that, she got up and went to the leader of the group. Full of bravado, she introduced herself.

"Are you the Commander?" she asked. "I'm Ces Drilon from ABS-CBN. I thought we were supposed to do the interview now, but Radullan's not with you. What will happen?"

"Change of plans," he said. "You'll interview Radullan tomorrow morning at the camp." Around them, the men began packing their belongings, preparing to march again. Ces took a second to think.

"We have to interview him by 5 a.m. so that we can be back in Jolo by 8:00 tomorrow night."

"That's okay. Should be no problem. It will depend on how fast you walk. I think you can make it."

"Commander, your men refused to give me back my cellphone. I have to let our office know where we are and what's happening to us so they don't worry."

"I can give it back to you, but we have to keep it off for your protection. You don't want to get caught in any crossfire if they trace us, right? Turn it on and text a message to your office." Ces nodded her head, and her cellphone was handed to her. She felt better with it — a connection to the outside world. Perhaps her fears were wrong and everything would go well after all. She would interview Sahiron in the morning and they could be back in Jolo that evening. She thought quickly about what she would tell the

June 8, 2008, Day 1. Screengrab from clandestine video shot by Jimmy Encarnacion.

office. She didn't want them to panic, but at the same time, she knew she needed to let them know they were okay. Her text was short: "I will get interview at 5 a.m. Will be in dorm where we're staying by 8 p.m."

The group packed and began to move. She joined Jimmy and Angel and told them what happened. By this time, it was after 1 a.m., and the group began walking. There were nearly a dozen heavily armed men with them now. The numbers would change as some left and others arrived, but they walked in a single file line with the ABS-CBN team near the front. Now they were walking deeper into the jungle. It was pitch black, and Ces took out her lighter with its tiny flashlight and used it to try to shine a pitifully small yellow circle in front of her. The men were making their own path through dense foliage. It was tough going, especially in the dark. She stumbled and slipped numerous times as they began to climb up a mountain, and walking became more difficult. Always, either Jimmy or Angel would help her, holding her arm if she needed guidance. The two men divided the tasks at hand: one carried the heavy camera; the other helped Ces.

Her mood alternated between hope and despair. She had plenty of time to replay past events in her mind. She questioned her decisions and her judgment — feeling guilty about what she had asked her team to do. This was supposed to have been a "picnic" — at least that's what she told them. They would buy food for up to 15 escorts — their security, according to Dinampo. Then they would travel by car to Indanan from Jolo. Get out and eat. Set up the equipment in a discreet location. Shoot the interview, and then return home. That's part of the reason they were so unprepared for the jungle trek. She stumbled again and felt Angel's steady hand. She thought about her team's unquestioning support and their faith in her decision. She never wanted to let them down. They had been through so much together.

\* \* \*

Since 2005, Ces had won all the news division's annual 20/20 Awards, when managers and team-members nominated colleagues who were the best of the best, those with 20/20 vision. Top anchors in the Philippines tended to act more like celebrities rather than serious journalists, but Ces' work restored prestige to hard-working field reporters. The awards called her 'inquisitive,' 'untiring,' the-top-of-mind choice of most people. Hands-down, she was included in nearly every nomination we received, and she got more than double the number of votes of anyone else in our division. She is a reporter's role model, a generous team player, working around the clock to bring in at least one major agenda-setting exclusive a week."[3]

I first met Ces in 1986, when we both worked for the government station: she was a reporter, and I directed the evening newscasts. I had just graduated from college and was on a one-year Fulbright fellowship to explore my roots. Ces stood out among the station's reporters because of her beauty and energy. In a class-conscious society like the Philippines, she knew how to move between different social circles, as comfortable with the upper elite as she was with cameramen and drivers, who tended to come from the lower income brackets. That's part of the reason there's a class divide at times between reporters and cameramen, but for Ces, it didn't exist.

She started working with ABS-CBN soon after it reopened in 1989 and built her reputation on exclusive stories, partly through luck and sheer hard work. She moved her way up the ladder, becoming one of the network's top anchors and the head of its business unit. She developed a reputation as a style maven, which sometimes worked against her on-air. In the end, news anchors wear clothes that are sleek, classic — and slightly boring. Ces' style was, at times, too distinctive.

By the time I became the head of ABS-CBN News in 2005, Ces had lived through numerous leadership changes which pushed the evolution of the news group. She gave me great insights into the people I would be leading, painting a picture of a disillusioned, sometimes cynical, news division buffeted by internal politics and a lack of commitment to journalistic values. I consulted her when I began thinking about how to change the culture, and she minced no words in listing the mistakes of the past and what needed to be fixed for the future. At that point, the network seemed to have a revolving door for the top post — with most news heads lasting two years or less. Disillusioned by the politics, turfing, the feudal styles of management and the corruption she had seen, she retreated to the background, rarely extending herself or doing any real journalism for years. Despite that, in the course of our conversations, I realized she nurtured a deep idealism about the Philippines and our profession.

I asked her to go back to reporting, the kind that only 20-year veterans can do, drawing on deep contacts and experience. When she did that in succeeding weeks and months, she became a force multiplier for the values I wanted our team to exhibit — a member of the old guard who began to lead from the middle. She helped ignite the culture change I wanted in our news

---

[3] Citation I wrote for Ces Drilon in ABS-CBN's 20/20 Awards, December, 2006.

group — inspiring and working with our younger reporters and pushing her peers to match the caliber and frequency of her work. I was all too aware that she worked 12 to 16 hour days — not easy to do when you're a mother of four. When we spoke about it, she always said how happy she was to rediscover journalism again, the exuberance apparent in her energy.

In order for her pieces to shine, she needed to work with a good cameraman with an artistic eye. Jimmy Encarnacion is a handsome man with a neat moustache and an impish smile that makes his eyes sparkle. Charming and good-natured, he is a ladies' man — easy and fun to be with. He is a quick thinker and an agile operator when he's working in the field — using his charm to get the video his reporter needs. He is also a fast learner. After he attended workshops run by my CNN cameramen,[4] I began to notice the stunning visuals of his camerawork. When his regular reporter left the network, I asked Ces to work with him, and that was how their partnership began.

The last member of their team is Angelo Valderrama, "Angel" for short. Self-effacing, quiet and humble, Angel is handsome in an altogether different way. Neatly dressed with his clean-cut hair, he watches more than he speaks, but he has a solid core, giving him an air of strength and dignity. He was also too aware of trying to live up to Ces' reputation, viewing her with quiet awe when they first began working together. He learned the ropes from Jimmy — always playing the straight man. He started as their driver, but soon began asking Jimmy to teach him how to shoot. He began to anticipate what Jimmy needed and at times would take the camera from him and shoot himself. Their combined initiative meant their team was nearly always first, matching Ces' drive and aggressiveness.

The three felt comfortable working in Mindanao because over the succeeding months, they were the team we sent when news broke, perhaps part of the reason why this coverage didn't ring alarm bells. Ces had made Mindanao her beat, she said, partly because she had gotten letters from these towns as a young girl from her father, a general of the Armed Forces of the Philippines. At one point, he was the commander in Jolo. Perhaps he was the reason she remained idealistic, her passion for reporting an extension of his life in the military. One night, she told me about his death in a helicopter crash in 1993 — heartbreaking for his family because they never found his body. Ces was the first of her family to learn of the crash — from a news

---

[4] The workshops for cameramen were led by two of the best cameramen I worked with at CNN, Andrew Clarke and Conrado Palileo.

room radio. She rushed home to comfort her mother and help pull their family together. When she was telling me about it 17 years later, she still had tears in her eyes. His daughter inherited his courage, and her team followed her like their commander.

2007 had been an eventful year for Ces, Jimmy and Angel. On June 10, Italian missionary Father Giancarlo Bossi was kidnapped by armed men in Zamboanga Sibugay. It became Ces' story, and she followed the developments closely. Near its end, she alerted us 24 hours ahead of time when sources told her he was likely to be released. She then immediately scheduled her team's travel plans — getting there six hours before he walked free after 40 days in captivity. [5] Instead of going to her hotel to sleep like most other reporters, particularly after her main source cut contact, she went to other sources looking for information and looped her managers in so we could prepare our organization for the story about to break (by sending a reporter to Italy to the family, another to get a church reaction, etc). That work paid off because she received a tip that he had just been released and would be brought to a military camp nearby.

She called me after midnight saying her team's car and driver had already left. Did I think it would be safe to take a tricycle to wait outside the military camp? I asked her why she didn't take her crew, and she said she wanted to let them sleep in case the tip was a dud. We assessed the situation, and off she went with her producer, Melay Masecampo. Using a handheld-camera, they waited outside the camp, and when she noticed activity, she called her crew. They got there just in time to tape the first video of Father Bossi's arrival.

The team stayed up working through the night and was first on-air to report the release — giving our network the exclusive. That was a 24-hour cycle for them as they followed the story and did live shots for our news programs on our flagship channel and three cable stations, radio and web. A few months later on November 14, Ces, Jimmy and Angel were in Basilan to report on the burial of one of the Abu Sayyaf's founder who crossed the lines and became a government official.

To weeks later, on November 29, 2007, the three were inside the Peninsula Manila Hotel as rebel soldiers took over the hotel, taking a stand against government forces outside. It was, to our mind, another coup

---

[5] "Italy priest freed in the Philippines," BBC, July 20, 2007. Available at http://news.bbc.co.uk/2/hi/asia-pacific/6907639.stm

attempt — the kind so prevalent in the late 80's. The most recent happened in 2003, dubbed the Oakwood Mutiny. More than 300 rebel soldiers demanding the immediate resignation of the leaders of the Arroyo adminis-tration occupied and threatened to blow up the Oakwood Premier, an upscale serviced apartment/luxury hotel high-rise in Makati (where CNN also had its Manila office so I saw the whole event unfold up close). The same group that led that coup attempt took over the nearby Peninsula Manila Hotel five years later on November 29, 2007 — making me joke that they really like luxury hotels. Their demand remained the same: for people to rise up against the alleged corruption of President Arroyo and her administration.

The siege began mid-morning and lasted until early evening. By late afternoon, the government was asking everyone to evacuate the hotel, making discreet calls to news organizations to ask us to pull our teams out. The last time a situation like this happened two years earlier, I agreed to pull out our people who had entered a high-security prison in Manila — Bicutan — during an ongoing jailbreak. After the press left, the police burst into the complex and killed all 23 members of the Abu Sayyaf who had been imprisoned in the facility — an event condemned by the Philippines' Commission on Human Rights and international legal groups as an example of "excessive force."[6] An independent study concluded it was "a premeditated and concerted effort to eliminate identified enemies of the state."[7] I remembered that bloody event when we received the second request to pull out from the Peninsula Hotel.

If we agreed to the government's request, there would be no eyewit-nesses, and we would have to accept the police's account of their actions. Given our past experience, I was wary. I wasn't alone. While some reporters left along with the hotel employees and guests, about 30 journalists from various news groups decided to stay, including twelve from ABS-CBN. We were in constant contact with our team and helped them prepare for the assault. I felt our team would be safer going up to higher floors of the hotel for shelter instead of going outside — an assessment Ces and our other jour-nalists on the ground shared.

---

[6] V. Datuinguinoo, "CHR finds police response to Bicutan siege 'excessive'," Philippine Center for Investigative Journalism, The PCIJ Blog, March 27, 2006. Available at http://www.pcij. org/blog/2006/03/27/chr-finds-police-response-to-bicutan-siege-excessive

[7] N. Reyes and M. Vaughn, "Revisiting the Bicutan Sige: Police Use of Force in a Maximum Security Detention Center in the Philippines," *International Criminal Justice Review*, Vol. 19, No. 1, March 2009, p. 5. Available at http://icj.sagepub.com/content/19/1/25.short

We decided to stay, and that's what we told the Department of Interior and Local Government who was in charge of the police forces storming the rebels. They asked us to move our teams to specific rooms, and we complied. Jimmy, Angel and Ces again showed inordinate presence of mind, retreating to the rooms but leaving their live camera rolling allowing television viewers to see the tear gas and the retreat of rebel soldiers and their civilian supporters. The government asked us to avoid showing the troop movements outside the hotel so we trained our outdoor cameras on the façade of a nearby building and switched to Jimmy's live unmanned camera inside the hall when the tear gas signaled the beginning of the attack. Ces, on a live microphone, kept reporting as long as she could. Outside, an armored personnel carrier burst through the front of the Peninsula, while SWAT teams wearing gas masks entered the hotel and captured the rebels.

What the police did next was highly controversial: they arrested not only the rebel soldiers but also the civilians and journalists who stayed to report the story. Our journalists, including Ces, Jimmy and Angel, were brought to Bicutan prison in police buses, but the government stopped short of charging them. Department of Interior and Local Government Secretary Ronaldo Puno said the reporters were "obstructing justice". It was an odd choice of words because this was an attempted coup, a political act, handled in the past by the military and Department of Defense. This was the first time the police took the lead and treated it like a crime scene, saying it was illegal for journalists to stay at "the crime scene" after being asked to leave. It was a novel approach and a new way to intimidate reporters and camera crews — a useful tactic for future scenarios.

Given what my teams reported from the hotel and the way they were treated by the police, I led our network in a strong public position when I was called to testify at the Senate Committee for Justice and Human Rights.[8] Many of us believed Seecretary Puno and his forces violated the Constitution because they were angry at the coverage and wanted to control the media. The arrests set a dangerous precedent. If there's another coup attempt in the future, would the police again arrest journalists for doing their work? Officials were using new interpretations of the law to redefine the journalists' role in conflict situations. All this was also happening against the backdrop

---

[8] M. Ressa, "*Media Position Paper for the Senate's Committee on Justice and Human Rights,*" December 13, 2007. Available at http://www.abs-cbnnews.com/sites/default/files/others/downloads/Media%20Position%20Paper%20for%20the%20Senate.pdf

of an atmosphere of impunity with an increase in the unsolved murders of journalists and human rights workers.[9] At some point, intimidation becomes the norm, and I saw moves like these as extensions of earlier attempts to control and curtail freedom of the press, perhaps setting the scene for similar conditions as the 2005 prison siege.

We felt it was dangerous to leave these actions unchallenged. So by December, Ces and I — along with more than a hundred journalists from at least 14 other organizations — filed a case challenging the arrests at the Supreme Court.

You have to know Ces is not easily intimidated.

* * *

By the time they were trudging through the dense vegetation of the jungles of Jolo, Ces, Jimmy and Angel had already been tested. They were about to be tested again. A little more than an hour into their uphill climb, Ces turned to the group's leader.

"How much longer will we walk," she asked. "It's very dark."

"We'll rest when we get to the top of the mountain."

"It seems so far. How will we get back?"

"Don't worry. You'll go back by a different route. Civilians will take you back so you won't have to go through the jungle. It will be much easier."

By that time, nearly everyone was walking in silence as they negotiated the steep incline. At about 2:30 in the morning, they reached the top of the mountain and found two huts. Here they would rest for the night. Again, Jimmy and Angel settled down on either side of Ces. They were so tired they immediately fell asleep.

Three hours later, Ces woke up to see the colors changing in the sky. Several of the men were already awake and talking nearby. She asked them when the interview was going to happen. They told her to have coffee first. So she did. It took another hour and a half before one of the men signaled to her and told her, "The Commander wants to see you over there."

She walked away from the main group towards the Commander. He was more brusque this time when she reached him.

---

[9] The United Nations filed a special report in 2007 that was damning. It accused the country's armed forces of killing leftist sympathisers in an effort to wipe out communist insurgents and their supporters. Full report and follow-up recommendations available at http://daccess-dds-ny.un.org/doc/UNDOC/GEN/G09/130/39/PDF/G0913039.pdf?OpenElement

"This is all I'm going to say," he told her. "We are kidnapping you for ransom."

Her heart sank, but she tried not to show it.

"Won't it be better to do the interview so you can tell people about your struggle? Don't kidnap. Don't ask for money. Tell me about your story. I'll tell the people. I'll air your story." Even as she spoke, she knew it was a feeble attempt. This was what she had feared, and somehow, she had known it all night.

"The government doesn't care," he answered. "Besides we've done interviews before, but they were never released or published." As they were talking, other men came closer. One was carrying Ces' cellphone and handed it to the Commander. He turned it on and handed it to her. "Call your office and tell them."

\* \* \*

Ces' call on that Monday morning telling me they had been kidnapped threw me into a living nightmare. After she hung up, I made two phone calls while I texted my assistants, Gina Jaculo and Anne Yosuico, to call an emergency meeting of my core management team. My first call was to the acting intelligence chief of the national police, Superintendent Winnie Quidato.[10] I needed perspective, and he would not only understand the threat, he would know how to deal with it. We met more than a decade earlier when he was an investigator for the Bureau of Immigration, unraveling the Philippine's links to al-Qaeda and Jemaah Islamiyah. He is a cool operator, balancing reality with politics. I outlined the problem and told him what I was going to do.

"Give me their numbers, Maria, and I can try to see where they are." he said.

"Can you pinpoint them exactly?"

"We triangulate. It's not precise because it will depend on the cell sites, but we'll have an idea."

"It's on this phone so I'll text it to you as soon as we finish. Will we get better information if I go directly to Globe and Smart?[11]"

"We might. You can ask them, but they may not give it."

---

[10] The Philippine National Police has a different rank system from the country's military, the Armed Forces of the Philippines. A Superintendent in the police is equivalent to a Lieutenant Colonel in the military.

[11] Globe and Smart are telecommunications companies.

"I'll try. I mean, I can explain the situation to them, right? I'll also call the U.S. to ask for help. They have the most sophisticated equipment, right? Can the Australians do anything the U.S. can't?"

"Well, call your contacts and ask them. You can ask them to call me to coordinate."

"If they don't want to get officially involved, they'll go through me. That okay with you?"

"*Bahala ka na* (It's up to you.). What about Ces' contact? Who's their guide? Send me that cellphone number too."

"I don't know who it is. Let me get to the office and get everyone together and I'll get you that information. I need a timeline. We need to set up barricades to prevent this group from either being taken over or handing over our people to a larger group. Remember what happened with Maan and Val? Do you have police forces in Jolo?" I asked. Maan Macapagal and Val Cuenca, an ABS-CBN reporter and cameraman, were kidnapped by the Abu Sayaff while they were reporting on negotiations for European tourists held hostage in 2000. The small group which kidnapped Maan and Val was then captured by a larger group that wanted a share of the ransom. Still others who were kidnapped in the past were given to the Abu Sayyaf or larger, armed groups for safekeeping — with the understanding that they would also have a cut.

"We don't have a lot. We just have SAF [Special Actions Forces]," replied Quidato. "You'll have to ask the military."

"So I talk to Sabban?" I ask, referring to General Juancho Sabban, the commander of the marines in Jolo. "I have his number. I'll call him. Do you know the local politicians in Jolo? Do you know whom we can trust?"

"The governor is Sakur Tan."

"Can we think of other names? I'd like to be able to present choices. I'm heading to the office now. Can you meet me there? Can you please help us through this?"

"I'll talk to my boss and get permission to help you."

The next call was to the owner of ABS-CBN, Eugenio "Gabby" Lopez, III. I was getting dressed as I was making calls, and my hand shook as I punched the speed dial. Energetic and smart, Gabby is a fascinating mix of East and West. With an MBA from Harvard, he is the CEO of the largest multimedia conglomerate in the country, the crown jewel of the Lopez empire. The Lopez family has long been intertwined in the history of the Philippines, long embroiled in the power politics of the country. In 1972 after Ferdinand Marcos declared martial law, he shut down ABS-CBN and jailed Gabby's father. Gabby helped break his father out of prison and flee into exile to the United States.

"Gabby, I have bad news. I got a call about 15 minutes ago from Ces. She and two of our men have been kidnapped in Jolo."

"What? Are they okay?" he asked.

"Yeah, they're okay. Ces is okay. She even asked if she was fired." I quickly told him the details of our conversation as well as my call to the Philippine police intelligence chief. "Ces said not to call the military or government. So I called the police."

"Should I call anyone? Should we go to the President? She may not like us, but she'll help us." There had long been an adversarial relationship between President Gloria Macapagal-Arroyo and ABS-CBN, but the added twist now is that a few months earlier, I — along with many of our journalists, including Ces — filed a case at the Supreme Court against the very men I would now have to ask for help: Department of Interior and Local Government Secretary Ronaldo Puno and the Philippine National Police Chief Director General Avelino Razon.

"Not yet, Gab. Let me find out all the details first, and I'll let you know. I've seen all of the major kidnappings, and I have an idea of how to approach this. I think we should go bottom up. I have sources and contacts we can tap, but I think it's important we move quickly. A lot depends on who exactly has them. So we have to figure that out." I repeated what Quidato and I had discussed. "I'm on my way to the office and will call you once we have a plan of action. Gabby, I'm going to do what I think is right because we have to act fast. Is that okay with you?"

"Yes, go ahead. Just let me know." That approval now meant that I was in charge, but the other side of that coin is that if anything went wrong, I would also be responsible. If anything went drastically wrong, I knew I would have to resign. I pushed the thought away and forced myself to think systematically. I was afraid for the safety of Ces, Jimmy and Angel, but I felt that if we acted fast, they could be home tomorrow.

I ran downstairs and told my driver, Domeng Magora, to get to the station as quickly as possible. While in the car, I made a list of the stakeholders we'd need to address, concentric circles that expanded to include more people the further you get from the center. The first circle, the core, are our three people: Ces, Jimmy and Angel. The next circle is composed of their families. We would have to notify them and help them handle their emotions and — I made a mental note — help them deal with the media. They would be besieged the minute news of the kidnapping got out. Which also reminded me that ABS-CBN would need to issue a statement.

After the family, we would need to deal with our own newsroom. First, we'd have to announce the kidnapping internally and lay some ground rules. I decided to create two separate teams: one I would head — the crisis committee to get our team home safely; the other, headed by my deputy, Luchi Cruz-Valdes, would do the news. We would set up a wall between the groups, with only Luchi and I communicating, and the understanding that our journalists were free to report anything it verified outside ABS-CBN. One of the hardest challenges facing any journalist is when the news becomes about you. I decided we would make it clear to our people they would get no preferential treatment and must do their own sourcing and reporting separate from the actions our crisis committee took. This step was crucial because it was important to keep the integrity of the news group intact.

The next circle is ABS-CBN itself — 4,000 strong. We would need to inform our executive committee, then the division heads, and go all the way down the line. After that is the journalism community. I knew that we would need to gather and control the flow of information in order to handle the kidnappers effectively. What do we tell journalists? When do we do that? The next circle beyond that is the local government. Whom do we work with in Jolo? How do we choose our negotiator? Whomever we choose would have to control a private army as well as command local law enforcement to make sure we can get them from the jungle back to civilization. Following that is the national government, represented in my mind by Secretary Puno and President Arroyo. I made a mental note to call them both after we dealt with the circles closer to the core.

Finally, the last and largest circle of stakeholders is the public. If we handle the journalists well, then the public mood will reflect what they write. In past kidnapping situations, what negotiators released to journalists set the stage for the success or failure of its plans because eventually what the public knows will reach the kidnappers — reaching back to affect the innermost core, the victims.

Both my phones were ringing incessantly, but I finished this crucial list before I took any more calls. I was trying to balance internal and external demands. I knew that if I was clear in identifying stakeholders, I could itemize the actions we needed to take and set our priorities. The overall goal is simple: get our people home safely. By the end of the thirty-minute ride, I had briefed Luchi and told her she would be in charge of looking after ABS-CBN News. Aside from running the news operations, Luchi would look at the information we would gather and pinpoint possible landmines because as the country's largest network, ABS-CBN carried an inevitable perpetual bulls-eye.

I wanted to focus solely on Jolo. I hung up the phone. Charie Villa, my Head of Newsgathering, wasn't answering her telephone. She exercised in the morning so she was probably still on the track. I hoped my assistants had gotten to her because I needed details of her last conversations with Ces. I spoke with Glenda Gloria, who heads ANC, our 24-hour English cable news network, and asked her to verify my number for General Sabban in Jolo. I told her briefly what happened and asked her to make a list of her military contacts we could go to for off-the-record A1 information. This is crucial. We can't act quickly if we don't have accurate information. Glenda has written several books, including one on Mindanao which she co-authored with the head of abs-cbnnews.com, Marites Vitug.[12] The two of them have some of the best and deepest sources in security, law enforcement and the justice system. Between the three of us, I was confident we could reach anyone and get immediate responses. I asked HR head for News, Libby Pascual, to find and collate the addresses and phone numbers of the families of Ces, Jimmy, and Angel. I went through my different circles and started listing specific actions that needed to be taken to address each stakeholder's concerns. Then next to each task, I put the names of people who would be in charge.

I also made several calls to sources — one to Malacanang to get a view from the top and make sure the President knew what we were doing, and another to General Sabban to ask him to set up barricades to prevent any possible handover of our people to another group. It turned out that he was in Manila so I asked if we could meet later in the day. He immediately said yes and that he would tell his men to set up the barricades.

As the car pulled into the station, I picked up a call from one of our anchors, Pia Hontiveros-Pagkalinawan. What she said alarmed me. News of the kidnapping was already spreading. She said her military and police sources were asking her about Ces. Is she missing? Was she kidnapped? I asked her to calm speculation. We tried to chart where the leak was coming from. It seemed Ces had been in touch last night with the military's Colonel Clemmens, who offered her security. When he couldn't find her or Dinampo this morning, he raised the alarm, and it had reached Manila.

---

[12] M. Danguilan-Vitug & G. Gloria, *Under the Crescent Moon: Rebellion in Mindanao* (Manila: Institute for Popular Democracy, 2000).

This is bad. No announcement of the kidnapping can come out before the barricades are up. Depending on where they are, it may take anywhere from six to twelve hours to do that.

By this time about an hour after Ces' call, I was walking into the newsroom. It's a large, open space with desk spaces in clusters: on the left near the editing rooms are the producers and writers for our newscasts. To the right are the reporter's cubicles. Further back are the writers and producers for ANC, the English cable news channel. To their left are the logistics team, and beyond them are the writers for abs-cbnnews.com. At the far right is the ANC studio, which uses the newsroom as its backdrop. In a small clearing in the center, I could see our desk editors starting to gather for the morning editorial meeting. This is one of the newsroom's quiet moments: the morning program had just ended; the night shift had left; and the day shift was just coming in. It was even quieter today because it was a holiday, meaning we were running with smaller teams.

I looked around as I turned the key and unlocked my office door. My office is to the right as you walk halfway into the newsroom. From my vantage point, I could see the whole space, part of the reason I could always sense the energy and mood of my news team. My heart was racing. As I walked behind my desk to sit down, I said a short prayer. I just want to get through this day. One step at a time.

\* \* \*

If only these walls could talk. When these buildings were built in 1968 by Gabby's father, Eugenio "Geny" Lopez, Jr., they were the most modern broadcasting facilities in the region, setting the standard in Asia. In succeeding years, the ABS-CBN compound played a crucial role in Philippine history, caught in a constant tug of war between political players for more than four decades. The reason is clear: whoever controlled this broadcast complex controlled public opinion.

This is where I began my career in the Philippines, right after the People Power revolution of 1986. During the days of coup attempts that followed, I was trapped several times in this compound as government troops held back rebel soldiers, so young (and so American) I didn't quite comprehend why the network was being attacked.

It felt right that after nearly two decades with CNN, I would return as head of this news group. I like circular journeys and when I walked into this office, I thought it was a perfect example of T. S. Eliot's haunting quote:

"We shall not cease from exploration, and the end of all our exploring will be to arrive where we started and know the place for the first time."

The man who brought me back to the Philippines is Gabby Lopez, who tried several times to recruit me from CNN. I thought I would never hear from him after I turned his offer down in the late 90's, but this charismatic, energetic man kept coming back until our paths finally converged.

For more than 200 years, the fortunes of his family intertwined with key moments in Philippine history, reflecting the country's colonial history and changing culture. There's a joke that the Philippines "spent 250 years in a convent and 50 years in Hollywood," referring to 250 years of Spanish colonial rule and half a century under the United States (America's only colony). Gabby is a living example: he carries a Spanish name but speaks, walks and talks like an American. From hundreds of hours of conversation, I know at heart he is deeply Filipino.

The Lopez family traces its roots to a Chinese-mestizo named Basilio, who took his Spanish landowner's surname in the 1800s.[13] He eventually became a wealthy sugar planter and miller known widely as Don Basilio Lopez. Among his 16 children are two who would determine the course of Philippine history — Eugenio and Fernando, who intertwined business, politics and media.[14]

Eugenio laid the foundation of the family's empire after World War II: he built Asia's first airline, ran the country's largest power utility (at a time when most companies were owned or operated by Americans) and became a media magnate. With an estimated net worth of US$300 million,[15] he was considered the wealthiest Filipino of that era. Eugenio became a political kingmaker. According to observers, he used his newspaper, the *Chronicle*, to degrade the popularity of then President Diosdado Macapagal (whose daughter, Gloria, would also become President) and help pave the way for the rise of Ferdinand Marcos. Eugenio bankrolled Marcos' presidential bid in 1965 with Fernando, Eugenio's brother, as Marcos' running mate. Fernando had worked his way up politically and had already won a term as Vice President from 1949 to 1953. He would be the only Filipino to serve a second term, this time under Marcos.

---

[13] "Origins of the Lopez family," Lopez family website available at http://www.lopezfamilytree.com/cgi-bin/hist.asp.

[14] "The Family Tree," Lopez family website available at http://www.lopezfamilytree.com/index1.htm

[15] E. Brazil, "Eugenio Lopez, Philippine Mogul," *San Francisco Chronicle*, July 2, 1999.

During succeeding years, relations between the Marcoses and the Lopezes gradually became strained and erupted in open battle. Soon the *Chronicle*, focusing on corruption issues, became Marcos' harshest critic. Marcos hit back: denouncing the Lopezes as oligarchs and attacking their businesses, ultimately trying to tear their family apart. It was vicious, and it was personal.

On September 21, 1972, Marcos declared martial law. It began with a media blackout after government troops marched into radio and television stations. A day later, Marcos shut down the ABS-CBN compound. Simultaneously, Marcos jailed the network's president, Geny, and used him as a bargaining chip against his father. Marcos pushed Eugenio to sign over his substantial wealth — companies worth hundreds of millions of dollars in exchange for Geny's release. Eugenio agreed, but Marcos didn't keep his word. Eugenio died in 1975 with his son still in prison.

In 1974, Geny and his cellmate, Serge Osmena (the grandson of the Philippine's fourth President, Sergio Osmena), went on a hunger strike to protest the detention of thousands of innocent Filipinos. Three years later, the two of them, with the help of Geny's son, Gabby, escaped from prison, and fled into exile in the United States.

During this time, the ABS-CBN compound was commandeered by a Marcos crony, Roberto Benedicto, who renamed it "Broadcast Plaza" and made it the headquarters of the government television station, MBS4. ABS-CBN would remain closed for 14 years. During that time, its transmitters pumped out government propaganda. Until 1986.

That was when I first walked through its doors. Although I was born in the Philippines, my family left for the United States soon after martial law was declared. Growing up in New Jersey, I became more American than Filipino, but in 1986, I came home in search of roots. As a fresh college graduate, I walked into the former government television station thrilled with the possibility of helping turn this former propaganda machine into a true People's Television network (reflecting the new name it adopted — People's Television 4 or PTV4).

From an instrument of repression, it became the voice of freedom. It was an exhilarating time full of endless possibilities. Excitement gripped our motley crew: potential anchors auditioning live, to be chosen by the people — who themselves were flush from an unimaginable victory ending Marcos' 21-year rule. That was the birth of "People Power," when hundreds of thousands of people gathered to protect a military in revolt and faced down a dictator with nothing more than prayers and songs. The iconic images of nuns stopping tanks and children putting flowers in the barrels of guns powered democratic dreams globally — in South Korea, Pakistan, China, Burma, East Germany, Bangladesh, Nepal and Indonesia.

People Power meant freedom of the press, something nearly forgotten for this generation of journalists, most of whom first labored under the outright censorship of martial law followed by something more insidious and damaging — self-censorship. In the government station, I struggled with the habits left behind — scripts so safe the words were devoid of meaning, but each word I rewrote was a death knell for the past.

Without the media, People Power couldn't have happened. After all, the calls to help, to assemble in the streets were broadcast on radio and later, messages of freedom came from the former government station. Military rebels targeted the broadcast compound in order to be able to control the airwaves. Again, the compound built by the Lopezes became a pawn in the struggle for power. Once rebel soldiers were in control, former ABS-CBN employees came to the compound and began to operate it, broadcasting the revolution and helping push more people out into the streets.

Euphoria infused the entire society: it was a moment of redemption. Spontaneously discovered, People Power was created by a failed military coup, the calls of the Catholic Church (in Asia's largest Roman Catholic nation) to help the soldiers, the journalists who risked their lives to get the message out, alternative political figures, and the hundreds of thousands of people from all classes of this economically stratified society who rushed into the streets. In those moments of uncertainty, Filipinos took a stand and risked all they had.

The woman who inspired the overthrow of a dictator was the gentle, self-effacing widow of Marcos' top political rival, Benigno Aquino, Jr. He was assassinated on the airport tarmac in 1983 when he tried to return home to the Philippines — a move many Filipinos believed was either instigated by or approved by the Marcoses. Three years later, his wife, Cory Aquino, was swept into power by a human sea of yellow in what had then become a real-life battle of good versus evil.

Soon after, she returned the companies which were illegally taken over by Marcos, including the Lopez companies. Geny and his family returned from the United States and, along with his brothers, Oscar and Manolo, began to rebuild their empire from scratch. ABS-CBN returned to its old compound, sharing it for years with PTV4. In a short period of time, ABS-CBN vaulted from the basement to first place among the country's broadcast networks, holding that place unchallenged for 14 years.

When I accepted Gabby's job offer at the end of 2004, ABS-CBN had just lost ratings leadership in the capital, Manila, to its rival, GMA7. For the news group, it was largely an issue of credibility, a problem I was hired to address. Back in power, the Lopezes again combined big business, media and politics. Although no Lopez would run for office in his generation, Gabby is perceived as a kingmaker like his grandfather, and often let his preferences be known publicly. In addition, several ABS-CBN news anchors ran for office and won: Loren Legarda became a Senator; Ted Failon became a Congressman; and top anchor Noli de Castro became Vice-President. The unspoken thought then, right or wrong, was that they would favor Lopez interests.

My solution was to professionalize the news group and operate independently of our owners' vested interests. Gabby agreed with me and helped me draw the line — in the process, giving up the power he used to wield in the newsroom and allowing professional journalists to call a spade a spade, regardless of whose interests the stories may hurt.

One thing about Gabby: he is not afraid. Perhaps it's because of what his family lived through. Regardless, we handled numerous crises of national importance which involved ABS-CBN directly. In 2005, a few months after I took over, President Arroyo accused our anchor, Julius Babao, of harboring a terrorist — a charge we proved false after an independent investigation I led, a conclusion later accepted by government agencies. In a closed-door meeting with President Arroyo, Gabby listened quietly while I explained the mistaken assumptions of the Intelligence Services of the Armed Forces of the Philippines (ISAFP) to Mrs. Arroyo. Later, Gabby told me he would have preferred I just avoid antagonizing the President, but he let me do what I felt was right.

In February, 2006, 71 people were killed while trying to get into the network's top game show, a tragedy now known as the Ultra Stampede. The lawyers asked Gabby to avoid making any statements, but Gabby immediately took responsibility on nationwide television and addressed the problems head-on. At a time when the executive committee was in disarray and the lawyers were concerned about potential liability, Gabby did the right thing regardless of his vested interests.

A few weeks later on the eve of the 20th anniversary of People Power, an armored personnel carrier parked outside our gates as the government threatened to shut down ABS-CBN during an attempted coup that never materialized — a time when President Arroyo declared a state of emergency with Proclamation 1017. When the government asked us to drop our live coverage, Gabby supported my decision to keep broadcasting even after other networks complied. One even started running cartoons.

In retrospect, this was the moment I felt the demonization of media began. Don't get me wrong. There's a lot to fix, but journalists were never officially targeted before. Now that was changing, and it would reach its peak with the police arresting journalists a year later.

To explain Proclamation 1017, Mrs. Arroyo claimed that the political opposition, elements of the extreme right and the extreme left, and "reckless elements of the national media" were working together to mount a coup against her government. Police immediately banned political rallies scheduled for the anniversary, but not everyone followed. Some respected leaders continued their plans and protested the declaration. It turned into a parody of People Power when police dispersed them with water cannons and carried out warrantless arrests on nationwide television. Then came the moves against media, starting with threats and the raid on a newspaper, the Daily Tribune.

This marked the height of President Arroyo's anger at media. She had been through a turbulent time: in 2005, a cellphone conversation was released which triggered calls for her resignation. On the tape, a voice sounding like hers gave an election official a command to cheat. She spent most of the year fighting for legitimacy and her survival. Forced by members of her cabinet to apologize on national television (in a move that backfired), President Arroyo blamed ABS-CBN and the Philippine Daily Inquirer, one of the leading newspapers, for "persecuting her." In several conversations, she and her advisers warned me that I was being used by vested interests to attack her administration.

The media is indeed powerful in the Philippines, and one incident during Proclamation 1017 brought that home to me again. At the height of uncertainty and the government's own loyalty checks among its troops, one of ABS-CBN's reporters, who had close links with anti-Arroyo forces, called. He was with the Army's scout rangers, and they were ready to march out in rebellion. They only asked we put them on air live. I made a quick calculation and said, "Tell them to march out first, and then we'll go live." They never left their barracks.

Still, I cringed when I heard government officials threaten to close print and broadcast media institutions, when I saw their efforts to divide and to intimidate journalists. Through it all — even after ABS-CBN itself was threatened, Gabby stood his ground and showed no fear. Because he did that, I could do my job.

Working with ABS-CBN and Gabby Lopez reminded me of the cycles of history, the excesses and failures of power, and the role journalists play in curbing human ambitions and building a nation.

# Crisis

A s soon as I sat down behind my desk, Luchi walked in. At 5'3", Luchi is a taut bundle of energy. Although she can sometimes be tactless, she says it like it is and possesses a sharp editorial mind. We've known each other since 1987 when we put together the country's first investigative television magazine program for ABS-CBN. A year later, the two of us, along with ABS-CBN's former head of public affairs, Cecilia "Cheche" Lazaro, resigned to set up a company called Probe Productions, which focused on investigative journalism and educational programs. It also became a training ground for investigative reporters and producers in our industry.

I gestured to the table while I punched the numbers on the speakerphone, called Glenda's office to ask her to get Marites and come to my office. Behind Luchi, Libby walked in. 46 years old, Libby is the perfect human resources manager for me. Reed-thin at 5'1", she worked the long hours with me, both of us often ending our days near midnight. She understands the systems and informal ways of getting things done in this network since she's been here since 1990, yet at the same time, she remains connected and empathetic to the people. One of the things I always wanted to avoid was to treat people like numbers, a danger in large organizations. Libby never did that because she never hid behind her authority and position. Close on her heels, Charie rushed in and started speaking as soon as she entered.

"What are we going to do? I told her not to go. I told her, but she wasn't listening any more." 46-year-old Charie Villa started her career with ABS-CBN as a reporter. Nine years later, she moved to Reuters. CNN was a Reuters client, and Charie often did advance work for me — giving me video and information before I landed in the Philippines on breaking news stories.

Heavy-set but energetic, she was one of my first recruits when I decided to take this job because she's driven by the adrenaline of breaking news. Logistically, she is among the quickest to react on any story.

"Wait, Charie, let's wait for everyone before we start. So you heard?"

"Yeah, I talked to Glenda. Sorry I missed your call."

"Luchi, do you have a recorder?" I asked. "I want to record what we say so we don't have to keep going over everything with all the different groups. I can get Anne to transcribe and distribute when we're done."

"Ah, yeah, I have a recorder in my office," replied Luchi. She pulled out her cellphone and texted her assistant to bring her recorder. "Why did you allow them to go, Charie?"

"No, I didn't," retorted Charie. "I told Ces to just give a camera to Dinampo, but I don't know what happened. She wasn't listening."

"Wait, wait, guys," I butted in. Energy levels were too high. Nervous tension, I guess. It was most evident in Charie. Glenda and Marites came in. It had taken me two years to recruit Glenda, an experienced newsroom manager and multi-awarded journalist who values independence. Revolutions and transitions shaped her temperament making her slow to boil and addicted to adrenaline. She worked for the *Philippine Daily Inquirer, The Manila Times* and the Philippine Center for Investigative Journalism as well as international news agencies. In the early 1990s, she co-founded investigative newsmagazine, *Newsbreak*, with Marites. Highly principled, Glenda lives her values and was turning out to be the best manager ANC ever had. Marites, also a multi-awarded journalist, had written several books and fought many lawsuits from power players she held accountable. Finally, ABS-CBN's online platform was adopting a more sophisticated editorial agenda under Marites.

"Okay, shut the door," I said. "The first thing we have to do is a chronology, but I want to record it so we don't have to keep going over it again and again with everyone else. I need as many names as you can remember and we can trace. Let's start with how this interview and coverage started."

By this time, Luchi had her recorder. She placed it at the center of the circular table.[1] Early in the year, Ces had asked us about pursuing this interview. Although I was dubious about the effort, I wanted to know more. I asked Charie to check Ces' sources so Ces introduced her to Dinampo in March. That's where I asked Charie to begin. She started to talk, going back

---

[1] The following conversation is transcribed from the digital recording of our first crisis meeting on Monday, June 9, 2008.

four months to her first meeting with Dinampo at ABS-CBN. Since then, Charie said she spoke with him at least five times on the telephone.

"He was trying to reassure me about the interview," said Charie. "I told him that we didn't feel good about this. He said, 'we've made this arrangement with the MNLF [Moro National Liberation Front]. Five of them will come with us, and Charie, there's another emissary from the MNLF, who initially didn't want to go but since we raised the issue about security, this guy agreed to go.' He never told me that guy's name but he said he's a top MNLF guy."

"So we have no names?" I asked. That's not good, I thought.

"No names. It's just Professor Dinampo. Ces kept pushing me. She said, 'Charie, it'll be on neutral ground. We'll not go inside the camp. Just to Indanan. There's a cellphone signal there. We'll just be at the entrance of their area.' I told her, 'But the fact that they're armed, Ces, they would still control you.' 'Well, they said they'll be in an ASG-controlled area.' I told her, 'Oh no, Ces, that's not good, and I told her 'you do not enter, Ces, without confirming with us.' So while she flew to Zamboanga, I spoke to Dinampo again."

"So let's focus on Thursday, when the three of us [Charie, Luchi and me] chatted, and we said, 'Okay, let's pursue it.'" I said, referring to our most serious discussion about the pros and cons of Ces' project. It happened five days ago.

"Yeah, no, Friday," said Charie.

"Yes, I thought that was Friday," overlapped Luchi.

"No, it's Thursday," said Charie.

"No, Thursday," I said, "Thursday night." I pulled out a calendar and placed it on the table so we could all see.

"Yeah, it was Thursday," said Charie. "That's right. That's right."

"On Friday, I called Ces in, and I told Ces ..." I continued.

"... because she left Friday," interrupted Charie.

"Yes, I talked to her around noon," I said. "Even when I had the ability to interview the Abu Sayyaf in their camp at the height of the kidnappings — I told her they specifically asked for me and offered an exclusive, but I never did because it's hard to trust these guys. Now they're not even in the spotlight, and we know their track record. 'What are you going to get out of it?' I asked her. Then she said, 'Okay, okay, I understand. I won't go in, but I'll meet with Dinampo.' A few hours after that, Charie called me and said, 'I'm going to give her a satphone, and I'm going to give her a little camera.' That's when we hatched the plan of the little camera."

"I told Ces, 'it's better to lose a camera than to pay for ransom,'" added Charie.

"So you were going to give the camera to someone else," asked Luchi.

"Yes," answered Charie. "They were going to give it to Dinampo."

"And he was going to do the interview?" interrupted Luchi.

"Yes, I told her to send questions and send the camera," answered Charie.

"But Radullan was going to surrender?" asked Luchi.

"Yes," Charie replied.

"But we didn't know that until Saturday," I said, pointing to the calendar and making a note.

"During the day on Saturday, Ces and I were talking," Charie continued. I told her, 'Ces, I don't think this is a good idea. Let's not do it anymore. She said, 'what's wrong with you guys?' She was starting to get defiant, but I told her, 'Ces, you have four kids. Are you thinking about your sons?' 'Of course, I'm thinking about my kids. *Anlabo niyo* (You're hard to talk to.)' She was already angry at me." Charie held out her cellphone and scrolled through their messages. Luchi, her glasses at the tip of her nose, looked at the phone with Charie. At this point, their sentences began to quickly overlap, and their voices began to rise in volume — although still controlled.

"Good, you have text messages," said Luchi.

"Oh, fuck, several!" retorted Charie.

"Because we have to be able to establish that we tried to stop her."

"Well, we really did."

"I need to establish that because we may be attacked here," said Luchi. I made a mental note that Luchi was already keeping track of possible vulnerabilities for our news group.

"I was talking to Maria on Saturday because I spoke to Mujiv Hataman," Charie continued after I tapped the calendar. Hataman is a former Congressman from Basilan, the birthplace of the Abu Sayyaf. His mentor was Wahab Akbar, a founder of the Abu Sayyaf who turned to politics, serving three terms as Basilan governor before getting elected to Congress. Akbar was one of four people killed by a bomb outside the congressional buildings in 2007. Police suspect Akbar was the bomb's target and that the bomb was planted by the Abu Sayyaf. Mujiv Hataman was implicated in the bombing, although the charges were eventually dropped. In 2011, Hataman became the governor of the Autonomous Region of Muslim Mindanao or ARMM, appointed by President Aquino as the OIC or officer-in-charge.

"Mujiv told me, 'Charie, I'm not recommending this.' See, the way Ces pictured it to me, Mujiv supported her. That he said, 'Radullan is different. He's an ideologue.'"

"Sorry," said Luchi. "Who's Mujiv? I'm not familiar with the personalities."

"This is the guy who did the party-list," said Marites. "And he's a suspect in the bombing at Congress. The one that killed Wahab ..."

"... Akbar," finished Charie.

"This is the first time you mentioned Radullan Sahiron may surrender," I reminded Charie. "Where did you get that from?"

"From Ces and Mujiv, and he was also sending feelers to Bert Gonzales [Philippine National Security Adviser] that he wants to surrender. Then Mujiv said, 'he was only driven to the Abu Sayyaf. He's a very respected leader of the MNLF until his wife and son were killed, and he didn't like the leadership of Nur Misuari and that drove him to the Abu Sayyaf. He's an ideologue — that's how I know this guy,' said Mujiv. 'But, Charie,' he said, 'I'm not recommending this. I don't want to be in the middle of this.' That's when I said, '*hay naku* (Good God), the people Ces said agreed it was okay are saying they're not recommending it. Dinampo texts me. He said, 'Charie, they're in safe hands. Don't worry.' It's all here." Charie shows her texts to me and scrolls down.

"Save that," I said.

"I have a lot. Then I called Ces. I said, 'Don't do this.' She said, 'Charie, you're making me nervous.'"

"*Talaga!* (You can say that again!)," interjected Luchi.

Charie finished her message to Ces: "'You know, it's instinct. I'm not comfortable with this so don't do it,' I said."

At that point, Luchi's messenger, Ed Acerada, comes in. Luchi had recently discovered that peppermint tea relaxed her, and she asked him to buy it before she came to my office. When we realized what she got, we all ordered peppermint tea. Some tension dissipated as we laughed, gave orders and looked for cash to give Ed. It was nice to think peppermint tea could relieve our stress. For a while, it seemed like any normal day, but it only lasted a few minutes. Charie picked up where she left off. "We argued, and she put the phone down on me. Then I called Maria. I said, 'Maria, I'm not going to allow Ces.' She said, 'Okay. Okay.' We were in agreement."

"But she was already where?" asked Marites.

"She was already in Jolo," I answered.

"I told her not to go to the interview, but she put the phone down on me!" said Charie. "I reminded her of her four kids, and I even told her what you told me, Maria, that we'd be offering them a plate of *hors d'oeuvres!*" Luchi and I overlapped at the same time.

"*Oo nga, e!* (That's true!)," said Luchi laughing.

"Precisely," I interrupted.

Charie kept recounting Ces' words: "She said, 'Oh, what Maria said — that was eight years ago. The people are different now! They're all dead. They're all dead — the people Maria's talking about. This guy is respectable. This guy is an ideologue …'" Luchi and I couldn't stop ourselves.

"He's not an ideologue!" I said emphatically.

"Yes! My God, she's so naïve," said Luchi. "To think he's an ideologue!"

"So after Charie and I spoke Saturday, I was relieved we'd just send the camera," I said, picking up the chronology. "By that point, it was a done deal in my mind: Ces would just give the hand-held camera and our team would be safe in Jolo. If we get Radullan Sahiron, Ces goes live from Jolo. So I called up Glenda just to make sure we all agreed, and I woke up Glenda."

"No, I was watching something," said Glenda.

"Ah, you were. Very good!" I said.

"You were watching XXX?" asked Luchi half nudging Glenda jokingly. XXX is a current affairs show produced by Luchi's team. The running joke is that Glenda only watches her channel, ANC.

Charie interrupted. "Aren't you guys worried?" There was a knock on the door and Ed came in with our cups of peppermint tea.

"Aren't you guys worried now," repeated Charie softly. We responded nearly simultaneously.

"Wait, wait, let's finish it, Charie," I said.

"Who's not worried?!" asked Luchi.

"We have to figure out what to do next," said Marites.

"Let's just do the chronology first," cautioned Glenda.

We spent another 20 minutes fleshing out the events, running down the last 24 hours before Ces' telephone call this morning. Ces was texting Charie until late Saturday evening. One of her texts said: "this opportunity will never come but that is your decision." Then it petered to nothing on Sunday morning. At 1 p.m., Charie said she got worried and texted Ces: "What's happening?" Ces didn't respond. So Charie texted Jimmy and Angel. Neither responded. Charie was scrolling through her cellphone, and it seemed like there was nothing else until early Monday morning. While I was taking notes, I wondered why Charie didn't alert us when she lost contact, but instead of pointing this out, I held back. This wasn't the time to bring this up. We needed to finish the timeline.

"Here," said Charie, going through her text messages. "June 9."

"She said she tried to call you in the middle of the night," I said.

"June 9, 1 a.m. 'Charie, I will get interview by 5 p.m.'— so this means she defied me," said Charie. Glenda was reading over her shoulders.

"So she's advising you — by 8 p.m. tonight, she'd be home," said Glenda.

"This was early this morning," Charie finished. Then I picked up and finished the timeline, starting with Ces' call this morning, telling them what was said and the succeeding calls I made.

By now, our meeting was increasingly punctuated by the ringing of our phones. Glenda and Marites were getting calls from other journalists asking about Ces. Other sources within the police and military were calling us. At one point, Charie picked up a call from Brian Yamsuan, who works for Sec. Ronaldo Puno, the head of the Department of Interior and Local Government, which controls the police. It was only 10 a.m. I took out my outline and told them about our different stakeholders and began giving assignments.

"Okay on the families: we need to tell them in person. We have to go to their houses. After we tell them, please bring them here," I said. "Two reasons: we need to brief them and we need to keep them away from journalists. Charie, you're in charge of Ces' family. Libby, can you handle the families of Jimmy and Angel?" I asked.

"Yes, I'll get help from HR if I need it," said Libby.

"Libby, please come up with the plans we need for the entire organization. I called Gabby and spoke briefly with Charo." Charo Santos-Concio is the former head of entertainment at ABS-CBN. At this point, she had just become the newly appointed president of our network. "How do we communicate this?" I asked Libby. "We should definitely meet with the news group today. Maybe a general assembly in the newsroom this afternoon once we know more. We have to brief our editorial team. Also once you walk out the door be careful what you tell our reporters. We're going to set up a wall between our news group and this crisis team," I continued, ticking my checklist. "Our biggest problem right now are the journalists. We need to ask for an embargo," I continued.

"Why?" asked Luchi.

"We have to give the military and the police enough time to set up roadblocks to prevent the kidnappers from handing them to a larger group. Remember the past kidnappings? So, let's list all the news groups and split them up. Call up the people you know well," I said.

"Do we include the foreign journalists?" asked Marites.

"Yes. Ask for a 12-hour embargo. We'll have a statement we'll release ..." — I counted the hours — "... at 6 a.m. Tuesday. Explain that doing this will help ensure our team's safety."

"What will the statement say?" asked Luchi.

"Uhm, I'll figure that out after this meeting." I responded.

"I'm uncomfortable with this," said Luchi. "Should we be doing this?

"I don't think we have a choice. You mean the embargo?"

"No, why don't we give this to the authorities?"

"We'll work with them, but we have great experience in this room. If we don't take charge, we'd also be responsible if anything happens to them. I don't think I can live with that if I don't feel we did everything we could. Look: Marites, Glenda and I wrote the books people are using as references. We can do this! We might even be able to do it better because we'll have no other agenda but to get them out."

"Yes, we can't wait," said Marites. "If we leave it to government, they'll take forever. We go local."

"Okay. I'll handle ABS then. Can you call the Inquirer?" Luchi asked me. I could sense Luchi wanted to say more but didn't. We didn't have time.

"Yes, I'll call Letty and explain."

"How much can we say?" asked Glenda.

"As little as possible but you can brief off-the-record if you trust them. Wait, only go as far as 'they're missing and we're looking for them.' Don't mention kidnapping yet. Let's stretch this out. The more time we can get to work quietly, the better. Also, please get information. What do people know and where are they getting it from? Who's talking? Let's make the calls then and regroup in about an hour." Everyone stood up to go to their offices. I opened the door and called my assistant and handed her the recorder.

"Gina, please ask Anne to transcribe. Can you get Mario and tell him to come as soon as he can? Oh, you already called him? Great!" Mario Santos is the legal counsel for the news division. He walked in. "Libby, Charie, you guys stay. Let's talk about how we're going to tell the families." We took 15 more minutes to discuss the families. I wanted to do this in the most humane manner possible and send people from our team who knew them personally. I also needed to know about possible legal liabilities so Mario outlined possible dangers.

"Bring them back to ABS-CBN because I want to talk to them," I said. "We need to consult them and make them part of this process. Plus, really, we need to brief them so they're prepared." They stood up to leave. "Good luck," I said. After they left, I made the call to the Inquirer.

"Hi, Letty, this is Maria. I have something I need to tell you off-the-record, and I'm going to ask for your help."

"Okay, Maria. What's this about?"

"Have you heard anything about Ces?"

"No, I haven't, but I haven't checked in yet." I remembered today is a holiday.

"Ces and our team went to Jolo last weekend, and we've lost touch with them. I've asked the military to set up roadblocks to hopefully find them, but it will take some time. Can you please embargo any story about them until we send a release to you?"

"Is this the Abu Sayyaf?" Letty asked.

"Yes, one of my embassy sources said they heard your reporter was also with my team. Is that possible?"

"Did your team pay them anything? Maria, Julie told me the Abu Sayyaf was asking for a cellphone as an 'entrance fee.'"

"No, they didn't ask for anything. Well, I think Ces asked to bring some food for lunch."

"Well, I didn't let Julie go because of that cellphone. Why? Has anything gone wrong? Have they been kidnapped?"

"I can't tell you that now. An embargo would help. It's really about their safety."

There was a slight pause.

"If it's about their safety, okay. I can't hold this for very long."

"I promise you'll have a statement from us you can run by 6 a.m. tomorrow."

"Okay, but I'm going to have Julie start working on a story. If it's about their safety, we'll hold."

"Thank you, Letty." I hung up and looked at the long list of action points. I ticked off what we had done. I sat down at my computer and began to write the statement we would release. I felt light-headed as I punched the speakerphone. "Gina, please ask Bong to come to my office." Bong Osorio is ABS-CBN's head of public relations.

The biggest question I had now is do we admit they were kidnapped publicly? Doing that would bring a rush of other questions. Who kidnapped them? Are they asking for ransom? Are we going to pay? These are questions I would need to be able to answer. I made a note to call friends from CNN and CBS who have dealt with ransom situations. It would also set all the armed groups and factions in Jolo looking for the kidnappers, perhaps even try to ambush them for a share of the ransom.

Since we had taken no concrete actions yet and couldn't answer these key questions and issues, I decided to hedge. Tell the truth that we can tell. I wanted to emphasize the uncertainty of the situation and our concern for the safety of our team. After all, it didn't affect the public because Ces and our team had been specifically targeted because of their interview. My cellphone rang. I looked at the caller number and picked up on the first ring. It was Quidato.

"Winnie, I have a timeline. I'm having it transcribed now."

"Maria, I spoke with General Añonuevo"[2] — the Director of Intelligence of the Philippine National Police and Quidato's superior — "and he's okay with me helping you. I'll be going there in a little while. I'm bringing Wed Iglesia from PACER."

"Remind me again what that is?"

"Police Anti-Crime Emergency Response. He's a negotiator. He's the best that we have. He can brief your people about what will happen next."

"So there'll be negotiations? Yes, of course. Will he negotiate?"

"Normally, no. He'll help the negotiator."

"Will I be the one to negotiate? I don't think I should be the one negotiating. If I do, it will be ABS-CBN, and they'll try to go for as much money as they can. Who negotiates in situations like this?"

"You shouldn't negotiate. You should step back, particularly if you're going to make decisions. Who do you trust? How about the family?"

"Is that right? The family?" Maybe it was only in the movies, but I remembered that the police seemed to keep families away from negotiations because they were expected to become emotional. I remembered this from an FBI briefing many years ago. Maybe western models weren't used here. I made a note to ask him about it later.

"Yes, do you know the family? Can one of them negotiate?"

"I'm bringing them all here. We can check."

"Good. We can brief everyone then. Winnie, reporters are calling. They don't have anything concrete yet, but they're asking questions. I don't want to give anyone anything they can write until we know the barricades are set up. Can you please ask the police not to make any statements? We're not speaking, but someone is. Who have you told?"

"Well we need to coordinate. Let me check. I'm just parking. Will be there soon."

"Okay. See you soon."

When I hung up, Bong, head of PR, stuck his head in.

---

[2] Rolando Añonuevo was the Director of Intelligence for the Philippine National Police.

"Come in," I said.

"Maria, I've been getting calls from reporters," he said before he even sat down.

"It's starting already. It's too soon. What did you tell them?"

"I said I didn't know but I would find out."

"Okay. Bong, we're asking for an embargo. Luchi, Charie, Glenda and Marites are talking to the news groups now and asking them to hold the story till early tomorrow morning. Please check with them and talk to the journalists you know well." Again, I explained why and gave him a briefing. I outlined the potential problems I saw and said he'd have to set up a media bureau because this may last a while, and — depending on events — there would need to be a steady flow of statements. I also asked that he set up a team to monitor media reports. I asked him what he thought we should say. He gave some ideas. I was typing as he was talking and incorporated his ideas with mine. This is the final statement:

"Three ABS-CBN journalists, Ces Drilon, Jimmy Encarnacion and Angelo Valderrama, are missing in Sulu. All efforts are underway to find them and bring them home. Until we learn more details, ABS-CBN News requests other media to report on this matter with utmost consideration for the safety of our news team. ABS-CBN is in touch with the families and ask that their privacy be respected."

It wouldn't be released until early Tuesday morning. I hoped that if no one gave concrete information — if there was no one to be quoted — there would be no story until after the checkpoints are up. I knew it was wishful thinking even then.

That was when I saw Quidato walking in the newsroom, and I got up to greet him as Bong left. I called Glenda, and together, we briefed Quidato on what we had done and the chronology we had put together. Doing something so concrete restored my confidence, and it felt good that we were piecing pieces of the puzzle together. Quidato told us about what he thought would happen next and what we would need to prepare for. He also explained what PACER does and why Iglesia is joining us. We agreed.

Charie came running into my office. She was holding her phone in front of her, and it was ringing loudly.

"It's Ces!" she said.

"Don't pick up," I said, thinking quickly. I looked at Quidato, and he nodded. The negotiator can't be anyone identified with ABS-CBN. It can't be me, Charie or Luchi. I looked at Glenda. I spent nearly two years recruiting her, and she had just joined ABS-CBN a few months earlier. She was not a public face for ABS-CBN yet. Charie's phone was still ringing. Then it stopped.

"Why?" asked Charie. My phone started ringing. It was Ces. Good. If I didn't answer the call, she would call Glenda.

"You have your phone?" I asked.

"Yes," said Glenda.

"Glenda, when Ces calls you, can you pick up and talk to her? We need to pull it away from ABS-CBN, and you're the face least identified with ABS right now. Can you do that?"

"Okay." Glenda didn't look happy, but she would be even-tempered and quick on her feet.

"Charie, when the families get here, we need to see whether any of them can possibly negotiate. We need someone who doesn't panic and who can think fast. Someone who's not emotional." Charie's phone began to ring and she ran out to take the call. Later I would find out she was talking to Ces' mom.

***

Although the armed men told her not to tell Jimmy and Angel they had been kidnapped, when Ces returned to the group, she found a chance to whisper the news to Angel. He wasn't surprised because he already suspected it but hearing it now made it real. She told him she wasn't supposed to discuss it, and they weren't supposed to know. Otherwise, the kidnappers threatened to tie up both men. With his heart pounding, Angel moved away from Ces and looked for Jimmy to tell him the bad news.

Ces sat down next to Dinampo and told him what had happened: they had been kidnapped. Part of her wondered about him. After all, he was persistent in bringing them here, and they seemed to treat him differently. Still, it's hard to say whether the special treatment he got was because of his age or because he was part of the group. He didn't seem surprised about their kidnapping, and they began discussing what they can do.

By that time, Angel had already spoken with Jimmy, whose face turned pale when he heard the news. Still, Jimmy continued what he had been doing since the walk began. He was secretly recording video of the walk, the men and the situation, telling his guards he was merely cleaning the camera. It's a dangerous gambit, one many Western cameramen would avoid, but for Jimmy, it was second nature. He had a camera and would document what they were living through.

Angel sat down near Ces, and she slid her notebook to him. Written on it, he read: "*Tatakas tayo sabi ni Prof Dinampo.* (We'll escape said Prof. Dinampo)." Angel looked at Ces and Dinampo and lowered his eyes. He didn't think this would be possible with the number of heavily-armed men who were closely guarding them. The discomfort lasted a few seconds, and then the mood shifted. Several of the men began packing. One of them came with three fatigue army jackets and handed them to Ces, Jimmy and Angel. They put the jackets on and began to walk.

The sun was moving up in the sky, the sweltering heat prompting many to shed layers, including — for the ABS team — the jackets they were given. The group passed through areas where people lived, and Jimmy noticed their guards would talk to people they passed, particularly their elders, whom they greeted respectfully. Angel whispered to Jimmy about the playing children they passed. After a few hours, they walked up a hill with a beautiful mountain stream that was feeding a bamboo open waterpipe system. It's an ingenious setup: open lengths of bamboo catch the spring water and act like pipes directing it to the next bamboo, gravity driving this delivery system. The air seemed cooler. The sound of the water flowing through the bamboo was soothing. The group decided to stop and rest. The armed men knelt and prayed. Jimmy and Angel sat on the side: Jimmy protectively covered his camera. After prayers, some of the men came over.

"So how are you guys?" one asked.

"We're okay. How much longer will we walk?" asked Jimmy.

"Well, you know we're not doing the interview, right? You're now with us."

"Who are you?" asked Angel.

"Lost command." There it was. They were kidnapped by a lost command. Around this time Angel and Jimmy noticed that the Commander and some of his men were talking to Ces on one side. They had given her back her cellphone.

"Radullan doesn't know we're doing this — that we're kidnapping you," said the Commander. Some of the men around him seconded him and started telling Ces that their Commander doesn't follow orders. "We're asking for ₱20 million ransom."

"That's too much. You have to make it lower," Ces recoiled back.

"It was originally supposed to be ₱50 million," said the man with an amputated right arm. By that point, because he seemed like the informal leader and was actually leading the group during the hikes, the ABS team nicknamed him Commander Putol, literally translating to Commander Broken. "Our Commander already agreed to bring it down to ₱20 million. That's as low as we go."

In the jungles of Sulu, June 2008.

Ces tried to bargain more until she felt the mood shift slightly. She noticed that some of the men were making fun of the Commander, and she realized that he was a decoy. The real leader of the group is Commander Putol, but he was using a decoy.

"Stop bargaining. Make the call and just follow what the Commander told you," said Commander Putol. Ces picked up the phone and dialed Charie's number. No answer. Then she tried my cellphone. No answer. Finally, she called Glenda.

\*\*\*

Glenda's phone began to ring. "It's Ces," she said as she took the call. I got up and came from behind my desk to the circular table where Glenda was sitting. Quidato moved his chair closer. My heart was pounding fast. "Ces, how are you?" asked Glenda. I brought my notebook. "No, wait, calm down, Ces. They're asking for ₱20 million." I wrote ₱20 million. Glenda took my pen and wrote: what do I say? I wrote: stall. I looked at Quidato. He nodded.

"Okay, I don't know." Long pauses punctuated the call. Glenda's voice was calm. "Wait. I'll have to tell Maria. I can't tell you that." I wrote: ask who's holding her. "Do you know who kidnapped you?" After a short pause, Glenda wrote: Amil's command. It meant nothing to me. I showed it to Quidato, and he shrugged his shoulders. Of course, it could just be a pseudonym. It gave us absolutely no leads.

I looked at my watch. A little after 11:30 a.m. — just about four hours after Ces called me, and it felt like I had run a marathon. I didn't want to think about worse things that could happen. For a second, I was deathly afraid because I still didn't have answers to basic questions. Was Luchi right? Were we in over our heads? The minute I thought that, I pushed it aside. I felt confident because it seemed my whole career prepared me for this. I know the feeling of being in a life and death situation — half scared, half excited. To make the right choices, you need to get clarity, which allows you to think and respond faster. You get that by draining emotions. It's an incredible state of being — the reason, I think, people get addicted to working in war zones. (Somehow though I realized it's easier when it's your safety you risk — harder when it's others). I leaned on those lessons from the past. I also knew what made Luchi uncomfortable. We crossed a line. We were no longer journalists, and the past few hours made that clear to me. We weren't sitting back watching and writing about what people were doing. We were acting — shaping events, but we needed to do that in order to get our people home.

What do we say? If we say yes now, we're assured of their safety. At least that's my assessment. After all, the bottom line is money. The rest are logistical details: choosing the right negotiator with a private army and local law enforcement to make sure they get from the jungle to civilization. My instinct is to agree, but the context pulled me back. It would put a permanent bulls-eye on all journalists in Jolo in the future, although this isn't the first time journalists had been kidnapped. Both major networks had dealt with this before. Still, I felt we had to publicly stick to a no-ransom policy. I understood even better why ABS-CBN couldn't lead negotiations.

That phone call turned out to be a pivotal moment when ransom was set. Ces was panicking, pressured by her kidnappers to deliver ₱20 million. Even having her do the negotiations was a stroke of brilliance because it meant we had no other voice to trace and identify. In the beginning, I hoped we would be able to pinpoint specific people. I remembered the 2000 kidnappings in Basilan when Muslim vigilantes in turn kidnapped the children of the kidnappers. Knowing the kidnappers opened possibilities for action (not that we would do that), but with Ces speaking, we had fewer leads.

There's another reason having Ces speak for the kidnappers worked against us: it's hard to bargain with the victim. When the phone call ended, Glenda's face was ashen. She had written a cellphone number that Ces had given her. Quidato copied it. When she left, I felt drained, but the door had barely closed when Luchi came in.

"They just asked for ₱20 million," I told her.

"What?!"

"Well, we expected a ransom demand. I have to call Gabby. Also, can you look at this statement I gave Bong? I need to know what ABS did in 2000 when Maan and Val were kidnapped. And wasn't there a GMA7 reporter also kidnapped a few years later?"

"Carlo Lorenzo. Both networks paid, Maria," said Luchi. Quidato nodded.

"Is that common knowledge?"

At that point, Charie, with tears in her eyes, barged in. She had just gotten off the phone with Ces' mother and seemed on the verge of crying uncontrollably. Luchi and I tried to comfort her, telling her people are relying on us to be strong. Charie's greatest strength is also her greatest weakness: her emotions. Perhaps I made a mistake in asking her to speak to the family, but she knew them personally, and I thought that would help the family. I didn't consider the manager. I hugged her and told her it would be okay. We'll get through this.

"I'm worried, Maria," she said.

"I know, Charie, we all are. Are you going to pick up the family? Where are her kids?"

"No, they're coming here. Her son is my godson!"

"Are you going to be okay?"

"Yeah, yeah," she answered. I punched the speakerphone. "Gina, please get Marites here." I turned back to Glenda, Charie and Luchi. "Okay, I need updates."

By this time, Libby had gotten an unmarked car, found Jimmy's address and was speaking with his wife, Eva, and daughter, Joy, in their living room. She told them that Jimmy's "provincial deployment had been extended and that communications were limited." She asked them to come with her to the office so they can get the full briefing. That early, Eva said she didn't feel good about this. Libby brought them to her office where her HR supervisor, Lulu Abrillo, stayed with the family while Libby went to Angel's house. Angel's wife, Rushell is a tall, pretty woman with long, black hair. A graduate from a computer college, she worked as a sales manager for a year until she gave birth to their three children. She stopped working to take care of them. Rushell readily agreed to come to the office.

On their way back, Libby called to ask where she should bring the families. I asked for a brief description of the wives, looking to see if any can help negotiate. I wanted to know how they were reacting. During the destruction of East Timor in 1999, I saw how quickly fear spread through the group of journalists staying together in a small hotel. Our team was able to avoid it a little longer because we set up our own house separate from the pack. It cemented in my mind that fear and negative emotions are highly contagious so I thought at this point, until I met them myself, it was better to keep them in separate rooms.

By this time, Ces' family was with Charie in her office. Her mother scolded Charie in the newsroom, prompting her to run in quickly and tell me about it. I asked to speak to Ces' mom and outlined the situation for her, attempting to reassure her that we would do everything we could to get Ces back. Charie looked shell-shocked. Ces' youngest son, 15-year-old Andre, a good-looking boy with wavy hair, arrived, followed shortly by Ces' sister, Grech (a nickname for Grace). Slim and petite, 41- year-old Grace Orena is a successful businesswoman with an air of understated confidence. Everyone called her Grech. The middle child, she seemed happy to take a supporting role around her more flamboyant sisters, Ces and Joyce, a former fashion model. The president and founder of a human resources company, Grech focuses on people — having developed more than 30 workshops and trained more than 16,000 people. Except I would learn this much later, long after I marveled at her literal grace under pressure. Without knowing her background, I watched her demeanor and thought she would make a good negotiator. By that time, Ces had called her family and spoken with her mom and son, Andre. They said Ces was crying and apologizing profusely.

I asked them to have lunch while Quidato and I met with Iglesia, who arrived around 12:30 p.m. and came straight to my office. Police Superintendent Edgar "Wed" Iglesia is the head of Intelligence, Research and Analysis for PACER (the Police Anti-Crime Emergency Response team), the group that handles negotiations in kidnapping cases, known as KFR's or kidnap-for-ransom cases. His nickname is Wed because he was born on Wednesday — or so he tells the story. A graduate of the Philippine Military Academy and a near two decades veteran of the police force, Iglesia has a master's degree in public administration and a studied way of maintaining the confidence of families. However, his daily contact with extreme situations sometimes makes him insensitive. I asked Iglesia about his experience and his thoughts about our situation.

About halfway through, Gabby Lopez came in. I introduced the two officers to our CEO, then walked with Gabby to quickly update him on how events were moving and the brewing plans. When I returned, Iglesia asked if he could brief the families on what would happen in the coming days. I asked our corporate head of HR, Mark Nepomuceno, to sit with them and give an assessment of the briefing next door.

While that was happening, Quidato and I went over the options in front of us — as well as clarifying how we would deal with the government, interagency potential conflicts and the media. By that time, I was starting to get reports about the journalists' source of information. Regional Police Chief Superintendent Joel Goltiao was talking liberally to reporters and speculating our team was kidnapped by Abu Sayyaf leader Albader Parad. That's a loaded statement because a little more than a year earlier, Parad and his men kidnapped seven people, most of whom were workers building a road, and demanded a ₱5 million ransom. When they didn't get it, Parad's men beheaded all of them and delivered their heads to the army camp, leaving the bodies to be found a few days later.

Quidato said it's still unclear exactly who the kidnappers are, but right now, he didn't believe it was Parad. If this Abu Sayyaf leader is verified, we would need a different tactic. I asked Quidato if we could tighten communication leaks. This only showed me the level of disinformation during times like these are extremely high, largely because law enforcement officers who speak do so prematurely and without central coordination. As a reporter looking for information, I loved this lax system. Officials speak for a combination of reason, partly personal, partly professional. Still, once we were the victims and the chances for a safe return were jeopardized by small mistakes like this, it made me wonder why clear lines of crisis communication had not been established as a matter of policy — both to protect the institution and the victims.

Quidato then joined Iglesia's briefing with the families while I met with Libby to prepare for the general assembly in our newsroom with our journalists.

"Where are we, Libby?" I asked.

"I've notified corporate," she replied. "I also made a list of some of the potential questions for your GA" — general assembly — "along with suggested answers."

"Wow, when did you have time to do this?"

"It's very brief, and I'm not sure how you want to answer the questions." I looked at the list and the questions were straightforward — similar to the questions I started asking myself.

"What about the briefing with the families? How's Wed Iglesia?"

"Well, I think he's offending Ces' family."

"Really? Why?"

"You should talk to them, Maria. He's just blunt."

"Okay. Here's what you need to work on next. We're going to have to create a crisis center. We'll need to find a hotel — but not someplace where people will notice us. I want the families to be there with us. Can you talk to them and see how many want to go? Wait, how about the Discovery Suites in Ortigas? We used to stay there with CNN, and they have complete apartments. Plus, it's out of the way. We'll also need to bring security because once the news is out, journalists will swarm the families."

"How many rooms?"

"Not sure, Libby. Maybe at least two floors? We'll need to include the police who'll work with us. We'll need computers, whiteboards. What else? Please think what else we'll need for a crisis center."

"Okay."

"So let's do the GA now, and then I'll talk to the families. Quidato also said their boss, General Añonuevo, is coming here to talk to us and the families." At that point, Luchi walked in.

"Okay, Maria, we're ready," said Luchi. My watch said 3:30 p.m. We walked out to an impromptu meeting in the middle of the newsroom. There was a somber mood. I briefed our journalists off-the-record and talked about the lines we would draw between the crisis team and the news group, which would be led by Luchi. I explained the need for the embargo, talking to them about past kidnappings I had seen. I said from this moment on, they are free to report whatever they can verify outside the walls of ABS-CBN. At least two people who worked closely with Ces, Jimmy and Angel had tears in their eyes. I took questions for about 20 minutes, then signaled for Luchi to take over. They were moving into crunch time for our primetime newscast.

When I walked into my office, Libby had already assembled the families. Glenda and Charie also joined us. I asked them how they were doing, and some started to cry. I started talking — telling them about the situation, what I knew of past kidnappings, what we had done and what we are planning to do. I assured them we would do everything we could to get the people they love back safely. Sensing their helplessness, the enormity of the situation hit me again. I asked them how their briefing with the police went. I told them it would be best if one of the family members negotiated. I asked if anyone wanted to volunteer. No one did. I asked the group if they would agree to have Ces' sister, Grech, be the negotiator. Although she looked surprised, Grech didn't say no, and the other families agreed.

Finally, I talked about how I wanted us to all be together as we lived through the crisis. I told them I wanted them to see what we were doing so they understand and are part of the decisions we make. All of them agreed to move to Discovery Suites tonight. I also warned them about controlling their emotions, mentioning that panic and fear would only cloud our collective judgment. I told them that we would choose a local negotiator by this evening and said one of us — either Charie or myself — would go to Jolo to decide on that critical factor. I realized how difficult it is to ask someone else to go to Jolo under these circumstances. Libby would be a good choice, but she wouldn't know the landscape well. The same would go for anyone in corporate, and if anything were to happen to that envoy, I would be responsible. While I was speaking, I made the call that it would be easier to do it myself and said so. In my head, I started preparing what I would need to do — to balance security with efficiency. I would ask Quidato to go with me.

I answered all their questions candidly, and the ones I couldn't answer, Quidato and Iglesia, who joined the meeting shortly before it ended, answered. After about half an hour, my assistant, Gina, knocked on the door to say General Añonuevo had arrived. It was a little after 5 p.m. The Intelligence Group Director of the national police is tall and bespectacled with a quiet authority of a man who knows a lot but doesn't need to brandish it. It was the first time I met him, and I liked him. Unlike most officials, he didn't move with an entourage. He walked in and started speaking to us in my office, reassuring the families that the police would work with them and with ABS-CBN. I looked around the room. They were listening, but I could see fear in their eyes. Quidato gestured to me and said Añonuevo would like to speak with me privately. When the briefing was done, Iglesia and Libby stayed with the families to answer questions. I walked with Quidato and Añonuevo to the adjacent office, ushered everyone out, and closed the door.

This was the time we took stock of where we are and what we would need to do. Añonuevo gave me a message from his superiors that they would support our initiatives. He said they wanted to meet with me. I said of course and we set the date. He also asked if we could officially make the Philippine

National Police the lead agency. To me, this was an issue of trust. The research and the work I did in writing about Jemaah Islamiyah showed me the police had better intelligence and stock knowledge about groups like the MILF and the Abu Sayyaf. They also handled kidnappings. The military, on the other hand, had deep experience in Jolo with its armed groups and partnership with the U.S. Special Forces. Inter-agency rivalry meant the military had more up-to-date knowledge about the Abu Sayyaf than the police. Still, I made the call and agreed. The police would take the lead.

Charie stuck her head in the door and said Ces' family wanted to speak with me. We ended the meeting, shook hands, and Quidato said he would walk General Añonuevo to the parking lot. When I walked into the newsroom, the studio lights were on, and the room was humming with energy. I stopped for a second and looked around, trying to absorb some of its energy. Everything had a different sheen today. Again, I said a silent prayer before I opened the door to my office. Grech and Libby were sitting at the small, round conference table.

"How are you, Grech?" I asked.

"I'm okay," she answered. "Maria, are you sure I can do the negotiations?"

"I don't know that much about you, but watching you with the families, I can see they already look to you for guidance. Also, you won't be alone. We'll have a police negotiator with us — you met Wed, right? Plus we'll all be sitting with you. You seem the best for this now, particularly since Ces is talking for the kidnappers."

"I spoke to my brother, and he'll be coming. I think he'll do a better job."

"Is he as calm as you?"

"Calmer. He's a lawyer."

"Okay, why don't we talk about that? When can he join us?"

"He's getting ready to come."

"And Maria, we want you to stay with the family. Can you please send someone else to Jolo? We think it would be best if you stay here with the group."

"But Charie can stay with you."

"We'd prefer you stay with us. So we know what to do."

"Okay, besides it may be hard to run our response from Jolo. Let me talk to Charie because one of us will have to make sure we get a negotiator we can trust on the ground. Grech, why don't you and Frank join our meeting tonight with General Sabban later? I'll also ask Winnie to join us." Glenda poked her head in the door, and I asked her to come in and tell Grech about Sabban. I looked at my watch. It was nearly 6 p.m. "Gosh, we'll have to leave in a short while because we're meeting him in Makati."

It turned out that Grech and her partner, Richard Eldridge, live in Fort Bonifacio, near the financial capital, Makati. They wanted to go home and make sure her mom was okay. The address was in Armed Forces housing and reminded me their father was an army general. We decided in order to save time, it was easiest to ask General Sabban to meet all of us there since he is coming from the military camp nearby. When Grech stood up to leave, we hugged each other. Glenda went to her office to finish pending tasks. Then I turned to Libby to iron out the final details for the move to Discovery. We went over the list of the ABS team and support staff, the families, the police and security. We'd block off two floors. We talked about other systems she would put in place and the role of other HR staff she'd ask for help. When Libby left, Luchi walked in and we discussed editorial issues and possible problems she could have. Luchi seemed nervous, but she said she felt better and would keep the fort. Glenda and Charie came to the office to pick me up.

During the 45-minute car ride, we updated each other on information we had gathered. Glenda gave a background and analysis of what the military had been doing. Charie talked about how other journalists reacted to our request — nearly all agreed but there was an interesting split between the foreign wire services: Reuters respected the embargo while the Associated Press did not. The headline of its piece released later that evening was "Suspected al-Qaeda-linked militants abduct three-person TV team in Philippines." It quoted Police Chief Superintendent Joel Goltiao saying that "armed men identified as being under Parad's command intercepted them as their vehicle passed through Kulasi village." Goltiao also said they "wanted to send feelers to negotiate with the abductors, but the abductors have not yet said anything." It's strange when you're in the middle of the news because you know exactly what's true and what's false, and you discern motives. Goltiao had not spoken to any of us. If he had, we would've asked him to be more circumspect, but public attention is important to many officers, even if the information may be harmful. It made me wonder how often situations like this happen. Soon after it was published, a former CNN colleague, Bob Dietz, now the Asia Head of the Committee to Protect Journalists called to offer his support in a statement.

We arrived at Grech's house at 7 p.m., but General Sabban was already there. He was in army fatigues and stood up when we came in. For some reason, his black, heavy boots caught my eye. They just seemed so solid. The Marine Commander in Jolo, he holds a masters degree in National Security Studies from the U.S. Naval Warfare College and has been awarded numerous medals. He works closely with the U.S. special forces and is incredibly media savvy. I asked him if he could give us an overview of armed groups in Jolo.

He said he ordered his men to set up barricades earlier in the day after our phone call then proceeded to brief us on what they discovered. Sabban said he believed our team was kidnapped by Albader Parad, one of the most vicious of the Abu Sayyaf commanders. That echoed what Goltiao had been telling journalists and hearing it from Sabban rattled me. I talked about the history of Parad and his last kidnap-for-ransom case, which ended in the beheading of all seven people kidnapped. I could see Grech, Frank, Glenda and Charie were affected. I asked Sabban for advice. At one point, Sabban and Quidato were talking about the forces they could muster. It was interesting for me to watch because I could see two men from sometimes rival organizations moving events through the strength of their personalities and a common motivation — to help us, the people they know. They began to break down walls fostered by rivalry and bureaucracy. For example, Sabban asked for support and technical equipment available to the police and Quidato said he would talk to the right people to get it to him. They offered ideal and pragmatic solutions.

When I asked him to recommend a negotiator, he thought of three people we discussed but quickly settled on one: Sulu vice governor Lady Ann Sahidulla. She's a flamboyant, quirky character able to move freely through all sectors of Jolo's male-dominated environment. At one point, she sang with a band and wrote songs. Still, the clincher for me is personal: Albader Parad is her cousin. In addition, she held an official title, second-in-command to Govenor Tan, and Sabban trusted her. He gave us her cellphone number, and I handed it to Charie and asked her to set up a meeting as soon as possible.

When General Sabban left, we kept building scenarios. Grech and Frank were getting their clothes ready and making arrangements for their younger sister, Joyce, to stay with their mom. I studied Ces' brother, Frank Orena. A lawyer by training, he had a quiet, calm demeanor. He asked for our plans, and I explained. I made the decision on a hunch as much as necessity: Frank would be our main negotiator. Near the end of our conversation, I got a text update from Libby. We were supposed to meet everyone at Discovery Suites in about an hour.

Then Grech's phone began to ring.

It was Ces.

***

# Roots

3

It's unclear exactly when he was born. His black hair is graying, and his goatee has flecks of gray. He lost his right arm fighting government troops in the 1970's when he was still part of the Moro National Liberation Front (MNLF), once the Philippines' largest Muslim separatist group until it signed a peace agreement with the government in 1996. His medium-build and athletic, wiry frame seem to belong to a younger man, part of the reason some people say he looks like he's in his forties. Most likely, he's older than 60. At 5'4" and 117 pounds, Radullan Sahiron was Khadaffy Janjalani's deputy[1] and is the most influential leader of the Abu Sayyaf today. He carries up to a US$1 million reward for his capture from the U.S. Rewards for Justice Program.[2]

Authorities have had little success getting him because he has a wide support base and a large family. Like al-Qaeda and Jemaah Islamiyah, the Abu Sayyaf is held together by ties that bind: an impenetrable network of family and friends, reinforced by intermarriages. Its founder and first *Emir*, Abdurajak Janjalani, had two brothers who joined the Abu Sayyaf, which began as a splinter group of the Moro National Liberation Front (MNLF). Sahiron was one of Janjalani's key allies and among the group's first members, part of the 14-man *majilis shura* or consultative council.

---

[1] According to documents recovered by the Philippine military on January 16, 2007, the Abu Sayyaf's key leaders meeting as its Majlis Shura or Consultative Council signed an agreement on April 4, 2006 on how to deal with kidnapping projects and its "war gains." The signatories were: Khadaffy Abubakar Janjalani (Emir), Raddulan Sahiron (Naib Emir), Dr. Abu Jumdail, Isnilon Hapilon, Hajan Sawad-Jaan, Jul-Asbi Jalmani, Tutuh Sahirin and Jainel Antel Sali (Abu Solaiman).
[2] Details from classified presentation, *Radullan Sahiron: Target Intelligence Package*, Joint Special Operations Task Force-Philippines High Value Target (JSOTF-P HVI), April 22, 2011.

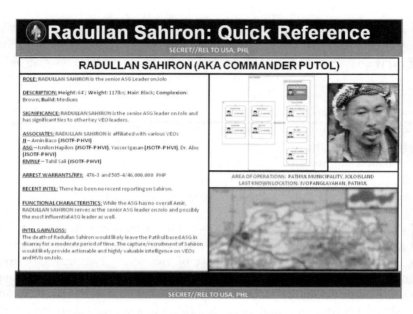

Classified document: Sahiron Quick Reference Card.

Sahiron's roots in the MNLF form the foundation of his network. Until today, his cousin, Tahil Sali, is a top commander of the MNLF. Another cousin, Mameng Biyaw, was a former MNLF member — the man referred to by Ces' contact, Dinampo, as the group's "safe conduct pass." Dinampo himself is a former MNLF commander. The negotiator Sahiron's men would later ask for is also a former MNLF commander. This shared history creates the trust necessary for transactions to work in a part of the world where institutions largely don't exist. Informal networks are necessary to get anything done.

Politician Mujiv Hataman says Sahiron joined the Abu Sayyaf after his wife and child were killed because of his differences with MNLF leader Nur Misuari. He is, according to Hataman, an ideologue. Perhaps it's all relative. Sahiron is one of the few Abu Sayyaf leaders who speaks Arabic and is known for his rational decision-making, which could turn calculatingly deadly. Sahiron was close to Janjalani and a power consolidator. When Janjalani's camp in Basilan was overrun by the military in 1993, he fled to Sahiron in Jolo. It was there in Sahiron's camp that the Abu Sayyaf held what members called a general assembly and officially named the group al-Harakatul al-Islamiyah.[3]

---

[3] R. Banlaoi, *Al-Harakatul Al-Islamiyyah: Essays on the Abu Sayyaf Group*. (Quezon City: Philippine Institute for Political Violence & Terrorism Research, 2008) p. 11.

By all accounts, Janjalani was an ideologue, an ustadz — Muslim scholar — as well as a warrior. The first 100 or so men he pulled together, including Sahiron, had similar training and ideas, but they operated in a landscape of poverty, corruption and crime — where the gun establishes order. So it was always a difficult balancing act, particularly after the group was infiltrated by government agents with their own agendas. Soon after Janjalani's death in a police shootout in 1998, the Abu Sayyaf lost its ideological moorings and degenerated into criminal kidnap-for-ransom gangs led by Aldam Tilao, its flamboyant spokesman more commonly known as Abu Sabaya, and Ghalib Andang aka Commander Robot.[4] Less than two years after Janjalani's death, they began a kidnapping spree that pushed Filipino officials to dismiss the group as bandits.

In March, 2000, the Basilan group, led by Abdurajak's younger brother, Khadaffy, kidnapped 55 people, mostly young students and teachers as well as a priest. Soon after, it made one of its first political demands: in exchange for the hostages, it asked the United States to release three terrorists held in U.S. prisons, including Egyptian Sheikh Omar Abdul Rahman, the blind cleric, and an Abu Sayyaf trainer and the bomber behind the 1993 World Trade Center attack, Ramzi Yousef. The United States and the Philippines ignored the demand.

A month later, the Jolo group, including Sahiron, hit international headlines by kidnapping 21 tourists, including Westerners, Malaysians and Filipinos, from a dive resort on the Malaysian island of Sipadan.[5] U.S. intelligence and the United Nations (UN) say Sahiron planned the kidnapping although negotiations were conducted by Commander Robot. The Abu Sayyaf demanded US$1 million ransom for each Westerner. Libya, which wanted to refurbish its international image, put together a fund of up to US$25 million. The government's chief negotiator, Roberto Aventajado, said US$10 million went into the Abu Sayyaf's pockets.[6] After that kidnapping, Sahiron held other hostages given to him for safe-keeping by other kidnappers in addition to kidnapping for ransom again. By

---

[4] Z. Abuza, *Balik-Terrorism: The Return of the Abu Sayyaf* (Carlisle: Strategic Studies Institute, U.S. Army War College, 2005), p. 13.

[5] UN Security Council listing, *Radulan Sahiron*, The Al-Qaeda Sanctions Committee. Available at http://www.un.org/sc/committees/1267/NSQI20805E.shtml

[6] Maria A. Ressa, *Seeds of Terror: An Eyewitness Account of Al-Qaeda's Newest Center of Operations in Southeast Asia* (New York: Free Press, 2003), pp. 112–115.

December, 2003, the UN estimates Sahiron received another $635,000 in ransom payments.[7]

Described as "a commanding presence among his men,"[8] Sahiron also provided sanctuary and worked with members of Jemaah Islamiyah (JI), al-Qaeda's arm in Southeast Asia. Funded and trained by al-Qaeda, JI is an Indonesian transnational group which carried out Southeast Asia's largest and deadliest terrorist attacks, including near-simultaneous attacks in Indonesia and the Philippines in 2000 and the Bali bombings in 2002. Since 2005, the ASG and JI were working so closely together in Jolo, Sulu that intelligence sources from three different countries considered them one group.[9] This was corroborated by JI member Rohmat, captured in the Philippines in 2005. He said, "I'm JI, but I was told to work with ASG, and we were all together. So my life is now ASG."[10] At some point, JI leaders Dulmatin and Umar Patek, both involved in the Bali bombings, gave commands directly to Abu Sayyaf members.[11]

Four senior Abu Sayyaf leaders operated on Jolo island in 2008: Sahiron, Ahmad Jumdail Gumbahali, better known as Doc Abu, Isnilon Hapilon and Yassir Igasan. Sahiron is largely acknowledged as the nominal leader, informally giving directions to all the groups in Jolo and Basilan.

On May 23, 2008, a few weeks before Ces arrived in Jolo, JI leaders Umar Patek from Indonesia, Muawiyah from Singapore, and Marwan from Malaysia[12] were training Abu Sayyaf members in the same area where Ces and our team would be kidnapped on June 8 — in Indanan, Jolo.[13] Back then, that was Sahiron's primary area of operations, and he commanded the island's largest armed group of about 50 men.[14] Less than a month later, Sahiron, along with other Abu Sayyaf leaders in Jolo met with JI leader and financier

---

[7] UN Security Council listing, op.cit.

[8] Classified JSOTF-P HVI presentation, April 22, 2011.

[9] Author interviews with intelligence sources from the Philippines, Indonesia and the United States, June 2005.

[10] Quoted in M. Ressa, "Infiltrating the MILF," *Newsbreak*, 28 October 2002, available at http:www.inq7/newsbrk/2002/oct/28/nbk_1–1.htm.

[11] Author interview with military intelligence, Manila, Philippines, March 4, 2011.

[12] Muawiyah and Marwan are each known by one name. Marwan is an alias for Zulkifli bin Hir, the head of Malaysia's Kumpulan Mujahidin Malaysia as well as a member of Jemaah Islamiyah.

[13] Classified Philippine Intelligence document: *Summary of Information — Umar Patek*, May 13, 2011, p. 9.

[14] U.S. classified presentation: *Radullan Sahiron: Target Intelligence Package*, Joint Special Operations Task Force-Philippines High Value Target (JSOTF-P HVI), April 22, 2011.

Umar Patek[15] to discuss "casing operations and execute the kidnapping plans targeting foreigners in an undisclosed beach in Palawan."[16] The plans never materialized, but it showed the activities and intent of the group.

The man Ces believed was the leader of their kidnappers is Sulaiman Pattah, who, because he also only has one arm, carries the same alias as Sahiron (and was coincidentally given the same nickname by the ABS-CBN team) — Commander Putol. Pattah works for Sahiron, and although he told Ces the kidnapping was his own initiative, others in his group claimed the planning and ransom demands went all the way to the top. Sahiron is considered a folk hero in Jolo and Basilan partly because he shares the ransom — giving him the reputation of a "Robin Hood". His best known picture shows him riding his white horse with a rifle slung over his left shoulder and a pistol in his right hand. He can also be ruthless, according to military reports — accused of beheading soldiers and suspected double agents within his ranks. On July 16, 2005, Sahiron married the former wife of Abdurajak Janjalani.[17] Observers say it was partly a way to protect her, a recognition of his strength as a warrior, and a sign of respect for the former leader.

"People respected Janjalani," says Mohammed, one of the founding members of the Abu Sayyaf. Mohammed is not his real name, which he asked to withhold for security reasons. A long-time Janjalani family friend, Mohammed helped set up the Abu Sayyaf's first base camp in Basilan. Shortly after he was captured, he wrote an appeal to his arresting officer because of the threats to his life. It shows us the personalistic nature of law enforcement and the incredible levels of distrust, even inside security forces. He wrote: "It cannot be denied that several individuals or groups want to kill me ... I am therefore begging you not to turn me over to other police or military units nor transfer me to any other place of detention."[18]

Shortly after his arrest, Mohammed gave his captors a history of the Abu Sayyaf, hand-written in a precise penmanship with a razor-sharp, black pen. According to Rohan Gunaratna, author of *Inside al-Qaeda* and the head of the International Center for Political Violence & Terrorism Research, he has

---

[15] Umar Patek was one of the field leaders and makers of the bombs used in the 2000 church bombings in Indonesia and the Bali 2002 blasts which killed more than 200 people.

[16] Classified Philippine Intelligence document: *Summary of Information — Umar Patek*, May 13, 2011, p. 9.

[17] Op cit.

[18] Undated, handwritten letter to arresting officer obtained from Philippine intelligence, December, 2002.

turned out to be the most important member of the Abu Sayyaf to be captured by authorities. Mohammed is one of the group's most learned recruits, a Muslim cleric and teacher who says he joined for ideological reasons. He had his differences with the group in later years, part of the reason, perhaps, that he is now a government informant under the witness protection program.

I knew he existed as early as 2002, when I was able to get a copy of his 32-page handwritten document, one of the few sources that talked about the origins of the group and gave a detailed breakdown and description of its members at that time. It took a few years before I could get to his handlers and develop the trust needed to actually meet him in person. Soft-spoken and humble, Mohammed speaks like he writes — using deliberate and precise sentences. We met in the second-floor of a restaurant at Fort Bonifacio, the old military camp turned into a commercial district in the country's capital. It was a sleepy Sunday. The sun was setting, and we were the only ones in the room. I noticed he sat with his back against the wall so he could see people walking into the room. It was hard to believe this quiet, unassuming man had intimate knowledge about the Abu Sayyaf's members and was, at times, part of its violent atrocities.

"Before the creation of the group, I was already with Abdurajak because I was very close to the Janjalani family," said Mohammed.[19] Calling him "Jack," he spoke about the group's charismatic founder. "He was only a high school student when he was sent to Saudi Arabia to pursue his Arabic studies." Janjalani graduated in 1981 then went to study Islamic jurisprudence at Ummi I-Qura in Mecca for three years.[20] In 1984, he returned to Basilan and Zamboanga to preach. "He became very popular among the people, especially the youth," said Mohammed. Janjalani then travelled to Libya for a master's degree in *da'wah* or Islamic proselytization in 1987. During that time, the MNLF asked him to head its *da'wah* movement. Two years later, he returned home and vowed to wage "*jihad qital*"[21] — armed struggle — merging *Salafi Wahhabism* with a drive to create an independent Muslim state in the southern Philippines.

"The MNLF was supported by the ulamas, the Muslim scholars, but then Misuari changed his direction and agreed to drop the demand for

---

[19] Author interview with Abu Sayyaf founder, Manila, Philippines, January 30, 2011.

[20] G. Gloria, "Bearer of the Sword: The Abu Sayyaf Has Nebulous Beginnings and Incoherent Aims," *Mindanao Updates*, June 6, 2000.

[21] Abuza, *Balik-Terrorism*, p. 2.

independence," said Mohammed, explaining why Janjalani lost faith in the MNLF leader and decided to form a new group. At that point, the secular, ethno-nationalist MNLF — which at its peak fielded about 30,000 fighters[22] — was starting to break into factions: with Hashim Salamat, the leader of the Moro Islamic Liberation Front (MILF) demanding a state fully governed by the Koran and Islamic sharia law. However, Mohammed said the MILF was perceived as soft then. "People will NOT support you if you are an MILF member because it was seen as a government organization — controversial issue during that time. We see the MNLF as a group that's already lost its way, and the MILF, although it shouts Islamic jihad, was sitting on the sidelines. It wasn't carrying out any offensives. So he was inspired to form a group, but Janjalani had difficulties convincing the ulamas to join him so he tried to ask the graduates of Darul Imam." He looked to see if I recognized the name. I nodded. "We were the first graduates of Darul Imam Shafi'ie, and Khalifa told him about us. Khalifa wanted us to be in the group. So I joined him."

Mohammed Jamal Khalifa is Osama bin Laden's brother-in-law, who came to the Philippines in 1988, the same year bin Laden formed al-Qaeda, to lay the foundation of a financial network to support a terrorist cell that would plot and, ultimately, carry out some of al-Qaeda's most imaginative and deadliest attacks around the world. Born in 1957 in Medina, Saudi Arabia, Khalifa said he and his best friend and roommate, Osama bin Laden, served together in the jihad against the Soviets in Afghanistan. Authorities around the world say Khalifa's work with al-Qaeda dates back to the beginning, a claim he denied until his death in 2007. Khalifa was behind at least two major Islamic charities which funded al-Qaeda and other Islamic terrorist groups: the Benevolence International Foundation (BIF) and the International Islamic Relief Organization (IIRO). BIF is banned worldwide by the United Nations Security Council Committee 1267,[23] which compiles a list of terrorist financiers which also includes IIRO in the Philippines and Indonesia.

In 1988, Khalifa created a web of numerous charities and non-governmental organizations[24] which funneled money to the Abu Sayyaf and

---

[22] "Moro National Liberation Front," *FAS Intelligence Resource Program.* Available at http://www.fas.org/irp/world/para/mnlf.htm.

[23] Previously known as the al-Qaeda and Taliban Sanctions Committee.

[24] Some of the other charities and non-governmental groups set up by Khalifa which were linked to al-Qaeda and/or terrorist financing: International Relief and Information Center (IRIC),

the MILF as well as laying the seeds for future recruits by creating Islamic centers which proselytized an exclusionary and violent vision for Islam. Khalifa started Benevolence International Corporation, an import-export company which later moved its offices to the United States and funded other terrorist groups around the world as the Benevolence International Foundation. By late 1994, its head was a known al-Qaeda member, who was arrested along with Khalifa in the United States. Although both were later released without any charges filed, the group would be designated for terrorist financing by the U.S. Treasury Department before being banned by the UN.

Khalifa also set up and became the chairman of IIRO in the Philippines, which — among other things — financed the creation of Darul Imam Shafi'ie (DIS), an Islamic center and school, which provided ideologically-driven recruits for the Abu Sayyaf and the MILF. Mohammed was one of his best students. Abdurajak Janjalani, Abu Sayyaf's founder, graduated two batches — or classes — later.

"Our education in Darul Imam influenced us a lot," said Mohammed. "I felt it was my obligation to take part in jihad after Darul Imam. Jihad means fighting to regain our lost homeland and living under a pure Islamic state. We were told that it is our obligation to establish *sharia* law and that we are sinners unless we do that. So we thought during that time that people who do not join us are all sinners and enemies. Janjalani was telling us God does not need numbers. He needs the pure in heart, and as long as we are sincere, God will help us."

Creating feeder schools and training centers to prepare potential recruits for its network is a successful al-Qaeda tactic, replicated for the networks of Abu Sayyaf, the MILF and JI. As Khalifa was doing this in the Philippines, JI founders Abdullah Sungkar and Abu Bakar Ba'asyir were doing the same thing in Indonesia, setting up feeder schools that would churn out future terrorists. Khalifa tested the waters in the Philippines. In May, 1989, he recruited "Muslim youths and ustadzes" in Basilan, Jolo, North and South Cotabato, Maguindanao and Tawi-Tawi and sent them to al-Makdum University in Pitogo, Zamboanga del Sur for a one-month commando

---

Islamic Wisdom Worldwide Mission (IWWM), Markazzo Shabab al-Islamiyah (MSI), the Muslim World League, the Darul Hijra Foundations, the Islamic World Committee Foundation (IWCF), Khalifa Trading Industries, International Islamic Efforts Foundation (IIEF), Darul Ehsan Foundation, Darul Imam Shafi'ie Foundation, Islamic Dawah Guidance Counci, Darul Hijra Foundation, Islamic Studies, Call and Guidance (ISCAG) and the Islamic Students Association of the Philippines (ISAP).

training.[25] After that, he used existing networks of the MNLF, MILF and the Abu Sayyaf as well as his charity and religious programs to identify recruits across ethnic lines for the 18-month course at Darul Imam. He told Mohammed key parts of his vision to unite Filipino Muslim groups and break ethnic boundaries.

"Khalifa was trying to convince Janjalani that his jihad should be patterned after the Muslim Brotherhood."

"Did he convince him?" I asked. Mohammed paused before he answered.

"It was very hard to convince Janjalani. He had his own ideas. To him, what the Brotherhood did in Egypt will be too long a process. It will take years — 10 years, 20 years — to build an Islamic community. Janjalani is very well-informed about the Muslim Brotherhood. He wanted something now. For him, it was necessary to purchase firearms and fight the government. He was very aggressive." Mohammed talked about the strain this difference created between Khalifa and Janjalani and pinpointed the crucial moments that gave the Abu Sayyaf its schizophrenic split between ideology and crime. Khalifa, who made funding contingent on his vision, wanted to indoctrinate Filipino muslim recruits — to make sure they were ideologically driven like Mohammed, but Janjalani was impatient.

"Khalifa was willing to lose millions provided that Janjalani will comply with his requirements. And when I asked him what requirement, he told me the Abu Sayyaf's members should be identified and trained — educated the way we were educated because we do not want anybody who has firearms not knowing whom they will kill or why. Or what they're going to do with the firearms." Mohammed grimaced. "This was the greatest mistake that I have observed with the Abu Sayyaf."

"When did that start to happen?"

"It started in the later part of 1992. There were negotiations, and Khalifa was being asked to donate millions of money, and he donated. Not only Khalifa but also some of our contacts, the Arab brothers who were with Khalifa, also sent money." According to Khadaffy, Janjalani's youngest brother, Khalifa gave the Abu Sayyaf US$122,000 or about ₱6 million.[26] In exchange,

---

[25] Classified Philippine intelligence document, "*Person Report: Mohammed Jamal Khalifa*," 1995.

[26] O. Dinampo, "Khadaffy Janjalani's Last Interview," *Philippine Daily Inquirer*, January 22, 2007. Also in "The Evolution of Terrorist Financing in the Philippines," presentation given by PCSupt Rodolfo Mendoza, Jr. to financing terrorism workshop in Manila, Philippines, 2008.

the Abu Sayyaf sent men to train and fight in Afghanistan. However, Mohammed pointed out the bulk of Filipinos, about 600 men,[27] who were sent to the Afghan training camps came from the MILF. Their experiences in Afghanistan laid the groundwork and created personal relationships among jihadists in Southeast Asia which made setting up training camps in the southern Philippines much easier later.

Khalifa provided the seed money for Abu Sayyaf to recruit and organize about 100 men, most of them former members of the MNLF and graduates of Darul Imam Shafi'ie. Mohammed said during that time, those who joined the Abu Sayyaf were "the defenders of the oppressed" — an image he was proud of. He talked about the people who came to Janjalani for help because they distrusted the military and the police. He spoke longingly of those days, and I could feel a deep sense of regret.

"The Abu Sayyaf would come to help those people, and they were very happy with what we did," he said. "This was the image that we had during that time before the coming of Edwin Angeles." A former MNLF member, Angeles came from Jolo and played a crucial role during pivotal transitions of the group. He was also a military double agent, commonly referred to as a "deep penetration agent." Angeles, according to Mohammed, also diluted the group by recruiting drug addicts. "Everything was ruined because of Edwin. Janjalani was convinced to engage in kidnapping — more so because Khalifa had a misunderstanding with him so funding was very difficult during that time. Khalifa stopped sending support, and I think Khalifa was trying to unite the MILF, the ASG and the MNLF because the students of Darul Imam were from different organizations."

It's unclear exactly how the group was named "Abu Sayyaf." It was Janjalani's *nom de guerre*, the alias he chose. From most accounts, it seems the Philippine military baptized the group. Janjalani's brother, Khadaffy, said Abdurajak took the name of a legendary Afghan mujahideen, Abdul Rasul Sayyaf — the founder of the Afghan Islamic movement. His camp would become a crucible of terror for most of the Southeast Asian Muslims who took what they learned back home. What Khadaffy remembered though was that Sayyaf "became famous for his practice of beheading traitors to the

---

[27] Classified Philippine intelligence documents, *The Islamic Fundamentalist/Extremist Movements in the Philippines and Their Links with International Terrorist Organizations*, a PNP-IC Special Investigation Group (SIG) report released December 15, 1994. Although the report claims 600 Filipinos went to the Afghan war, anecdotal evidence seems put the actual number lower.

Taliban — whether Muslim or Christian."[28] When the Abu Sayyaf discovered spies in their midst they beheaded them. "The marines called us the Abu Sayyaf Group, perhaps referring to us as 'the group of beheaders,'" said Khadaffy. The irony, of course, is that Angeles was so good as a double agent that he not only evaded discovery, he rose to become the second-in-command and the Abu Sayyaf's operations chief.

In the summer of 1991, key figures who would soon arrive in the Philippines were in Pakistan. All were linked to Sayyaf. Future World Trade Center bomber Ramzi Yousef attended Sayyaf's school. His uncle, Khalid Shaikh Mohammed, who would bring down the towers of the World Trade Center 10 years later, was Sayyaf's secretary. Wali Khan Amin Shah, who fought with bin Laden in Afghanistan, was working for the charity International Islamic Relief Organization (IIRO), the same group Khalifa set up in the Philippines. Khalifa himself was also in Peshawar, reporting progress after he had been ordered by bin Laden to help Janjalani create an Islamic state in the southern Philippines.

Khalifa took a two-pronged approach in creating his schools and indoctrination centers, much like Sayyaf and the Afghan training camps: a focus on religious study combined with intensive military training. By December, 1991, Khalifa was back in the Philippines, followed shortly by Ramzi Yousef, who came to the Abu Sayyaf camp in Basilan at bin Laden's request. Yousef introduced himself to Angeles, Janjalani's deputy, as an "emissary from bin Laden."[29] He trained about 20 Abu Sayyaf members in bomb-making and was known as "the Chemist." In January, 1992, Yousef was joined by Wali Khan Amin Shah, who taught demolition and tactics at Darul Imam for "30 Muslim youths from different tribes: Tausug, Marana-Sangil, Maguindanao, Yakan" along with Christians who converted to Islam.[30] The program included weapons training as well as boarding and hijacking airplanes. At some point though, Yousef became frustrated and complained to his high school friend that the Abu Sayyaf's "members only know about their assault rifles and nothing more. He called them illiterates."[31]

---

[28] Ibid.

[29] Classified Philippine intelligence document: "Interrogation reports of Edwin Angeles, former Abu Sayyaf founder turned double agent." Undated transcript. Also quoted in Abuza, "Balik-Terrorism," p. 3.

[30] Classified Philippine intelligence document: "Interrogation report," Abu Sayyaf operations officer, p. 2.

[31] Classified Philippine intelligence document, "Debriefing Report No. 2," February 13, 1995.

He decided he would set the bombs himself and claim credit for the Abu Sayyaf, still matching Khalifa's goal: to make the Abu Sayyaf "gain notoriety and popularity" and for "Abdurajak Janjalani to be recognized as an emerging leader of the newly born Islamic fundamentalist movement in the Philippines."[32]

"The idea there was for al-Qaeda to build up the reputation of the Abu Sayyaf," said Rafael Alunan, III, who worked closely with his Pakistani and U.S. counterparts when he was the interior secretary in charge of local governments and the national police in the mid-90's. He said there was no doubt the group was working with al-Qaeda, which had sent numerous operatives to the Philippines at that time. "Even if they were the ones involved, they give credit to Abu Sayyaf and, hopefully, enable the Abu Sayyaf to gain more adherents."[33] Under Alunan, the Philippine police documented the rise of radical Islamic fundamentalism in a classified report released in 1994.[34] The findings were alarming, charting a dramatic rise in the number of mosques, charities and groups linked to what the Philippine National Police (PNP) report called the Osama bin Laden organization.[35] That was accompanied by an increase in terrorist acts of nearly 150% in three years from 1991 to 1994.

Mohammed said the group began its attacks in 1991, with most attacks directed at churches, missionaries and non-Muslim communities. Other members talked about one particular meeting between Yousef and the executive committee of the Abu Sayyaf. It was the "17th day of Ramadan in 1993," and the group agreed on a plot presented by Janjalani and Yousef to assassinate Pope John Paul II during his visit to the Philippines.[36] "The ASG will

---

[32] Classified U.S. report shared with the Philippines, *Mohammed Jamal Khalifa*, December, 1994, p. 2.

[33] Author interview with former DILG Secretary Rafael Alunan III, Manila, Philippines, August 12, 2005.

[34] Classified Philippine intelligence documents, *The Islamic Fundamentalist/Extremist Movements in the Philippines and Their Links with International Terrorist Organizations*, a PNP-IC Special Investigation Group (SIG) report released December 15, 1994.

[35] Osama bin Laden and Muslim cleric Abdullah Azzam established a "Bureau of Services" (Mekhtab al Khidmat or MAK) which channeled recruits into Afghanistan, men known as the Afghan Arabs. After the Soviets pulled out in April, 1988, bin Laden and Azzam agreed to turn it into a base or foundation (al-Qaeda) for future jihad. Bin Laden sent Khalifa to the Philippines shortly after.

[36] Security presentation by Col. Rodolfo Mendoza, Jr., "The Evolution of Terrorist Financing in the Philippines," International Center for Political Violence and Terrorism Research, 2010.

be the prime planner and supporter," states one interrogation report, "Yousef will be the co-planner but because of his experience in making human bombs, the ASG decided to let him lead."[37] The suicide bombers will be "one Filipino, one Jordanian and one Palestinian." Neither the Abu Sayyaf nor Yousef will state publicly they were involved. Instead, it will be the work of "all Muslim fundamentalists under the Islamic movement" — Al Harakat al-Islamiyyah. So Khalifa was working on a build-up of local, home-grown groups and simultaneously financing foreign operatives.

1993 was also the year Mohammed said he met a fourth, key member of this terrorist cell. He was among a group of Abu Sayyaf members who travelled to MILF's Camp Abubakar for training. "It was Khalifa who facilitated everything," he said. "He was the only person who could unite the Muslim organizations." The training was led by two Arabs introduced to him as Abu Haidar and Abu Khalid. Years later while he was in custody, FBI agents showed him video of their training at Camp Abubakar, the MILF's main headquarters. "We were not aware that there were videos," said Mohammed. "I was told that this video was taken from the camera of Wali Khan. I told him, 'I did not meet Wali Khan. I only met Abu Haidar.' Then he showed me a picture. That's when I learned that Abu Haider and Wali Khan is the same man." Abu Khalid was more of a surprise. After looking at more pictures, he realized that their trainer was Khalid Shaikh Mohammed, known as KSM in intelligence circles — the man who conceived and carried out the 9/11 attacks which he proudly admitted in a clandestine interview in 2002.[38]

In 1993, KSM and his nephew, Ramzi Yousef, tried — but failed — to bring down the World Trade Center. Yousef was an expert and an innovator; the bomb he set off then ripped a 200-by-100 foot crater into the building's foundation and had been used only once before in 73,000 explosions recorded by the FBI.[39] A year later in Manila, with the help of KSM, Yousef would develop and test both liquid bomb explosives and the shoe-bomb[40] — basics later taught in al-Qaeda training camps and plots which would later

---

[37] Author interviews with former Abu Sayyaf member and Philippine intelligence official, who gave notes from a 1995 interrogation of another Abu Sayyaf member.

[38] Y. Fouda, 'We Left Out Nuclear Targets, For Now,' *The Guardian*, March 4, 2003. For a fuller treatment of Shalid Shaikh Mohammed's activities, see M. Ressa, *Seeds of Terror: An Eyewitness Account of Al-Qaeda's Newest Center of Operations in Southeast Asia*.

[39] S. Reeve. *The New Jackals: Ramzi Yousef, Osama Bin Laden and the Future of Terrorism* (London: Andre Deutsch, 1999), p. 75.

[40] M. Ressa, *Seeds of Terror: An Eyewitness Account of Al-Qaeda's Newest Center of Operations in Southeast Asia*, p. 28–29.

resurface. Al-Qaeda was a learning organization, and from 1993 until his arrest in 2003, KSM kept track of lessons learned and revisited old plots in an attempt to perfect them.

KSM's terror cell had many more plots aside from what it shared with the Abu Sayyaf. Aside from targeting Pope John Paul II, it also planned to assassinate U.S. President Bill Clinton on his trip to the Philippines. There were attacks planned on nuclear facilities in the United States as well as attacks in France, Britain and Sweden. More interesting though were its plans to use airplanes for terrorist attacks.

The fifth member of the Manila cell is Yousef's high school classmate whom he introduced to KSM in 1993, Abdul Hakim Murad, perhaps the first commercial pilot recruited by al-Qaeda. Murad trained as a commercial pilot in four schools in the United States as well as in Dubai and at the Air Continental Flying School in Manila. He said he recommended "the World Trade Center to be the best target for bombing" and helped Yousef's 1993 attack by doing "structural studies"[41] of the buildings. Murad also said KSM was obsessed with airplanes for terror plots, like using a crop-duster plane to assassinate the Pope. The cell ruled this out after police announced there would be a no-fly zone in Manila during the Pope's visit. A second plot involved a light plane loaded with explosives, which they would ram into the CIA headquarters in Langley, Virginia. The third, though, is the best known: Operation Bojinka, using small, lethal bombs from liquid explosives developed by Yousef to blow up 11 airplanes headed to the United States from Asia. It was supposed to be 48 hours of timed, near-simultaneous explosions that would've killed more people than the 9/11 attacks. "It was meant for Hollywood," said Alunan. "It was a best-seller thriller. The assassination of the Pope was more or less scheduled for the middle of January and Bojinka would be unleashed about a week later."

By the end of 1994, Yousef and his co-conspirators had tested his liquid bomb three times. The first was in a mall in Cebu when Yousef successfully detonated a small contact-lens bomb. The second was in Greenbelt Theater in the financial capital, Makati. U.S. court documents later revealed the bomb was planted under a theater seat by Wali Khan. I was having dinner in a nearby restaurant and heard the explosion. By the time I got to the theater, the police had cordoned off the area. The impact seemed small: no casualties but there were several injured.

---

[41] Classified Philippine intelligence document, "Significant Revelations of Murad: Tactical Interrogation Report," February 20, 1995.

The third and final test was set for 10 days later. Yousef boarded a Philippine Airlines flight to Cebu. He successfully evaded airport security and carried with him liquid explosives hidden in a contact lens bottle. Mid-air, he put the bomb together and planted it inside the life jacket under his seat. Then he got off the plane in Cebu. Two hours later, with the plane on the way to Japan, the bomb exploded, tearing a hole in the plane and killing one Japanese passenger. The plane made an emergency landing in Okinawa. The test run was a success, each of the three tests bringing larger explosions. With a little more tinkering, Yousef planned to cause a blast large enough to destroy a commercial jet and kill all the passengers onboard.

Aside from testing the explosives, they also had to test airport security to make sure they could bring the explosives onboard the planes. KSM and Yousef did these tests themselves on a flight from Manila to Seoul, South Korea. They took "concentrated nitromethane, which is readily available in the Philippines and poured out the contents of 14 contact lens solution bottles"[42] and carefully refilled them with the liquid explosive. Yousef stabilized it using cotton wool. KSM carried 13 bottles while Yousef carried one. KSM also worked out how to clear airport security with a detonator. For the PAL flight, Yousef hid the metallic components of the bomb in the hollowed-out heels of his shoes, which fall below the area the x-ray examined. KSM finetuned it further. He taped a steel bolt to the arch of his foot and put a sock over it — lucky because airport security asked him to take off his shoes. He carefully placed his foot down when he was walking so the bolt would make no sound while the agent scanned his shoes with a metal detector. He made it through security.

They were ready for Bojinka. Like the Philippine Airlines test run, their operatives would board flights with liquid explosives and set bombs to explode after they got off the plane. However, the FBI was closing in on the co-conspirators for the World Trade Center bombing in 1993. As the case moved toward trial, KSM and Khalifa would both be named as unindicted co-conspirators supporting the terrorist cell. Neither name, though, was ever disclosed publicly then.

In December, 1994, Khalifa left the Philippines to escape growing suspicions about his involvement with the Abu Sayyaf. Shortly after, the U.S. revoked his visa, and he was arrested in San Francisco as he was preparing to return to the Philippines. His travelling companion was a senior al-Qaeda

---

[42] Classified U.S. intelligence documents, "Revelations of Khalid Shaikh Mohammed," April 2003.

operative who had tried to purchase uranium for al-Qaeda a year earlier, according to court testimony. Khalifa's luggage contained a treasure trove of information, including terrorist training manuals, addresses and phone books listing al-Qaeda's leaders, including bin Laden himself. The FBI also found the address of the apartment building in Manila where Wali Khan lived (and where Khalifa called him several times). Yousef was building bombs in a different apartment a few floors up. Three weeks after Khalifa's arrest, the Philippine police raided Yousef's apartment. Authorities said a freak apartment fire helped uncover the Manila cell and its plots, but the FBI forwarded its Khalifa intelligence to its Filipino counterparts two days before the raid.[43]

Murad was arrested by the police and interrogated for three months before he was turned over to the FBI. Ramzi Yousef escaped the dragnet in the Philippines but authorities caught him a few months later at a bin Laden guesthouse in Pakistan. Wali Khan was arrested in the Philippines, but he escaped from police custody. 11 months later, he was captured in Malaysia. Both men were rendered to the United States. All three would be tried and convicted in a U.S. court in 1996. The FBI and CIA closed its case. Filipino authorities heaved a sigh of relief. Both countries called it a great victory against terrorism, but they celebrated too quickly.

There was one plot so fantastic no one paid attention, not law enforcement and intelligence agencies, and not journalists like me. Murad told his Filipino interrogators about a suicide mission involving planes: "he will board any American commercial aircraft pretending to be an ordinary passenger ... there will be no bomb or any explosive that he will use in its execution. It is simply a [suicide] mission that he is very much willing to execute." Among the targets named: the World Trade Center and the Pentagon. Authorities in the Philippines called it the blueprint for 9/11.[44]

Two men would escape the dragnet in 1995 and build the terror networks of Jemaah Islamiyah and al-Qaeda. The first is Indonesian Riduan bin Isamuddin, better known as Hambali, the man who became JI's operations chief and would later mastermind Southeast Asia's deadliest terrorist

---

[43] J. M. Berger, "Mohammed Jamal Khalifa: Life and Death Secrets," *IntelWire.com*, January 31, 2007.

[44] Author interviews with Concepcion Clamor, National Intelligence Coordinating Agency, Rodolfo Mendoza, Jr., Philippine National Police, Rafael Alunan, III, former DILG Secretary, General Avelino Razon, former chief of national police. These officials, along with others, called this plot the blueprint for 9/11.

attacks, including Bali in 2002. An Afghan war veteran, Hambali became the lynchpin holding JI and al-Qaeda together, a senior member of both groups. In 1995, he helped Khalifa funnel money for the Philippine plots. He also helped Wali Khan escape from his Philippine prison and gave him shelter in Malaysia.

The second is KSM, who would take the lessons learned from the Philippines and build on them. That's largely why every single major al-Qaeda attack between 1993 and 9/11 had some connection to the Philippines. In 1998, KSM took lessons from the World Trade Center truck bomb, fine-tuned it and successfully set off two truck bombs in U.S. embassies in East Africa, killing 224 people. One of those involved, Mohammed Sadiq Odeh, allegedly planned part of that plot while he was in Davao in the southern Philippines. KSM went scuba diving in Puerto Galera near the capital, Manila. Authorities said he and Yousef seemed to be plotting an underwater attack, which al-Qaeda developed and carried out in 2000, bombing the USS Cole in Yemen, killing 17 sailors and nearly sinking the US$1 billion American warship. KSM passed on lessons he learned avoiding airport security at the Manila airport to another operative who worked for him — Richard Reid, the shoebomber, who tried to bring down an American Airlines flight in 2001. He successfully evaded airport security, but the attack failed because he couldn't light the bomb. In 2006, Bojinka resurfaced in London, which triggered a worldwide alert for liquid bombs intended to cause mid-air explosions in airplanes. And, of course, there was September 11, attacks which finally brought down the World Trade Center six years after the first commercial pilot recruited by KSM told Philippine police about his plot to hijack planes and crash them into buildings.

\*\*\*

All of this was unknown to Abu Sayyaf members like Mohammed, who realized he was trained by KSM only after the 9/11 attacks. By this time, it was dark outside, and others had walked into the restaurant. I could see he was aware of each person who entered, looking them over carefully while speaking. He continued to tell his story in an understated manner — his nearly monotone rhythm providing a sharp contrast to the events he was describing. Shortly after that 1993 training, he decided to leave the Abu Sayyaf because he felt kidnapping-for-ransom was contaminating the group's ideological mission. However, you can't just decide to leave the Abu Sayyaf. Like the mafia, once you're in, it can be dangerous trying to get out.

"You cannot say I am turning my back against the group because as long as you are still in the place, you will be killed," he said matter-of-factly. "You will be called *mortad* — turning your back against the organization." He never completely escaped. He told Janjalani he would "marry a local woman," left the camp and worked in the city for Khalifa's IIRO. After a few months, he asked Khalifa for seed money to start a bakery. However, the Abu Sayyaf seemed to be extorting money from him — although he didn't call it that, instead saying the group "asks him for money and support." He said he couldn't turn them down because it was a way to protect his business. At some point, he became a public school teacher and when he was captured, he had been a government employee for at least five years. In 1995, he was already working for the Department of Education — teaching and running a high school in Basilan. He said he had no choice but to continue to help the Abu Sayyaf to protect the teachers in his school. "Otherwise, they will be kidnapped," he said. "I have to protect them."

Soon after the discovery of the Bojinka plot in Manila, the Abu Sayyaf began to mobilize and recruit for a large-scale attack. Mohammed said the plan began in early 1995 to attack what he thought was a military detachment in Ipil, a town which sits at a crucial junction of the two provinces of the Zamboanga peninsula — Zamboanga del Norte and Zamboanga del Sur. Most of its 70,000 residents are Catholic. The organizers told him to buy his own uniform and weapon and then join them. He made his excuses and was shocked later to hear what happened on April 4, 1995. It was gruesome.

At about 10:00 in the morning, about 100 men arrived with Abdurajak Janjalani on Mangrub Island. They went to Ipil onboard a three-engine boat and arrived at Ipil "at exactly 12 noon."[45] They joined another group that arrived by land. They "positioned themselves in the bank, police and military installations and the market." They waited for the signal: a single shot from Abdurajak Janjalani. From the shoreline, they went to the center of town onboard tricycles. Once they got there, they commandeered an army truck.

---

[45] Account of events by Yacob Basug alias Sumayya, one of the Abu Sayyaf members recruited by Janjalani. Memorandum from the Commander of Task-Force Sanglahi, "1st Dev Report on the Arrest of Yacob Basug @Sumayya, December 5, 2003.

They demolished the city center, where buildings and stores were looted, burned and razed to the ground. Armed men were shooting randomly, setting buildings on fire, including the police station, where two corpses still in uniform were left burning. The town police chief had just taken his post that day. He was among the 53 people who died in the rampage.

Eyewitness accounts chronicled indiscriminate killings of men, women and children. An army brigade based in Ipil tried to help the victims. Led by Colonel Robert Santiago, 14 soldiers ran out to try to stop the attack but pulled back when confronted with an overwhelming number of armed men holding hostages in front of them. All told, the marauders took about 30 hostages, many of whom died as the Abu Sayyaf retreated. Alunan, who was in office then, called the violent attack "the opening shot in the war to establish an Islamic state in Mindanao."[46]

Authorities long thought the Ipil attack was in retaliation for the arrests of the Abu Sayyaf's Arab backers in Manila. It turns out, according to Mohammed, to be part of a master plan that included exploiting religious and ethnic fissures to foment chaos, a formula that would later be used in plots in Singapore and Indonesia.

"It's an order from the higher up — from the Arab brothers," explained Mohammed, "so that the Abu Sayyaf would be known internationally. They needed to do something big. Kidnapping was not very sellable outside, but attacking a Christian community would result in Muslim-Christian conflict. So it was the project of Janjalani to create religious strife."

"It's the same thing JI did in Ambon and Poso," I said, remembering nearly 10,000 people killed in Muslim-Christian wars from 1999 till 2000.[47] In the midst of reporting it, I wondered why the conflict flared among religions and communities that had peacefully co-existed for decades. Only much later, while tracking the growth of JI's network, did I realize that JI and its associate groups fomented and inflamed religious conflict to gain more recruits. "They fuelled Muslim-Christian violence."

"Yes, because Janjalani was expecting that after the Ipil raid Christians would take revenge and attack Muslim villages, but the ulamas during that time were very strong. The Christian priests and the ulamas were united because they knew that if this would happen, Janjalani will be successful in creating

---

[46] ABS-CBN television interview with then DILG Secretary Rafael Alunan, III, April, 1995.
[47] CNN death toll count maintained by the Jakarta bureau, which I headed.

religious strife in Mindanao, and it will become a religious war." Mohammed stopped short of condemning his group's actions in Ipil, particularly after the leaders told him they could do it again. "They were very happy after the incident," he said. "They told me it's better to do a similar attack rather than fight with government soldiers in the jungle. I told them, 'Why? What's the advantage?' 'Many things, material benefits and big impact outside. So they were very optimistic that they can do a similar attack in the future."

"Are you glad you decided not to go?"

"It's not what I wanted to do. I want to do what we have been told about the Afghan war, military operations like the NPA, ambush of the military. That's okay, but not attacking civilians." This idea seems to be a driving force for Mohammed, part of the reason, he said, he returned to the Abu Sayyaf to take care of a long-standing problem. I was taken aback when he confessed he led the assassination team that targeted Edwin Angeles, Janjalani's deputy, less than a month after the founder's death. Mohammed was afraid Angeles would gain control of the Abu Sayyaf.

"Ma'am, the group was on the wrong path with kidnappings, extortions and bombings, but things got worse, particularly when Wahab Akbar became governor. The Abu Sayyaf abused and harmed people. The government oppressed its own people, and Edwin Angeles came back to Basilan. I was a teacher at that time, and I didn't feel safe. I had to do something about Edwin." Mohammed's energy increased when he described how Angeles was preparing to organize an urban death squad much like the New People's Army's ABB, the Alex Boncayao Brigade. Mohammed put together a three-man assassination team to target Angeles. Then he contacted the military, who turned out to be family — an example of the intricate interconnections and the complexity of Basilan. Mohammed spoke with the brother of his brother-in-law, who's a scout ranger in the military. He told Mohammed some members of the military had tried to kill Angeles but failed. This situation shows how good and evil lose meaning in the heartland of the Abu Sayyaf: a soldier plotting to have a government double agent killed by an on-again, off-again member of the Abu Sayyaf.

It was January 14, 1999. Angeles' wife was waiting for him at an open-air market in Isabela, the capital of Basilan, near the mosque where Angeles decided to pray.

"Actually, I talked to him before he went in to pray," said Mohammed. "I shook hands with him."

"What did you do then?"

"He had to be killed. Look, Abu Sayyaf already wronged the people of Basilan, and with this brigade he's creating — most of whom are drug addicts — he had to be killed. Edwin Angeles did so many things that demoralized the organization, and Janjalani listened to him because he needed the money."[48]

After Mohammed shook hands with Angeles, he left and walked to his house, which was only a few meters away. When he turned around, he — along with Angeles' wife — watched as Angeles stepped out of the mosque and walked towards the market where his wife was waiting. Two men working with Mohammed began to follow him and, with 0.45 caliber automatics, pumped six bullets into him at point-blank range. He absorbed the bullets, stumbled towards his wife and died in her arms.

\*\*\*

The death of Angeles didn't stop the kidnappings. For nearly a year, no clear leader took control. By 2000, Abu Sayyaf went on its wildest kidnapping sprees and captured international attention. The three largest cases showed a progressive learning curve and a voracious appetite for ransom. On March 20, the Basilan group, led by Khadaffy Janjalani, kidnapped more than 50 teachers and students in Basilan. About a month later, that was overshadowed by the Jolo group's kidnapping of 21 Western and Asian tourists from the Malaysian resort of Sipadan. The succeeding hostage negotiations marked the peak of Abu Sayyaf's power: for five months, it dictated terms to the Philippine government and held the foreigners and their European governments hostage. After a US$10 million ransom was paid through Libya,[49] the Abu Sayyaf literally became Robin Hoods — contributing more to their local economies than any government program. That swelled its ranks from about 600 members to more than 1,000 and allowed it to buy more advanced weapons and speedboats. On the day the last

---

[48] It's widely known that it was Angeles who pushed Janjalani to kidnap for ransom and carry out extortion operations. Since he was also a government operator, was he told to do this in an effort to discredit the Abu Sayyaf? It's not completely farfetched. If so, it's another case of blowback.

[49] Author interview with Philippine government hostage negotiator, former Secretary Robert Aventajado, Manila, Philippines, June 20, 2005.

Sipadan foreigners were freed, Khadaffy and his men, including the volatile Abu Sabaya, announced Abu Sayyaf had kidnapped American Jeffrey Schilling and demanded a US$10 million ransom. Mohammed said this was another turning point for him: he argued with several leaders, led by Abu Sabaya, against kidnapping Schilling.

"I told them Schilling shouldn't be kidnapped because he's Muslim," said Mohammed. "Sabaya was convincing me — 'No, he is a CIA.' I told him, 'why?' 'He's a very knowledgeable person. He knew about Kosovo. He knew about Serbia. He knew about Afghanistan, Palestine. He must be CIA.' I told him, 'No, anybody can be knowledgeable because of the Internet.'" According to Mohammed, Schilling met the widow of an Abu Sayyaf member online and came to the Philippines to marry her. Schilling said he was invited to join the Abu Sayyaf, which promptly kidnapped him soon after he walked into their camp. The U.S. government refused to negotiate for ransom, and Abu Sabaya was sorely disappointed when little happened for months, and Schilling escaped. For Mohammed, the disagreement opened a fundamental rift. He also disagreed with Abu Sabaya's moves to keep about 130 armed men together without using its size for a military attack. He proposed they break the group down into smaller, more mobile groups of 12 men or so. Abu Sabaya rejected his idea, and Mohammed left the group again.

On May 27, 2001, Khadaffy took one of the new speedboats they purchased with ransom money from the Sipadan kidnappings. His group travelled about 30 miles across the Sulu Sea to the Dos Palmas resort on the island of Palawan. There, they kidnapped 20 people, including three Americans. Khadaffy handed them to Abu Sabaya, who less than a month later, announced he beheaded one of the Americans. Taunting authorities in a chilling telephone interview, Abu Sabaya told Radio Mindanao Network, "We chopped the head of Guillermo Sobero. They better hurry the rescue. Otherwise, there will be no hostages left."[50]

Abu Sabaya called me and offered a videotape of the beheading to CNN. Horrified, I declined, a decision immediately seconded by my superiors. In the following months, more hostages were beheaded, but most of the others were freed after ransom was paid. By November, 2001, only three hostages remained: Americans Martin and Gracia Burnham, Christian missionaries from Wichita, Kansas, and Filipino nurse Ediborah Yap.

---

[50] "U.S. official: Indications of Rebels Beheading Hostage," *ABC News*, June 12, 2000. Available at http://abcnews.go.com/International/story?id=80949&page=1

Five months after they were captured, Martin Burnham wrote to the government that they had been caught in 16 firefights — or "encounters" with the Philippine military. Copies of his letter were given to journalists. It outlined the dangers of the government's "rescue operations," saying his wife, Gracia, was "emotionally very stressed." "We have learned to 'drop,' 'crawl' and 'run' as bullets whiz past our heads," he wrote. "These encounters are terrifying to us and it is impossible for us to see how they can be called 'rescue operations.' I fear that the next gunfight might make our children orphans." He appealed to the government to negotiate with the Abu Sayyaf and pay ransom.

After nearly a year of exploring options (including offering a Delta Force strike team, which was turned down by the Philippine government),[51] the Bush Administration reversed its long-standing policy against negotiating with terrorists and created new guidelines that allowed ransom payments in certain situations. In May, 2002, the FBI, working with the Philippine police, delivered a ransom of $300,000 to Khadaffy Janjalani, according to U.S. and Philippine officials.[52] Khadaffy, however, refused to give Abu Sabaya, who held the hostages, his share of the money. Abu Sabaya, in turn, refused to release the hostages.[53]

On June 7, 2002, Philippine troops attacked the Abu Sayyaf in a rescue attempt code-named Operation Daybreak. What Martin Burnham feared would happen did: all three hostages were shot during the mission — not by the Abu Sayyaf but by bullets of the soldiers who were trying to rescue them. Only Gracia survived, largely because when he was hit, Martin fell on top of her and pinned her down, helping protect her from stray bullets from the ongoing firefight. After 376 days — one year and 11 days — in captivity, Gracia went home to their three children alone. A few days after she was released, I spoke with her and was surprised at her generosity and grace. "It's unfortunate that Martin died in a gun battle like we thought he would, but that wasn't the fault of the Philippine military. It was the fault of the Abu Sayyaf. They were the bad guys."[54]

About a year after she left the Philippines, Gracia published a book, *In the Presence of My Enemies*. She wrote: "The soldiers were clearly upset, realizing

[51] R. Bonner, "Philippines Terror Group Seeks Money for Couple," *New York Times*, March 9, 2002, p. A10.

[52] Author interviews for CNN, Zamboanga City and Manila, Philippines, April 25, 2002.

[53] M. Lerner, "Hostage's Father Says Abu Sayyaf Broke Deal," *Washington Times*, April 26, 2002, p. A15.

[54] Author interview with Gracia Burnham for CNN, Manila, Philippines, June 10, 2002.

that in their rescue attempt, they had shot all three hostages ... Eventually, the Lieutenant-in-charge came over to talk with me. 'Mrs. Burnham, I know that you're probably very angry with us,' he said. 'But we were just doing our jobs.'" Gracia told him, "I know. We never forgot who the bad guys were and who the good guys were. I don't think of you as the bad guys."

Such clarity isn't always easy in the southern Philippines. Several lessons stayed with me in reporting these hostage situations: first, neither the military nor police have the ability to control the situation. A no-ransom hard-line position only works if it's backed up by strong law enforcement. If the hostages are harmed, the kidnappers should be afraid of repercussions, possible only if there are systems in place. There must be a deterrence factor. It's clear this is not the case in Sulu and Basilan, where men with guns have relative impunity to do what they want — time and time again. More telling for me is that after nearly a year of grappling with the crisis, the U.S. government reversed its long-standing no ransom policy. Even the U.S. caved in to a reality it couldn't change.

Second, avoid military action: a rescue could just as easily become a death warrant.

Third, be careful who you give your money to. It was clear even conduits skim money from the ransom. You have to be certain that whoever you trust gets the money to the kidnappers. Many groups have had to pay twice because they trusted the wrong people.

Fourth, cut out as many middlemen as you can. Go directly as possible to the source because every middleman is a possible leak or spoiler. It's hard to know whom to trust because power is in the hands of the kidnappers. In the end, you have no choice but to rely on honor among thieves.

Finally, paying the ransom doesn't always mean you'll get what you paid for. Given the patchy infrastructure and weak law and order situation, you'll have to make sure you are working with local officials and/or residents who have the power to make sure that after the release, the freed hostages aren't kidnapped again by another group.

As you can see, despite the best-laid plans, the risk remains high that you're throwing the ransom money away. The worst part is when it does work, you'll realize you've just given the kidnappers more experience, more money and more power ... to do it again.

*\*\**

# A Piece of the Action

**4**

The phone rang.

I was trying to prepare different scenarios in my head when Grech's phone rang on Monday, June 9, 2008. I looked outside the window and saw the trees swaying with the wind. The crescent moon was strangely bright. How fitting. It was a little less than twelve hours since I received Ces' phone call telling me she and her team had been kidnapped in Jolo. Now we were in her sister's home, afraid our team was kidnapped by one of the most notorious leaders of the Abu Sayyaf, Albader Parad. This is where terrorism meets crime: Parad is better known as a criminal — a kidnapper whose acts of violence are just simply shocking. By joining the Abu Sayyaf, he gained added credibility, and in turn, signalled the Abu Sayyaf would be further blurring the nexus between terrorism and crime. Grech lifted her cellphone and showed me who was calling. It was Ces.

"Pick up," I said. "It'll be fine." She was standing by the dining room table. I could feel she was nervous but resolved. I pulled out the chair near her and sat down. Glenda sat next to me. Frank took a seat next to Grech. Candy, Frank's wife, had prepared food for us and was walking in and out of the kitchen, but when the conversation started, she also sat down. Although we could only hear one side of the conversation, we were transfixed.

This call seemed to officially mark the bargaining process. Shortly after we finished meeting with General Sabban, we were able to speak quickly with Lady Ann Sahidulla, the vice-governor of Jolo. She recommended payment of about ₱2 million or US$37,735.85.[1] The conversation was quick

---

[1] Using 2008 conversion rate of US$1 to ₱53. By 2011, the conversation rate was fluctuating between ₱42–44, for US$1.

83

because as soon as Grech named that much lower figure to Ces, the call was abruptly cut. It left all of us worried. In my head I was wondering: should we even bargain? Are we risking the lives of our people by doing this? It was an extremely difficult situation: I was in charge of getting them out safely; yet at the same time, I needed to look out for ABS-CBN. What if something goes wrong? Can we afford to pay again? Do we need to set aside more money if we do? What does this mean for the future? I was lost in my thoughts until I looked at the faces of Grech and Frank. Then I realized they needed help to deal with everything that was happening. We would all have to fight our inner demons.

By 10:00 that evening, I was walking into the three-bedroom suite that would become our crisis center. Ever-efficient Libby met me at the door. We walked into the dining area, which had a wooden dining room table for eight people. It opened into a large living room with a deep couch on the wall to the right, two armchairs on either side — all in front of a television set. On the long wall on the right, Libby and Anne, my assistant, had set up whiteboards and canvases with rolling paper. To the left of the living room, adjacent to the dining area is a small kitchen. I looked inside and saw Gina, my secretary, putting food and drinks away. We would need a stocked refrigerator. The open hallway connecting these areas led to the three bedrooms: on the right is the smallest room with two twin beds. I dumped my things there, thinking I would share it with Gin de Mesa, who would take care of our messaging. The room next to it, linked through an interconnecting bathroom, I would give to the police: Iglesia and his team would have this room. Across the hall was the master's bedroom, which I gave to Frank. Libby walked through with me, and we agreed on the room assignments.

She quickly gave me a rundown of events and who was where: the families of Ces, Jimmy and Angel were assigned rooms. We went over the room assignments, making sure those on 24/7 call were assigned to this suite and floor. I realized Bong and his corporate PR team would not be able to quickly identify and flag stories that could impact us immediately so I set up another news team to monitor the media. That's in addition to the news officers who would be handling government, military and police sources. I wanted to see all updates at a glance. Anne and Gina were buzzing around the rooms, taking care of transportation, check-ins, anticipating what we may need in the coming days.

We sat down at the table and called our first meeting. I began outlining each task and identified what each person would be responsible for. The families listened carefully. The immediate concern was to get someone I trusted in Jolo so we could gauge the situation on the ground. I didn't get a chance to speak privately with Charie, and in the meeting when I assigned her to go to Jolo, I realized in retrospect she couldn't have said no in front of so many people. I wanted someone on the ground with money and a direct link to me just in case we could make the deal quickly and directly. I asked Quidato, who had come in a bit later and was on the outer edge of the group around the table, if he could go to Jolo with Charie. While he wasn't prepared, he took the challenge.

Asking him to go was one of the best decisions I made because when things became difficult, Quidato had the confidence to improvise and react to each new development in a calculated manner. More importantly, he balanced the sometimes competing interests of our team with what his bosses wanted. I would be anxious sending Charie alone, but I felt confident when

Inside the Discovery Suites crisis room. From left to right: Mark Nepomuceno, Nestor Cusi, Frank Orena, Wed Iglesia, author (back turned on cellphone), Richard Eldridge (Grech's partner), Glenda Gloria (on cellphone), part of Andre Drilon (behind Gloria), Grech Orena.

Quidato agreed to guide — and guard — her. I told them I wasn't sure how long they would need to stay in Jolo so they should bring clothes. Their primary task: to identify the people we can trust and make sure we take the safest route both for the money and, once our team is released, to get them out of Jolo safely. Glenda called Sabban, and he promised to have soldiers help them on the ground. While we were meeting, staffers prepared flight plans and permits for ABS-CBN's corporate plane. They would leave as soon as they could the next morning.

We updated everyone on the events of the day. We wrote each development on the board so we could see it visually and reiterated our ground rules to the families: they can be part of the entire process and listen to the phone conversations, but they cannot speak directly during these calls. By this point, I was getting information from the telephone company and foreign intelligence agencies. I gave the coordinates to the police tracking team for verification. I asked for a map so I could see where they potentially are. That's when I realized that tracking by cellsites is imprecise. You can track to a general location, but precision is near impossible given the number of cell sites in Jolo.

I also knew that the U.S. had the most sophisticated tracking and surveillance equipment, but asking for their help officially would be futile. It would have to come from the Philippine government, something I was certain wouldn't happen. If they didn't allow the U.S. to help with the Burnhams, why would the Philippines treat our team's case any differently? Also, what would the U.S. stand to gain by risking the progress of their own priorities by getting involved in ours? After our meeting, I called Colonel Bill Coultrop, the head of the U.S. Special Forces and the Joint Special Operations Task Force-Philippines, more commonly known by its initials, JSOTF-P, and asked for his advice. He said they would help us and asked for someone they could work with behind the scenes. I told him about Winnie Quidato — how he had been assigned to us and the decisions we made that day. If this had been done through official channels, he may not have been given these operational details and wouldn't know the precise information we would need. I knew we were circumventing the system and working around the hierarchy, risking the egos of men and nations, but it was more important to get all who have the power to act on the same page. I had no illusions. I knew the U.S. could not — and would not — take action on its own, but they had access to valuable intelligence the Filipinos would not normally have. So if men I knew and trusted (and who knew and trusted me) were to look for what we would need and coordinate with the Filipinos on the ground, then we would've accomplished something all the bilateral treaties would spend months and years arguing about. All of this would have to happen below the official radar screen making me realize the value we journalists can add to this process.

I couldn't help but think of the Burnhams. I had spoken to many of the American soldiers whose unit was flown in precisely to rescue and evacuate them. Months later, during a conference at West Point in New York, they spoke to me candidly about their individual and collective frustration because they were never allowed to act. Imagine, there was a team whose training, equipment and expertise could've saved the lives of Filipino and American hostages. Instead, standing on sovereignty issues, Filipino troops alone began their attack mid-afternoon on June 7. Gracia wrote about her regret: "I've learned just how badly the American military wanted to launch a special operation for us! I've been told how they sat around conference tables in Zamboanga City just itching for the opportunity. They would, of course, have done the job far differently. They would have moved into action at, say, two in the morning instead of two in the afternoon, wearing night vision goggles and all the rest to snatch us to safety."[2]

She pointed to another hostage situation, which happened a few months later: when rebels took over a school for missionary children in the Ivory Coast in West Africa. Authorities there gave the U.S. special forces team permission to launch a rescue and in a few hours, "the students and faculty were roaring down the highway toward safety, waving the Stars and Stripes out of bus windows. But nothing like that happened in our case," Gracia wrote. "The local authority said no, and the Pentagon felt it could not trample upon an ally's national sovereignty."[3]

What I had learned from decades of reporting is that affairs of state, when disconnected from the people on the ground, lead to illogical, testosterone-driven decisions. It's what bureaucracies teach people: if you don't do anything to rock the boat, then there will be no problem. Forget that people may be saved or could die! Nor that the people themselves from those nations would have said yes if they had been asked. I wrote this in 2002 and reread it the day Ces told me our team had been kidnapped: "I wager that if you tell any Filipino on the street today that letting U.S. troops handle the

---

[2] Gracia Burnham with Dean Merrill, *In the Presence of My Enemies* (Wheaton, Ill.: Tyndale House Publisher, 2003), p. 303.
[3] Ibid., p. 304.

rescue mission could have saved the lives of Martin Burnham and Ediborah Yap, he or she would agree that they should have been allowed to try. Filipinos have generous hearts, and the hostages' ordeal has made an impact on the national psyche."[4] This is how I connected it with global terrorism then: "What has become clear is that the further international politics gets from the people affected on the ground, the less effective it has been in dealing with the problem. The diplomacy has been cloaked in so much double-speak that it has become difficult to address the root problems in a linear manner. It starts with the internal rivalries among the individuals involved, aggravated by the politics of the organizations they represent, the institutions they belong to, and the leaders they report to. Self-interest at every level has obscured and twisted every step of the global war on terror, and these are the cracks al-Qaeda continues to exploit."[5]

Egos and vested interests prevent more effective action against common problems. In the coming days, I would live through this first-hand, but these ideas meant nothing to me that evening. All I cared about was harnessing the available resources and people to help me get our people home. I wanted no regrets. So I called sources and friends within the U.S. special forces team: aside from Colonel Coultrop, I called the head of his intelligence team, Major Matt Worsham, along with others much lower on the totem pole who, I felt, would have access to information and live through events we may need to know about. I shared information with them off-the-record. They shared information with me off-the-record, and in our crisis center, we wrote it down in neat lists on our whiteboard.

Glenda was doing the same thing with her trusted sources inside the Philippine military, leaning on relationships of trust she had built in decades of reporting. Plus, we were working directly with the police and had access to the information they had and could help shape the response. This process verified what I had long suspected: often law enforcement gets information AFTER the journalists on the scene. For the first time ever, three vertical silos that operated in the same space but rarely shared operational information openly with each other were doing so now through the journalists the individual sources trusted. Using the vocabulary and techniques of journalists, we were able to cut horizontally through their processes and link them all together. We built trust into a process normally filled with distrust through our professional relationships. In our crisis center on our

---

[4] M. Ressa, Seeds of Terror, p. 123.
[5] Ibid.

whiteboard and on my yellow pad, we listed what each source told us and began to piece the whole picture together.

***

The more I spoke with Mohammed, the more I realized how intertwined his life was with the history of the Abu Sayyaf. He linked together many groups, largely because he would come and go whenever he wanted. He is what social network theory would call a "boundary spanner." He was one of Khalifa's favourite students, interested in understanding how Muslim movements around the world operated and gained strength. At the same time, he was a trusted friend of Abu Sayyaf's leaders. He tried to always find a better way because he believed in revolution, not crime. When he got disillusioned, he tried to leave several times, but he was always pulled back by the needs of his friends. Because he carried out attacks, he knew where the money came from and could help define the money trail, crucial to keeping any rebellion or movement afloat. It turns out Mohammed also played a role in connecting the Abu Sayyaf, the MILF and Jemaah Islamiyah and was actually part of the group's first joint attack. You can see the role of social networks in the spread of terrorism clearly looking through the life of Mohammed.

Let's pick up the thread of the Abu Sayyaf's development where we left off — soon after the spate of kidnappings in 2000. While the foreign hostages were being released from August to September, 2000, a 24-year-old American walked into the Abu Sayyaf camp because he wanted to join them. Jeffrey Schilling converted to Islam in 1996 and was fascinated with the Islamic revolution. He met his wife, Filipina Ivy Osani, online. She had been married to a member of the Abu Sayyaf. Her cousin, Aldam Tilao, is better known as the Abu Sayyaf's flamboyant spokesman, Abu Sabaya — who had been negotiating publicly with the Philippine government for the release of the hostages. Schilling said Abu Sabaya invited him to join their group, and he did on August 28, 2000.[6] His presence sparked a debate: Schilling was an American, part of the group's enemy. Why shouldn't they kidnap him and demand ransom?

Mohammed was at the camp when Schilling arrived and argued against another kidnapping. He lost the debate, and soon after, Abu Sabaya demanded a ransom of US$10 million for Schilling. Mohammed said he

---

[6] D. Lamb, "Philippines, Libya Doubt U.S. Hostage's Credibility," *Los Angeles Times,* September 23, 2000.

tried to protect Schilling, but he had other complaints about the way they were operating. They were a large group of 130 people, yet Abu Sabaya was not staging any attacks that could justify keeping that large a group together. Aside from giving radio interviews, Mohammed pointed out, Abu Sabaya wasn't doing much of anything else.

"Abu Sabaya talked on the radio, but he kept on running," said Mohammed. "We were 130 people, and I am *emir* of one group. I have 12 with me. So why don't I bring Schilling with me, and we can hide without being traced?" The group turned his proposal down. For Mohammed, it was the last straw but again he had to find a way to leave gracefully. He asked Khadaffy if he could bring his wife and child to safety in Zamboanga City. Once he got there, he planned to never return, but it was hard to cut his roots, particularly because he needed a job. He contacted bin Laden's brother-in-law and his mentor, Mohammed Jamal Khalifa.

"I admitted I was wrong," said Mohammed. "I asked Khalifa if I could go back and reorganize the graduates of Darul Islam in order to propagate the religion without using arms." Khalifa sent him to another Arab, who paid him a monthly stipend to write propaganda. That was what he was doing when he got a call from the Abu Sayyaf member in charge of finance, Borhan Mundus, nine months later. It was June 1, 2001, and the military had surrounded Khadaffy and his men in a hospital and church compound in Lamitan, Basilan along with their 20 hostages. It was a few days after they kidnapped hostages from the Dos Palmas resort in Palawan. Martin Burnham and Guillermo Sobero were still alive. It was the only time in three years that the military had the Abu Sayyaf's top leadership completely surrounded. Khadaffy called for help — asking Borhan Mundus to find Mohammed, whom he wanted to create "diversions" to pull military forces away from Basilan.

"It hurts when you hear that some of your comrades are being cordoned off and they need help," said Mohammed, who admitted he felt guilty about leaving Khadaffy's group. "So Khadaffy contacted Borhan looking for me and asked me to do something. The Arab people also contacted Borhan. That was the time we moved to central Mindanao."

This was a pivotal moment that, ultimately, began the transformation that would bring the Abu Sayyaf back to its ideological roots because it would bring it together not just with the MILF but also with Jemaah Islamiyah.

At the center is 33-year-old Borhan Mundus, who also attended Darul Imam Shafi'ie in the class following Mohammed's. After he finished, he went to work for Khalifa's IIRO in Zamboanga City. The 5'4", 136-pound balding man of medium build has a thin face and trustworthy eyes. In the mid-90's, he left for Saudi Arabia where he met two Arabs who began to funnel money to the Philippines through him.[7] This, according to Mohammed, is partly how the Abu Sayyaf was funded after Khalifa's networks were discovered in 1995.

"Borhan had two bosses in Saudi Arabia during that time: Al-Sughayir for charitable institutions and Abu Abdulrahman for jihad," said Mohammed, who executed a public affidavit in a Quezon City court naming the two Saudi financiers in 2005.[8] For jihad, he pinpointed a shadowy figure who still baffles intelligence agencies in the region, Mossad and the CIA: Abu Adulrahman Qasamollah, an Afghan war veteran from Saudi Arabia. Little is known about him until today. Borhan admitted the first of many instances when he funnelled money from Abdulrahman to the Abu Sayyaf in 2001 — 20,000 Saudi riyals or about US$5,300 slated, Abdulrahman told him, for Radullan Sahiron's group.[9] Borhan said Abdulrahman asked him to come to Kuala Lumpur, Malaysia, where Abdulrahman gave him the money as well as ₱150,000 or about US$3,000 for himself.

Despite that, when Borhan was captured in Malaysia in 2006, he denied any connections to the Abu Sayyaf, but testimony from captured Abu Sayyaf members as well as agents like Mohammed tell a different story. Borhan's family is intertwined with terrorist financing. His brother, Khair, is one of the Abu Sayyaf's key leaders. Arrested by authorities in May, 2004, he escaped from prison in a daring jailbreak ordered by Jemaah Islamiyah and is now leading the Abu Sayyaf group in Basilan. The U.S. claims he has ties to Middle Eastern and Malaysian funding sources.[10] Another brother, Gulam, is a leader of Markazos Shabab, another front organization allegedly funneling money to the MILF, according to Philippine intelligence sources. All three brothers, Filipino authorities say, have a wide network

---

[7] Classified Philippine intelligence document, "Debriefing Report: Borhan Malban Mudus/Mundos," December 15, 2006.

[8] Quezon City Court Document: Affidavit of Identification, January 19, 2005.

[9] Classified Philippine intelligence document, "Debriefing Report: Borhan Malban Mundus/Mundos, " December 15, 2006, p. 8.

[10] Classified U.S. intelligence document, "Khair Mundos: Target Intelligence Package, JSOTF-P HVI," April 17, 2011.

among NGO's and provide terrorist financing using money from Saudi institutions.[11]

The second man Mohammed named was also identified by Borhan as his financial backer, Mohammed Saleh Sughayer also known as Al-Sughayir. According to intelligence sources from three nations and leaked U.S. State Department cables, Al-Sughayir is a "known financier of al-Qaeda and Jemaah Islamiyah."[12] He helped make arrangements for employment that brought Khair Mundos and his wife to Saudi Arabia. More importantly, Filipino officials say Al-Sughayir asked Borhan to set up a charity called Safinatun Najah (the Ship of Salvation) in Isabela City, Basilan. That essentially became a front to fund the Abu Sayyaf,[13] the first NGO set up specifically to do that. When Al-Sughayir was finally arrested by Filipino authorities in 2005, then Saudi Ambassador Mohammed Amin Wali interceded and pressured the Philippines to deport Al-Sughayir to Saudi Arabia, highlighting worrisome connections between Saudi officials and terrorist financing.[14]

After Borhan called him about Khadaffy Janjalani's request for help in 2001 (during the Lamitan siege), Mohammed immediately contacted another Darul Imam Shafi'ie alumni, Yacob Basug, a former member of the Abu Sayyaf who had now joined the MILF.

"I went with Yacob Basug who is also engaged in bombing activities and extortion in central Mindanao. So the diversionary activities were planned and executed with the help of Basug, and he introduced me to bomb experts of the JI." This was the beginning of the expansion of JI with the Abu Sayyaf, mandated by the JI leadership in Indonesia. The first operation, however, had to be immediate and included only the Abu Sayyaf and the MILF.

Borhan gave Mohammed ₱40,000 or about US$750 for a terrorist attack meant to siphon attention and troops away from Basilan. Mohammed and Basug recruited two more men: one from Jolo who arrived with Mohammed; the other an MILF member from Cotabato, who helped them purchase explosives. Their target: the ConStar Lodge in General Santos City, chosen because they believed it was a prostitution front. According to Basug,

---

[11] PCSupt. Rodolfo Mendoza, Jr., "The Evolution of Terrorist Financing in the Philippines," International Center for Political Violence & Terrorism Research, 2010.

[12] Wikileaks, "Deportation of Saudi Terror Suspect at Behest of Saudi Ambassador," Secret/NoForn, May 4, 2005. Available at http://www.wikileaks.org/cable/2005/05/05MANILA2042.html

[13] Classified Philippine intelligence document, "Debriefing Report: Borhan Malban Mundus/Mundos," December 15, 2006, p. 7.

[14] Op cit.

it had a disco on the top floor and rooms for the "sex trade" behind it.[15] They successfully set two bombs, a smaller one on the roofdeck to funnel people towards the staircase, where a second, larger explosion was set to explode three minutes after the first one.

Mohammed then moved to Cotabato where he met JI's leader, a 23-year-old, 5′4″ Indonesian known as Zulkifli.[16] "They had been planning to meet some members of the Abu Sayyaf as directive from their higher-ups. So we became acquainted with each other," said Mohammed. "Every day, they come to our safehouse, and we also come to their safehouse until such time that trust was established. Zulkifli wanted to go to Khadaffy so I wrote a letter to him. After the diversionary activities we had, Khadaffy was very happy that I am still working with the group, and I have a connection with JI."

Mohammed said although he wanted to focus more on extortion to raise money, JI had different ideas. "They don't want money. They want bombings. They conducted the actual bombing in General Santos!" The first joint JI-MILF-Abu Sayyaf operation happened less than a year later at the FitMart mall in General Santos City. Mohammed said he represented the Abu Sayyaf; Basit Usman was there for the MILF; and JI leader Zulkifli actually set the bomb. "Zulkifli was very happy. A day later, he was summoned to meet his senior officer in Malaysia. The meeting was about the funding for the JI for the next year. They have this annual budget, and they have allocations for operations." Zulkifli had been training militants in the MILF's Camp Abubakar since 1998.

The relationship between JI and the Abu Sayyaf was critical in changing the group's bipolar orientation between ideology and crime. There have been four concrete cycles of evolution since its founding: from 1991 until 1998, the Abu Sayyaf was largely driven by ideological goals, partly because of the funding and behind-the-scenes manipulation of al-Qaeda. From 1998 till 2002, it turned to crime: kidnappings-for-ransom and extortion operations, largely because of the loss of its ideological moorings after the death of its founder. The third cycle ran from 2002 until 2008 when JI helped reorient the group again towards terrorism. During that time, it carried out the region's worst maritime attack — the Superferry bombing in 2004. A year later, the Abu Sayyaf reached out from its lairs in the south to the

---

[15] Classified Philippine intelligence document, "1ˢᵗ Dev Report on the Arrest of Yacob Basug @ Sumayya," December 5, 2003.
[16] Zulkifli is different from Malaysian Zulkifli bin Hir alias Marwan, a Malaysian. This Zulkifli is Indonesian, and his real name is Ahmad Faisal bin Imam Sarijan.

capital, Manila and carried out near-simultaneous, coordinated attacks, including the Valentine's day bus bombing. Finally, the fourth cycle began with the kidnapping of Ces, Jimmy and Angel in June, 2008 when the Abu Sayyaf degenerated into kidnapping-for-ransom again.[17] Members trained in terrorist and bomb-making tactics became "terrorists for hire" — growing the nexus between terrorism, crime and politics. By the end of 2011, one intelligence officer told me "there was a United Nations" in the southern Philippines, referring to the growing number of nationalities kidnapped and being held for ransom: Filipinos were joined by an American, an Indian, two Malaysians, a Japanese and an Australian.[18]

There is one last crucial element that contributes to the complexity of the problem: the continuing allegations that the security forces in charge of running after the Abu Sayyaf may be colluding with them. In her book, Gracia Burnham wrote about how the military would send food to her kidnappers, the Abu Sayyaf. "The Armed Forces were feeding us!" she said. "A group of them met our guys and handed over quantities of rice, dried fish, coffee and sugar. This happened several times over the course of a few weeks. Why in the world did President Arroyo's troops provide the Abu Sayyaf with their daily bread? We were told that it was because Sabaya was wheeling and dealing with the AFP [Armed Forces of the Philippines] general of that area over how to split up any ransom that might be paid."[19] There's a certain practicality behind the Abu Sayyaf's moves. "Sabaya was willing to give the general 20% of the action. But the messenger reported back that this wasn't enough. The general wanted 50%." Although the general in the area denied these allegations, residents in Basilan largely regarded his denial with disbelief.

Allegations of military collusion and corruption have been constant through the years. The most high-profile case which was investigated by the Philippine legislature happened in 2001 in Lamitan, Basilan — the standoff which prompted the Abu Sayyaf's leader, Khadaffy, to ask for diversionary

---

[17] R. Banlaoi, "The Sources of the Abu Sayyaf's Resilience in the Southern Philippines," *Combatting Terrorism Center at West Point,* May 3, 2010. Available at http://www.ctc.usma. edu/posts/the-sources-of-the-abu-sayyaf%E2%80%99s-resilience-in-the-southern-philippines

[18] The Filipino-American would be released before the end of 2011. In January, 2012, a video of Australian Warren Rodwell was given to me. He asked for a US$2 million ransom. Clips and photos were released by Australian media as well as Rappler, available here http://www.rappler. com/nation/703-kidnapped-australian-appeals-for-help

[19] Burnham, *In Our Presence,* p. 222–223.

tactics from Mohammed. After an 18-hour firefight, Khadaffy and his men were surrounded by soldiers in a church and hospital compound. Strangely, at sunset the large group and its hostages escaped through an unguarded backdoor — a fiasco that spotlighted either the incompetence of the Philippine military or collusion and corruption on a massive scale. The walled compound had only two points of entry and exit: the front door and an alley that led to a small back door. The commanding officer called for backup, which was ignored by his superiors. Surprisingly, the soldiers guarding the back door were pulled away, allowing the 40 kidnappers and their 28 hostages to walk out single-file through a narrow corridor, walk out the back door and disappear into the jungle.

Several members of a civilian militia group known as the Civilian Volunteer Organization or CVO were the only ones at the back door. The Abu Sayyaf added four new hostages, hospital staff members they thought they might need, including nurse Ediborah Yap. "As we were being taken hostage by the Abu Sayyaf, we heard the words, 'It's okay — it's okay at the back,'" said nurse Sheila Tabunag. One of the members of the CVO, Eligio Cordero, explained, "The military told the CVO's and the PNP [police officers] to stay away from the area, but we disobeyed their orders."[20] Some of the militia fired on the group and hit at least one of the Abu Sayyaf as well as Americans Martin Burnham and Guillermo Sobero, both of whom received minor wounds. "We overheard them saying to each other: 'They said it was clear. Why are they firing!?'"[21] said Eligio's brother, Paterno. The two brothers, along with several Lamitan residents, later testified in front of a Philippine Senate hearing. On August 24, 2000, however, a military fact-finding board found "no collusion."

Ransom creates an informal economy that underpins much of life in this part of the Philippines. Soon after the escape at Lamitan, the Abu Sayyaf became angry because they received less money than they expected in the first ransom payments. While the world heard about the beheading of American Guillermo Sobero, little was written about their revenge attacks that followed in the next two months, aimed at making the Philippine military look ineffective. After Sobero, they went on a killing spree, beheading more than a dozen Filipinos. The Abu Sayyaf's indescribable brutality

---

[20] P. Mykannen, "Greed of Philippines Army Elements May Be a Security Hazard for U.S. Troops," *Helsinging Sanomat*, February 3, 2002.
[21] Ibid.

gouged out a deep well of anger and hopelessness, seemingly impermeable to change on all fronts.

Until today, allegations and documentation of military corruption exist. A book written by Glenda Gloria, Gemma Bagayaua-Mendoza and Aries Rufo titled *The Enemy Within: An Inside Story on Military Corruption* documenting institutionalized corruption in the Armed Forces was published in 2011. Using euphemisms like "conversions" for fake receipts and expenses and "PS" for money for troops which never existed, military officers received perks and cold cash.

One of the latest charges pinpoint General Sabban, the military commander who worked with us on our team's kidnapping. According to leaked U.S. State Department cables, then Defense Chief Gilberto Teodoro told U.S. ambassador Kristie Kenney that Sabban "had managed to profit personally" from the kidnapping of three humanitarian workers from the International Committee of the Red Cross,[22] — a charge General Sabban immediately denied.

Military collusion, says Mohammed, happens — from ransom to weapons. He says the Abu Sayyaf buys some of its guns from soldiers and policemen, and some of the guns allegedly find their way to terrorists in neighboring countries.[23] Victims complain they don't know whom to turn to for help, particularly since the kidnappers are sometimes protected by the police and military as well as the politicians, all of whom demand a piece of the action.

***

It was 1 a.m., early Tuesday morning, June 10 — Day 3 of the kidnapping — when I got word that Jolo's Vice Governor Lady Ann Sahidulla would like to meet with ABS-CBN at 11 a.m. at the Capitol Building. I talked to Charie then texted Quidato that she would pick him up on the way to the airport around 8 a.m. The permits and crew as well as arrangements on the ground were set.

It was raining hard when the plane landed on the Jolo runway. Quidato called to let me know they were there. I also sensed a note of complaint: he asked why Charie didn't bring any clothes. He seemed worried he would be

---

[22] Wikileaks, "Defense Secretary Discusses VFA, Washington Visit, and Election Prospects with Ambassador," August 28, 2009. Available at http://wikileaks.org/cable/2009/08/09MANILA1845.html

[23] "PNP gun used by Indonesian terrorists?" Rappler.com, September 13, 2012. Available at http://www.rappler.com/nation/12368-pnp-gun-used-by-indonesian-terrorists

left alone and accountable. I understood the complications, but since he also did everything by the book, he had the full approval and knowledge of his superiors. Charie had money with her, and only later would she tell me how frightened and pressured she felt. I emphasized how Quidato was also there to protect her. He said he was confident since he also mobilized the police Special Action Force (SAF) as well as an intelligence team. At this point, though, no one knew what would happen next. I hoped that if all went well, we could do a quick swap and our team would be home soon. I knew the faster we acted in the beginning, the greater the chances they would be safe.

They were picked up at the airport by Juancho Sabban's men and brought to City Hall for their meeting with Lady Ann. They had lunch and waited at least an hour. When they met her, she assured them she would send someone to her cousin, Albader Parad, to determine whether he had the hostages and ask him what he wanted. She said she also sent emissaries to other groups to try to get more information. Governor Sakur Tan was in Manila, and as the acting governor, she offered to negotiate for the family. She told them again the ransom shouldn't be more than ₱2 million or about US$40,000. Lady Ann is a flamboyant character: a woman who moves in a man's world. She seemed like someone from "the Wild West" and told them stories about how she dealt with armed men: by carrying guns herself and outshooting them if necessary. She is also extremely empathetic and struck an instant connection with Charie, whose strength lies precisely in creating those quick bonds. She asked Quidato and Charie to stay at her home so they could avoid the reporters.

Back in Manila, Day 3 began before 6 a.m. with our official release confirming our team missing in Jolo. Soon after, radio, television and online reports were out, alerting armed groups in the area about a possible ransom scenario. This worried me, but I knew we had no choice. Regional police Chief Joel Goltiao continued speaking to media, giving them erroneous information. It reminded me of vested interests. This is a high-profile case, and it could make the career of a regional police officer. It was a morning of politics. My next call came from the Palace. Someone from my team was speaking about our confidential plans, and the information was being distorted before reaching President Arroyo. I could sense the powerplay in her cabinet and the tug of war for the President's ear. I traced one source of information and found our leak was Charie (which she admitted haphazardly when we spoke about it later). I knew how important it was to constrict the information flow to allow us to act quickly. I offered to explain everything to President Arroyo, but I was told she was not happy with the situation and blamed Ces and our team for interfering with military operations in Jolo. It didn't help that both the police and military had their own internal politics — with their leaders jostling for information and control. I told them we were working with both police and military on the ground, essentially bypassing Manila decision-makers. I promised to keep Manila informed of any developments and made a mental note to speak with the Secretary of Interior and Local Government Ronaldo Puno. I looked again at my list of concentric circles and realized I needed to keep broadening contacts.

The Palace was at the top of the government pyramid, and I addressed some of the misinformation that was reaching officials there. I also asked for advice on how ransom should be treated. While officially, the Philippine government's position is to pay no ransom, everyone, including the President, knows the only way to assure the safety of hostages is to pay. I wanted to know the nuances: is there a better way than paying cash? One of the ideas from the Palace was to offer specific livelihood projects which could be coursed through local government officials. This made me slightly nervous though because it would mean trusting what I knew to be a corrupt system.

Which brought me to other political considerations. Behind the scenes, numerous people were volunteering their services. A former cabinet secretary working with the Lopez Group of Companies called and gave me a list of three local government officials who wanted to handle the situation on the ground as a group. I wrote down their names but felt wary. Not only were they probably too plugged into local vested interests, they could also avoid liability as a group. Jolo Governor Sakur Tan, a powerbroker, is in Manila, and I knew I would need to deal with him at some point. Otherwise, he would — in the words of a common acquaintance — "feel slighted." I called him and set an early evening meeting at our safehouse. He could be either a powerful ally or a dangerous enemy.

Senator Loren Legarda, a former ABS-CBN anchor and journalist, also called to offer her help. She had helped negotiate the release of hostages in the past from the communist New People's Army as well as other situations in Mindanao. I took down notes, thanked her and told her we would call if we needed help.

I called Secretary Puno and thanked him for allowing Quidato and Iglesia to work closely with us. He asked me to promise him we would coordinate with him, and I gladly gave my word. I told him what we were doing in our safehouse and promised his men would have access to all the information we were also gathering. It was important to me that anyone actually acting would have accurate and timely information. I had seen too many instances in the past where the wrong information led to deadly decisions.

Puno also told me the head of the national police, General Avelino Razon, seemed upset I had not called him. I told him I knew Charie was coordinating closely with him. I had known General Razon since 1995. He was the head of the Presidential Security Group during the discovery of the al-Qaeda cell in Manila. Immediately after the collapse of the World Trade Center towers, he was the only official to publicly link 9/11 to 1995, until, he told me, he was asked by President Arroyo to stop speaking about it publicly. However, since those days, we had run into situations of conflict like the Peninsula Manila Hotel. I found myself sitting across both these men, actively challenging their views of the role journalists played in society. I decided to discuss it directly with Puno to make sure he didn't harbor any grudges. I think he appreciated my frankness and gave his assurances we would see this through together.

I walked outside into the living room where Iglesia and his team were having coffee along with Frank and Grech. Gina and Anne were making sure everyone had eaten. Even my driver, Domeng, had been drafted: he was in charge of the food delivery brigade. He was in the kitchen leading the clean-up. The news was on television. Gin was monitoring the radio and preparing future releases. Ory, Ces' son, had set up a wifi that distributed broadband from the living room's one Internet link. There was a flurry of controlled activity buzzing on top of a sustained note of anxiety. Every now and then, you could see people comforting each other — Grech holding the hand of Jimmy's wife; Libby speaking in hushed tones to Angel's wife; Ces' sons, coming in and out of the room, as they searched for news.

Last night, Ces' middle son, Gian, had a fight with his father, Rock. Gian wanted to go to school, but we discouraged this because we knew the reporters would deluge the children with questions. Rock asked me to speak with Gian. The quietest of Ces' sons, Gian came into the room with Rock. I asked him why he wanted to go. Despite his efforts for control, he became emotional when he said he needed to go to school because it's important to his mom. It was clear this was his way of doing something so we found a middle ground: we notified school administrators to prevent journalists from entering school grounds.

Thinking about Gian, his halting explanation and the emotions that powered the importance of going to school today, made me duck back into the room and get a tissue. Ces is very lucky: her boys are handsome, smart, and they love her. It made me even more determined to do everything we could to get her back to her family. Gian's heartfelt effort to do something, anything that could help, touched me. That was the feeling that permeated our rooms: every person was trying to find what they could do to help, trying to think about what Ces, Jimmy and Angel would want.

There was a knock on the door. Grech's phone was ringing. There was an explosion of activity as I rushed out. Grech handed her phone to Nestor Cusi, the second member of the police team embedded with us. He put the phone on the table in front of Frank and punched the button activating the speakerphone. Iglesia took the seat next to him with his pad and paper. I sat opposite Frank.[24]

"Hello, Ces?"

"Yeah."

"It's Frank."

Ces in Jolo talking to Frank on the cellphone.

---

[24] What follows is a full transcription of the telephone conversation at 11:33 a.m. on June 10, 2008. The Tagalog parts have been translated to English.

"I'm so sorry, Frank. I tried to convince them that we're not rich ..."

"Can you speak louder?"

"I tried to convince them that we're not rich. So I proposed that we get a loan from the company or from other sources — someone who can help our family to raise the money they want. They don't want to bring it down. If we don't agree to that price, they'll cut contact. They'll give an ultimatum."

"Yeah, yeah. We're trying our best. We now have ₱2.5 million [about US$47,000] on hand. You tell them that. That's the only money we can raise now. The loan you want — we need more time to talk to ABS. Can you tell them — we can't get money from thin air! You tell them ..."

"I told them, but they don't want to listen."

"Huh?"

"I told them naturally, our plans — where we are ..." As Ces was talking, I reached over to Iglesia's paper and wrote — "can we talk to kidnappers?" Frank looked over and nodded. Iglesia pointed to what I wrote and nodded as well.

"Can I talk to somebody there?" Frank asked.

"They don't like," said Ces. Then she spoke to her kidnappers in Tagalog. "Can they talk to you?" She paused then came back on the phone. "Just me. Speak to me."

"Yeah, but can you tell them initially that we were able to raise ₱2.5 million?"

"Actually, they were very angry when I told them that. Very angry. So I tried to say ₱10 million, but they still didn't want it. They threatened to give an ultimatum." Ces' voice was agitated, trying to communicate the urgency she felt. We understood.

"And the ₱10 million you mentioned to Grech last night? We don't have that."

"I know," Ces interrupted.

"Yeah, and the loan — you'll have to give us more time."

"Well, you know ..." Ces paused. "How much more time on the loan?" Frank and Iglesia looked at me. I signaled two then three fingers. Frank wrote "hours?" on the pad. I nodded.

"Two to three hours," said Frank.

"Okay. Two to three hours."

"Yeah, tell them.

"That's 11, 12, 1, 2" — I could see Ces counting her fingers in my mind. "Two o'clock?"

"Yes, let's make it two o'clock."

"Okay, two o'clock."

"Who'll call," asked Frank.

"I'll be the one to call. There's a number I gave Glenda yesterday who was supposed to get the money. There's a number I gave her."

"Okay," said Frank. He looked at Jimmy's wife and daughter as well as Angel's wife. "How are Jimmy and Angel?"

"They're okay. They're with me. I'm in front of them. We're all together. They managed to take a bath in a nearby well."

"Yeah."

"So again, two o'clock — whether the money's in place ..."

"Of course, we'll need guarantees that you're safe."

"Yeah, what they will do."

"That should be very clear," reiterated Frank as he read my writing. "Tell them." There was a slight pause while Ces talked to her kidnappers. Then she started talking even as we heard men talking behind her.

"What they will do is bring us to a place where you will bring the money. When you contact the person I gave Glenda, this person will contact them, and they will bring us to a place that's nearer town. Right now, we're very far from the city — about, I don't know, maybe three hours. I don't know. Then they said they'd bring us to a place and when the money's counted then we will be brought to you. They guarantee that we'll be safe. You'll have to talk to me by the time the money's brought to that location." On the pad, I wrote "assurances" and gave it back to Frank.

"They should give you assurances — give us assurances that you'll be safe," said Frank, looking at me. I nodded. Ces spoke to her kidnappers in Tagalog. "What assurances can you give that we'll be safe," she said in Tagalog away from her phone. "Promise? What if you kill us once the money's with you? How will they know that we're still alive? You'll have me call and I can speak with them once you've counted the money? You'll let me talk to them? But what if there's no signal?" Listening to Ces gave us all courage. She didn't sound like a victim. She sounded in control. She was making demands and somehow hearing the certainty in her voice was making us all feel better. I wrote "negotiator" on the pad, and Frank nodded.

"Frank?" said Ces.

"Tell them we can talk to a third party we both trust. Ask them if they'll agree to have a third-party negotiator."

"But they don't like politicians. Okay," she said to Frank and turned to her kidnappers, speaking to them in Tagalog: "Can we agree on a person we both trust? Someone you know. Someone we know. This third party will make sure to tell our families we're safe. Someone who you'll choose whom I also know. Let's agree. That person is a guarantee to our families. Yes ..." There was a slight pause while men spoke in a dialect I couldn't understand. Ces continued: "A person we all trust. Who is that? Let's think about it now." During this time, I wrote: "Lady Ann."

"We suggest Lady Ann Sahidulla ... the vice-governor of Sulu," Frank said.

Ces responded quickly. "But they don't like politicians." Then she asked the kidnappers in Tagalog: "Do you want Lady Ann?" There was a discussion and voices were raised. We looked at each other around the table. Perhaps this would be easy. Then Ces came back: "They said no." I wasn't prepared. Frank looked at me. I pointed to the phone.

"Ask them — who do they want?"

"Is there someone you want?" Ces asked them in Tagalog. "Talk about it. Yes." I wrote on the pad: "Get number again." Then she turned back to us. "They will discuss it then I will give the name to you later."

"Can you send the number again — the one you mentioned a while ago? Just to make sure — send it again," said Frank.

"Okay, bye bye."

"Wait, wait, wait! So you'll call us about the person?"

"Yeah, we will call you when they have a suggestion." I wrote "Aventajado" — the former cabinet secretary who negotiated the release of the Sipadan hostages in 2000.

"What about Aventajado?" Frank asked.

"Wow, that was a long time ago," Ces said and laughed. It was good to hear her laugh. "How about Aventajado?" — she asked the kidnappers — "No, they don't want him."

"Okay. Okay." Ces kept talking to her kidnappers in Tagalog: "I should also know this person — an ordinary person I also know" — she told them.

"Of course," Frank agreed. "There should be mutual trust."

"I'm telling them" — they spoke to her again — "Okay, they'll talk about it then I will call you at two o'clock. Wait" — she turned to her kidnappers again — "Are we giving them the name at two o'clock or we tell them as soon as you decide?" She turned to her phone again. "Okay, as soon as they decide — even if it only takes 30 minutes ..."

"Yeah, as soon as they decide…"

"Wait, they're changing their minds. They don't know, but we will call you."

"Yeah, we'll give them time. But try to …

"… bring down the money …"

"… yes. We cannot handle the ₱20 million." Ces started to cry. I looked around the table while we listened. When she spoke, she sounded angry with herself. I could only imagine what she was feeling.

"God, I'm starting to cry."

"We're doing our best here," Frank tried to comfort her while looking at me. I nodded. "We're doing our best here."

"They can't be swayed. They want the ₱20 million." Ces started to break down then caught herself.

"Hang on. Hang on. We're doing everything we can."

"Frank, remember the abaca bag I like so much? I saw them making abaca here in this area." It took me a second to realize that Ces shifted once again. She was giving us clues to her location! I looked at Iglesia and Cusi, and they were taking down notes.

"Okay," Frank responded. "Yes?" I could sense Ces pulling herself back together.

"Okay, so we'll wait for them to decide on a person. Then see if we agree with what they suggest. Then I'll call you."

"Ask them to keep it affordable. ₱20 million is really too high."

You could feel something break in Ces. "Frank, they get really angry if I try to bring down the amount." She started to cry. "I'm so sorry."

"Don't be," Frank quickly responded, trying to comfort her. "Don't be. Hang on."

"Yeah." Ces took a deep breath. "Yeah. We are. We're being strong. They'll guarantee … They have to agree to this third person." Then she really started to cry. "I'm sorry, Frank, I'm really sorry." I looked around the table, and I saw all of us — with the exception of Iglesia, Cusi and Frank — were emotional. Someone started passing a box of tissues. I marveled at Frank, who kept Ces on the phone with smooth, even tones.

"We're doing everything we can," he promised. "We're all here. Everybody's behind you here."

"Bye," said Ces, and she hung up.

\*\*\*

When they weren't walking, they didn't have much to do so they were forced to really observe their surroundings. Ces noticed how large the plants were, and only much later when they were resting did she realize how the blades of grass sliced sharply through her skin. Time moved slowly in the jungle, and Ces was impatient at the beginning until she learned to accept it. She kept a journal, trying to stay busy. She felt incredibly guilty and kept looking for signs from her companions that they blamed her for their predicament, but not once did Jimmy or Angel show that. In fact, they seemed so concerned for her, and she felt that the respectful way they treated her kept the kidnappers at a distance. She thought of her four sons, Ory, Mico, Gian and Andre. Again, she felt guilty because she realized she took their time together for granted. She wanted to hold them again and tell them how much she loved them. More than anything, Ces could hear and feel the forest breathing. It had its own rhythm, its own life — one that was changing hers.

The wildlife was like nothing they had seen before. Everything — from insects to plants — were so much larger than expected. They called them 'jurassic.' On their first night, they noticed huge, red ants on the ground. Jimmy told Ces and Angel to find something to cover their ears so the ants wouldn't be able to enter while they lay sleeping on the ground. Ces rummaged through her bag and found her pantyliners. She tore them apart and gave each of them enough to stuff in their ears.

On Tuesday, June 10, their third day in captivity, their kidnappers woke them up at 5 a.m. They prayed, packed up and again began to walk. Soon, they stopped because they were worried about planted bombs so they sent scouts ahead to check while the group waited. They climbed a short while longer to a clearing with many trees. Angel felt it was a secluded crossroad of sorts in the jungle. There was a nearby water source, and the team was allowed to bathe. They set up tents and pitched camp. This is where the negotiations began in earnest and where they would spend the next six days.

Jimmy had begun his daily ritual — borrowing the camera from his kidnappers so he could clean it. While he was cleaning it, he would secretly take pictures of the makeshift camp and the men holding them hostage. Many of the kidnappers in his video were children. Ces noticed that they handed out many small packets of crackers, which she hid in case she needed food for an escape. She and her team would keep their garbage in a small pile near their tent, but the kidnappers would randomly litter the jungle floor with their wrappers.

Ces preparing to walk again in Jolo.

Shortly after Ces spoke with Frank, she called him again. Jimmy had the camera rolling and you could hear parts of their conversation on the tape. He was shooting up so you could sense that Ces and the one-armed Commander Putol were on elevated ground above the tent. It was starting to rain. Ces realized her kidnappers spoke limited English so she began to drop hints about their location liberally during her conversations. Speaking to her brother was strangely comforting but also an emotional rollercoaster.

"They're still choosing. They haven't decided, but I asked that I be allowed to call so you don't worry."[25]

"Yeah, that's good," said Frank. "How are you doing?"

"We're okay. How about the families of Jimmy and Angel?"

"They're okay. We're communicating with them."

"You need to warn Jimmy's mother who lives abroad. She might have a heart attack when she finds out."

---

[25] Transcripts of telephone conversation, 4:50 p.m., June 10, 2008.

"I overheard earlier that she already knows, and she's okay."

"Frank, please tell Rock" — Ces' husband — "to update my insurance payments. I took loans on them, but I have money in our joint account. Please make sure they're paid. Just to be safe ... but we'll be okay."

"Yeah, of course. Positive thinking. How are the living conditions there?"

"Not great, but we're surviving. We're managing. It's cold. It's been raining. Frank, we're facing the sunset. We're facing the sunset in a mountain that I climbed before. Ask Melay." Sitting next to Frank, I marveled at how quickly Ces shifted from thinking and preparing for the worst to becoming proactive and giving hints about their location. I took notes and handed them to Gin so she could check with Melanie "Melay" Masecampo, Ces' producer. Frank asked again about Lady Ann.

"No, they really don't want a politician," answered Ces.

"Why?"

"They said politicians take a piece of the pot. They said they would make the negotiations last longer, then they'll also take a large chunk of the money." Ces began to talk to her kidnappers, urging them to choose. I wrote on the pad: "Sakur Tan" — thinking about testing the water.

"How about the governor, Sakur Tan?" asked Frank.

"What came out in the news?" Ces was talking to her kidnappers. "They said it came out in the news that the government wants to appoint Sakur Tan."

"Do they want that?"

"They're still talking about it." She turned away from the phone again. "You don't want Sakur Tan?" She turned back to the phone. "They said we should just agree on who we'll both choose. Otherwise, the price will increase if Sakur Tan's involved." I tried to figure out what I would say to Tan in our meeting that evening.

Strangely, these phone calls began to take a rhythm of their own. After all, there's comfort in hearing Ces' voice, knowing at that moment, all of them are alive and well.

The head of the U.S. forces, Bill Coultrup called Quidato and gave him leads. Shortly after, Matt Worsham also texted Quidato — a text forwarded to the PNP's Director of Intelligence, who gave his approval for the police to coordinate with the Americans. Classified Philippine documents recorded the careful, formal manner help was offered and accepted: "Sir, Major Matt Worsham JOSTF-P Intel Director here. Colonel Coultrup put me in touch with you to see how or if we can support you in any way for this kidnapping on Sulu. We have some fairly specific intel on locations that may assist. Please feel free to contact me. I will keep trying to call you. Thank you for your time."[26] This was the first time the police would be working directly with the Americans on an operation, and it set the stage for further collaboration in the future.

By the end of the third day of the kidnapping — what the police called "the nego cell," our crisis team at Discovery Suites, and the kidnappers had chosen negotiators: the family stuck with Lady Ann while the kidnappers chose Indanan Mayor Alvarez Isnaji and his son, Jun. By late evening, I met with Sakur Tan and came out feeling the governor's disapproval ostensibly because we didn't immediately appoint him our negotiator. I pointed out that we were working with his deputy in Jolo. Tan said we could continue coordinating with Lady Ann. The negotiator chosen by the kidnappers, Mayor Isnaji, was also not in Jolo — travelling out of the Philippines. In the meantime, the kidnappers gave the cellphone number of his son, Jun. They told Ces they chose Isnaji because they know "where he lives."

It was a confusing day finding the elements and links between the concentric circles I mapped on Monday — pushing me through a tour de force of Philippine society, government, law enforcement and journalists. Despite the myriad players and interests vying for a piece of the action, one thing became clear: at the core, there existed two disparate, diverging expectations — between the kidnappers and Lady Ann. She was preparing to negotiate the ₱20 million demand down while the kidnappers seemed to believe the only thing left was to deliver the money. It was set for a confrontation, which is exactly what happened the next day.

---

[26] Text sent to Winnie Quidato around 7 p.m., June 10, 2008. Recorded in police notes and report submitted to the Director of the Intelligence Group of the Philippine National Police.

# The Virus

**5**

---

Seventeen-year-old Sali Said was lazing in his makeshift hammock, waiting for the sun to rise. At 5'9", he stood out, his long, curly hair pulled back; his youthful brazen walk full of bravado. He had a bright smile and was one of the first two to approach the jeep carrying Ces and her team — making him, by default, the leader of the team which physically kidnapped them.[1] He was one of eight men sent by Radullan Sahiron to "fetch" the team. He and Sahiron's nephew, Kimar, were the first to greet Ces. Now, guarding Jimmy, he was closely aware of how the three were feeling. He liked Jimmy. In many ways, you could say it was predetermined he would do exactly what he's doing today.

Born in Indanan, Sulu, he knew the jungle well, and he felt at home in Sahiron's camp in the Kan Baddal area, where the ABS-CBN team was being held. After all, he had been going in and out of there since he was seven years old.[2] He was still a child when he began to run errands for Sahiron and soon worked his way up to become a lookout. At 14 years old, he learned how to drive and became more useful when he began driving four-wheel drive vehicles. Soon after, he got a job driving a passenger jeep from Jolo to Umbol Kura, Indanan. Picking up and dropping off passengers was an easy cover for his covert purpose — to buy food and supplies for the Abu Sayyaf. Later, he began moving weapons and ammunition from the MNLF camps in the area

---

[1] Author interview, undisclosed location, Manila, Philippines, June 9, 2011.
[2] The details are from agent interviews and classified Philippine documents, among them "Custodial Debriefing Report of Sali Said @Abu Miqdad," Naval Intelligence and Security Group of Western Mindanao, March 1, 2011. Some details are from a classified U.S. intelligence document "Task Force Sulu Significant Reporting," Joint Special Operations Task Force-Philippines, Joint Intelligence Support Element, INTSUM, May 1–8, 2011.

to the Abu Sayyaf. He then began buying and transporting weapons from an established supplier, allegedly a police officer still on active duty.

This is what "terrorism" actually looks like from the ground, and Sali's life shows the interpersonal links which power the social networks behind it. A closer look shows labels change quickly: one man can be Abu Sayyaf one day, MNLF or even MILF the next. Even more disturbing, the forces which are supposed to fight them also often switch sides. Sali has worked with — and for — both policemen and politicians. The glue of trust which holds them together is far stronger than the labels of groups. Individual zeal is strong because it comes from often hard-to-penetrate social networks which power terrorist organizations around the world: a dense interrelationship of family and friends.

Sali didn't have much to prove since he comes from Abu Sayyaf blue-blood: his father, Mohammed Said was one of the original members of the group, working directly with founder, Abdurajak Janjalani. To show you how it works within the communities, the recruiter of Sali's father was actually a village official, barangay Captain Hadji Solaiman, who actively supported the Abu Sayyaf by recruiting men and helping the group find sanctuary. Both men travelled to Basilan to pledge their oaths to Abdurajak and later joined him when he called for troops to carry out the Ipil massacre in April, 1995, a bloody rampage which killed 55 people and left the city center in smoldering ruins.

Mohammed Said carried out one of the first kidnappings instigated by Abdurajak. The targets then were three Hong Kong nationals kidnapped from Barangay Adjid, the same place where Ces, Jimmy and Angel would be taken nearly two decades later. Classified documents from the Philippines and the United States say the Abu Sayyaf received ₱8 million or about US$160,000 in ransom.[3] From that, Said received ₱130,000 or about US$2,700, enough to buy a new M16. This is significant if you live in one of the country's poorest areas, where stable jobs are hard to find.

This is very much a case of "like father, like son." Sali and his father received explosives training separately. For Mohammed Said, that began as early as 1995. Perhaps he was part of the group trained by Ramzi Yousef and Wali Khan — both of whom are now in a U.S. prison. During one of these training sessions, Sali's father accidentally detonated an Improvised Explosive Device (IED) and damaged his right eye and his arms. Despite that, Sali followed his father's footsteps and studied bombmaking in 2006.

---

[3] 1999 conversation rate of US$1 dollar to ₱50.

Sali's patience, loyalty and perseverance attracted the attention of other Abu Sayyaf leaders like Albader Parad, who tasked him to buy weapons like M14, M16 and M203 rifles from a member of the Philippine National Police. More disturbing is that these transactions allegedly took place publicly "along Lily military supply in front of Planet Pluto."[4] Parad actually named Sali — giving him his alias, Abu Miqdad, a name more popular than his real one.

Technically, Sali reported to another Abu Sayyaf leader named Juhurim Husin. Looking at these interconnected groups show that relationships, whim and availability determine who gets assigned specific projects and tasks like kidnappings and weapons procurement. These often random decisions determine the changing composition of each Abu Sayyaf group at any given time.

Again, it's "like father, like son" when it came to kidnappings. Following his father's successful kidnappings and ransom payments, Sali carried out his first kidnapping in 2006 — one of eight men who kidnapped Jolo businesswoman Caring Sinuro and her son, Beltran. Sali was the "spotter and lookout" — riding a motorcycle around their house in the run up to the kidnapping. Once the men had grabbed their targets, they loaded them onto a passenger jeep with Sali as the driver.[5] They received ₱800,000 or about US$16,000[6] in ransom. Each of the eight men received ₱25,000 or nearly US$500.

As we saw with the case of Edwin Angeles, what you see on the surface hides an underground world of agents and double-agents. In 2007, Sali said he was tapped by a government agent who offered him amnesty and a reward if he assassinated a member of the Abu Sayyaf using the alias of Abu Black. Sali took the offer and after he carried out the mission, he received a partial payment of ₱5,000 or about US$100. He went home to Indanan to wait for the rest of his money and his amnesty papers. That was where the man Ces,

---

[4] Classified U.S. intelligence document, *Joint Special Operations Task Force-Philippines, Joint Intelligence Support Element, Intsum,* "ASG UTG member (Sali Said) apprehended by AFP in Jolo City," May 1–8, 2011, p. 6.

[5] Details from classified Philippine and U.S. intelligence documents: *Joint Special Operations Task Force-Philippines, Joint Intelligence Support Element, Intsum,* "ASG UTG member (Sali Said) apprehended by AFP in Jolo City," May 1–8, 2011, p.–4. Also *Naval Intelligence and Security Group — Western Mindanao,* "Custodial Debriefing Report: Sali Said @Abu Miqdad, March 1, 2011.

[6] 2006 conversion rate of US$1 to ₱53.

Jimmy and Angel called Commander Putol — whose real name is Sulaiman Pattah — found him. Pattah asked Sali to join a kidnapping they were planning for June 2008.

Sali said Sahiron, the Abu Sayyaf's most senior leader, planned and pulled together the core kidnap group, which included Sulaiman Patah, Mameng Biyaw, and another relative, Amrin.[7] On the Sunday when Biyaw was walking with Ces, Jimmy and Angel, the person he spoke to on his cellphone was Amrin, who told him to go home because the team would be kidnapped. Biyaw left and the group kept walking until they reached the Kankitap area, where they were picked up by Amlon's group of about 10 fully armed men. They stayed at Kankitap for a night then walked to the Kan Baddal area — Sahiron's main camp. Although Ces, Jimmy and Angel never met Sahiron, the Abu Sayyaf leader was there a few meters away observing them. It was years later that I learned every move in the negotiations in those first few days were brought to — and approved by — Sahiron himself.

I tell you these details so you begin to understand why Sali Said joined the Abu Sayyaf and helped in the kidnapping of the ABS-CBN team. Studying terrorism through a social network paradigm highlights a key moral question: does a person's position in their network as well as their connections to others necessarily cut down the individual capacity to exercise free will? New technology now allows us to pull out to a much broader, larger perspective — God's eye-view — in order to examine patterns of behavior and emotions of a human superorganism. This allows us to examine entire societies, which may show characteristics missing in individual people — like observing an anthill and focusing not just on individual ants but on the entire colony and its various activities. Several fundamental "laws" — recurring traits — that emerge are surprising. What's clear is that groups modify the behavior of individuals, and the larger the group, the larger the pressure stifling free will. Under this paradigm, Sali had no choice but to be exactly what he was — one of our team's kidnappers — at that place and time.

***

---

[7] Classified U.S. intelligence document, *Joint Special Operations Task Force-Philippines, Joint Intelligence Support Element, Intsum,* "ASG UTG member (Sali Said) apprehended by AFP in Jolo City," May 1–8, 2011, p. 4.

When I first began studying terrorism in Southeast Asia, I focused on individuals — the people who carried out the attacks. As a journalist, I stumbled onto what intelligence agencies called link analysis because it was a methodical way of finding leads to the next story. How was this bomber connected to the next one? How did they get together? How did the plans develop? Because I travelled so much in Southeast Asia,[8] I was often able to piece together information that intelligence agencies didn't share with each other, allowing CNN to break exclusive stories. When intelligence agents in the region received the first software that computerized link analysis, I helped input who was connected to whom. This was why when the name of Khalid Shaikh Mohammed surfaced, I was the first journalist to reel off his activities and connections in Southeast Asia.

Then I began to study the groups they belonged to, but I realized the labels often lost meaning because terrorists are not card-carrying members and the groups are far from static. They're extremely dynamic and are buffeted by their governments' and people's actions as well as global conditions. I realized early on that the intelligence agencies gathering the data often had the wrong paradigms for analysis. In the beginning, they were still trying to fit their information into a post-Cold War scenario. With time, particularly after Singapore arrested Jemaah Islamiyah members and published its white paper[9] outlining the covert group's purpose, paradigms changed, but it happened slowly. Singapore moved quickly and tried to take its neighbors along, but the level of denial was very high, particularly in Indonesia and the Philippines.

Bureaucracies don't take paradigm shifts well so in my reporting, I found the best analysis often came from outside governments. Rohan Gunaratna provided a global perspective and analysis of al-Qaeda while analysts like Sidney Jones from the Brussels-based Crisis Group International focused on Southeast Asia's historical and cultural factors as well as what the terrorists and members of overt and covert Islamist groups in Indonesia said. Yet, I also thought that Marc Sageman, a former CIA officer who began his own terrorist database, was correct when he said we need to look "beyond the self-justification of terrorists and look at the facts, rather than their

---

[8] News events would take our team to three or four cities a week in Southeast Asia from 1995–2005. From 1998–2005, I spent a total of less than three months of every year in my apartment in Jakarta.
[9] "The Jemaah Islamiyah Arrests and the Threat of Terrorism," *Ministry of Home Affairs,* Singapore, January 7, 2003.

claims." Very often, the terrorists lie. For my purposes, I focused on the ideology as well as shared goals and projects.

It all came together in a coherent whole when I began to study social network theory, which shows insights may come not from individual psychology but from understanding group dynamics. In the past decade, technology has allowed us to study networks in a way never before possible, giving added insights through a new paradigm, resuscitating an iteration of the nature versus nurture question. Studying the links between individuals and groups actually show that connections to people matter most, allowing the science of social networks to explain a lot about human experience, including how and why ordinary people become terrorists.

Social psychology has provided numerous studies about how good people can turn evil — conformity experiments where "normal" people placed under social pressure either agree to obviously wrong conclusions or actually harm others, doing things they would never have done if they had been making decisions alone.

In 1955, psychologist Solomon Asch investigated what a person would do when confronted by a group that insists wrong is right. A group of people were shown lines drawn on paper and asked to choose the shortest. Only one subject is actually being tested; the rest were told to choose the obviously wrong answer to see how it would affect the subject's choice. 75% of the subjects tested agreed with the group and gave the wrong answer — suggesting that peer pressure plays a large role in the individual person's perception of reality.[10]

A decade later, Stanley Milgram performed a series of experiments designed to test a person's reaction to authority under conditions where that person is helping others learn. When the "learner," hidden by a screen, failed to memorize word pairs fast enough, the "helper" was told to apply an electric shock (and to increase the voltage with each wrong answer). It turns out most people follow instructions to give what would have been potentially lethal shocks despite their subjects' screams and pleas.[11] (The "learners" were actors who deliberately got the answers wrong, and no electric shocks were actually used).

Finally, an experiment done 40 years ago with Stanford students playing roles of prison guards and inmates was cut short less than a week later after the "guards" became sadistic and the "prisoners" pathological. Philip

---

[10] S. E. Asch, "Opinions and Social Pressure," *Scientific American*, 193 (1955). For a description of his experiments, see http://www.experiment-resources.com/asch-experiment.html.

[11] S. Milgram, *Obedience to Authority: An Experimental View* (New York: Harper & Row, 1974).

Zimbardo's Stanford Prison Experiment was later used to help explain the behavior of American military prison guards in Abu Ghraib.[12] It turns out people are highly affected by their environment, generally follow authority and can do unspeakable acts if pushed to do so gradually.

In 2007, social scientists Nicholas Christakis and James Fowler began publishing ground-breaking research that allowed them to define the Three Degrees of Influence Rule, which show how a broad range of attitudes, behaviors and feelings spread through groups of people.[13] Using available survey data from the Framingham Heart Study,[14] they charted the contagion of emotions and behavior through a densely interconnected social network. The data collection of the Heart Study began in 1948 and followed three generations of 12,067 people from Framingham, Massachusetts, assessing them repeatedly from 1971 to 2003. By mining and analyzing this data trove, Christakis and Fowler were able to come up with broad conclusions that applied across the board when talking about social networks.

The Three Degrees of Influence Rule says social networks transmit emotions and subliminal signals that influence behavior up to three degrees. Researchers mapped the spread of emotions like happiness[15] and loneliness[16] and studied the spread of complex behaviors like political views and voting behavior;[17] sexual behavior and disease contagion;[18] smoking and drinking;[19]

---

[12] P. Zimbardo, "The Stanford Prison Experiment," www.prisonexp.org. See also P. Zimbardo, *The Lucifer Effect: Understanding How Good People Turn Evil.* (New York: Random House, 2007).

[13] N. A. Christaks & J. H. Fowler, *Connected: The Amazing Power of Social Networks and How They Shape Our Lives* (Great Britain: HarperPress, 2010), p. 28.

[14] T. R. Dawber, *The Framingham Study: The Epidemiology of Atherosclerotic Disease,* (Cambridge: Harvard University Press, 1980).

[15] J. H. Fowler & N. A. Christakis, "Dynamic Spread of Happiness in a Large Social Network: Longitudinal Analysis Over 20 Years in the Framingham Heart Study," *British Medical Journal,* 337 (2008).

[16] J. T. Cacioppo, J. H. Fowler & N. A. Christakis, "Alone in the Crowd: The Structure and Spread of Loneliness in a Large Social Network," *Journal of Personality and Social Psychology,* Vol. 97 (2009).

[17] J. H. Fowler, M. T. Heaney, D. W. Nickerson, J. F. Padgett & B. Sinclair, "Causality in Political Networks, "*American Politics Research,* 39: 437 (2011).

[18] P. S. Bearman, J. Moody & K. Stovel, "Chains of Affection," *American Journal of Psychology,* 110 (2004) and J. J. Potterat *et al.,* "Sexual Network Structure as an Indicator of Epidemic Phase, *Sexually Transmitted Infections,* 78 (2002).

[19] N. A. Christaks & J. H. Fowler, *Connected: The Amazing Power of Social Networks and How They Shape Our Lives,* (Great Britain: HarperPress, 2010), p. 114.

and even obesity.[20] In short: everything we say or do ripples through our social network, affecting our friends (one degree), our friends' friends (two degrees), and our friends' friends' friends (three degrees). All influence falls aside by the fourth degree.

Take obesity, for example. A person's chances of being obese increased by 57% if a friend became obese, 40% if a sibling became obese, and 37% if a spouse became obese. The types of friendships are important: between mutual friends, the risk of obesity increases 171%, even if you live far away from each other. Your faraway friend has even more influence on your weight than neighbors or even relatives who live with you. There are many reasons why this may be the case: friends eat together, mimic each other's behaviors, weight gain may become more acceptable or less acceptable in a social circle, etc. The results of the study show the recent obesity epidemic in the U.S. has more to do with social ties than with genes or physical proximity. Christakis and Fowler conclude: "Network phenomena appear to be relevant to the biologic and behavioral trait of obesity, and obesity appears to spread through social ties."[21] They add that "both bad and good behaviors might spread over a range of social ties."[22]

Several years later, they combined the study on obesity with numerous others and outlined fundamental principles as well as the structure and function of social networks. The structure of the social network is determined by the connections, which have to do with who is connected to whom. Another, more famous experiment by Stanley Milgram in the 1960's showed that people are connected to one another by an average of "six degrees of separation" — meaning that between any two people, between you and me for example, there would be six people or less connecting us to each other. Using Milgram's famous experiment, if you send a letter (or an email today) to someone you know who then forwards it to someone he knows, it would take an average of six hops before it reaches me.

The network's function or purpose can be seen in what flows through its ties. Contagion determines what flows through the links of the network because networks magnify what they're seeded with. Contagion determines influence, which according to Christakis and Fowler, is governed by the Three Degrees of Influence Rule. So any social network's structure is

---

[20] N. A. Christakis & J. H. Fowler, "The Spread of Obesity in a Large Social Network over 32 Years," *The New England Journal of Medicine*, 375 (2007).

[21] Ibid., 370.

[22] Ibid., 378.

governed by six degrees of separation, and its function is determined by three degrees of influence.

Christakis and Fowler outline universal rules for all social networks, and it's important to understand them so we see why the whole is greater than the sum of its parts. This helps explain why terrorist networks behave in unpredictable ways not seen when studying the individual people in it.

First, we determine the shape of our network. Like attracts like. They cited homophily, our conscious or unconscious tendency to gravitate towards people like us. This is a fundamental element in how we shape our network, and we do this in three ways. First, we decide how many people we are connected to and how many friends we have. Are you a loner or do you like parties and social events? Second, we decide whether we introduce our different groups of friends and family to each other; we determine how densely interconnected our friends and family are. Finally, our choices in the first two determine how central we are in our social network. Obviously, the more central you are, the faster you receive and pass on the information or emotion. These three choices determine the quality of our lives — from our emotions; to the amount of money we make; to whether we smoke or gain weight, among other factors.

Interestingly though, the very fact that we are part of the social network automatically strips some of our individual decision-making powers. It's clear — as some of the conformity experiments cited earlier showed — that our networks and peer groups shape us.

Then there's the Three Degrees of Influence Rule, which show that not only do we consciously or unconsciously copy our friends but that we are also affected by our friends' friends and our friends' friends' friends. It's only recently that we've discovered the tools to be able to see this on a large scale, allowing us to observe the whole network at once.

All this allows us to see emergent properties of human social networks that we have never been able to quantify before. Emergence is when the network begins to act in ways the individual parts could not have anticipated nor may even be aware of because a higher-level pattern or behavior emerges out of parallel complex interactions of the individual parts in the network. Again, these properties can only be understood by studying the whole group and its structure, not by studying isolated individuals. An example cited by Christakis and Fowler is the human wave in sporting events which first appeared in the 1986 World Cup in Mexico. If you only study an individual, you'd see a person stand up and then sit down, depriving you of the larger view of the actual wave washing through the sports gallery. When scientists looked at patterns in the entire network of people in the stadium, they found a predictable behavior which the individuals could not have known: the wave usually rolled in a clockwise direction and consistently moved at a speed of 20 "seats per second."[23] There was no central group controlling the movement. Each person adopted a rhythm from the group, which manifested a kind of instinctive collective intelligence.

We find examples of emergent behavior in nature: when the group has a life of its own — in ant colonies or flocks of birds or schools of fish which exhibit a collective intelligence that allow it to avoid a predator or find food. Christakis and Fowler point out "flocks of birds deciding where to fly reveals that they move in a way that accounts for the intentions of all the birds, and even more importantly, the direction of movement is usually the best choice for the flock." This is nature's crowdsourcing, something humans have only recently been able to harness because of the Internet.

New technology now allows us to find the "wisdom of crowds," which posits that the group's collective decision is better than any single member's if certain factors are in place. James Surowieki wrote: "Large groups of people are smarter than an elite few, no matter how brilliant — better at solving problems, fostering innovation, coming to wise decisions."[24] Here are the four criteria that need to be in place for this to happen: (1) Diversity of opinion — each person should have private information; (2) Independence — people's opinions aren't determined by the opinion of those around them; (3) Decentralization — people are able to specialize and draw on local knowledge; and (4) Aggregation — some mechanism exists for turning private judgments into a collective decision. That mechanism is the Internet, and it has given birth to endeavors like Wikipedia, an online encyclopedia which has no central core giving assignments and organizing reporters, writers and editors. People create an entry when they feel like it, or edit and correct another, acting from different parts of the world. If Wikipedia were made into a book, it would be 2.25 million pages long.[25] The most interesting thing is that it has the same number of errors, on the average, than

---

[23] I. Farkas *et al.*, "Mexican Weaves in an Excitable Medium," *Nature 419,* (2002: 131–132).

[24] J. Surowiecki, *The Wisdom of Crowds,* (New York: Doubleday), 2004. Excerpt available at http://randomhouse.com/features/wisdomofcrowds/

[25] E. Qualman, *Socialnomics: How Social Media Transforms the Way We Live and Do Business,* (Hoboken: J.Wiley & Sons), 2009, 2011. Statistic can be found online at http://www.social-nomics.net/2012/01/04/39-social-media-statistics-to-start-2012/

Encyclopedia Britannica, which hires and organizes a large bureaucracy to accomplish the same task.[26]

I studied social networks and the Internet closely when I was designing the elements of ABS-CBN's citizen journalism and election campaign program, which marries traditional broadcast media with new technology and crowdsourcing for social change. Our lessons from the five-year program with evolving iterations backed the findings of Christakis and Fowler.

We started our citizen journalism program in 2005 and combined it with a crowdsourced election campaign in 2006 to prepare for mid-term elections in 2007. The campaign, *Boto Mo, iPatrol Mo* (Patrol Your Votes), was successful because it mitigated rampant violations of election rules.[27] It was the first instance globally where a news organization called on citizen journalists to act for a very active, political purpose — to patrol their votes and push for clean elections. We moved one step ahead of Western media groups because of our unique political situation: a country of nearly 100 million people in a chaotic democracy which still used manual voting and counting, and where charges of fraud, cheating and violence in elections are constant and consistent. No candidate ever admits losing in Philippine elections. They just say they were cheated! As far as violence — well, in 2007, the Philippine police said it was one of our country's most peaceful elections ever — with nearly 130 people killed in 217 incidents of poll-related violence.

*Boto Mo, iPatrol Mo* was our reaction to survey results that showed Filipinos were apathetic about governance and elections. The campaign was simple: get the people to care and to take action. If you see something wrong or something good, tell us about it. If you see someone trying to buy votes, snap a picture on your cellphone and send it to us. If you see a town mayor using public vehicles for his campaign, shoot a video with your cellphone and send it to us. If you see violence, tell us about it, and after a verification process, we will put it to air. Just two months into the campaign, we received reports that *Boto Mo, iPatrol Mo* helped level the playing field after an incumbent was caught on cellphone video using city resources for his campaign. So cellphones were effective weapons.

---

[26] D. Terdiman, "Study: Wikipedia as Accurate as Britannica," *CNET News*, December 15, 2005.

[27] Parts of my description here of *Boto Mo, iPatrol Mo* were used earlier in speeches and journal articles describing the citizen journalism campaign I led.

The sheer volume of messages we received — about 500 a day leading up to the 2007 elections and one a minute on election day — showed us not only the public's distrust for our institutions and the electoral process, but also more importantly, it showed a hunger for change and highlighted individual battles for integrity. Their fears — because it is dangerous to fight power — were balanced by their own clamor to make things work. When we gave them venues to do something about it, they did. While our 2007 campaign was successful, it focused on technology rather than spreading emotions.

It's clear the process of thinking and decision-making requires feeling. Brain imaging scans show that our feelings actually allow us to understand the subliminal information we can't directly process or comprehend in order to make daily decisions. Studies of brain-damaged patients whose capacity to process emotions have been impaired show they are incapable of making routine decisions like what clothes to wear or where to eat.[28] Very often, they cease to function in society, losing their jobs because they are unable to cope with the myriad decisions we consciously or unconsciously make everyday. Reason without emotion leads to inaction and an inability to decide. Some studies show that up to 80% of our decision-making process is influenced by how we feel.

This is why I felt Christakis and Fowler's work seemed intuitively correct and immediately applicable. When I read their first studies in 2007, I wondered whether their findings applied to the virtual world. I decided to test it and incorporate it into our 2010 election campaigns which began in 2009. We ran daily stories and infomercials at least four times a day through all our broadcast channels, special monthly drives, concerts, workshops coordinating mass market and individual elements of the campaign. Each element was infused with the emotion of hope embedded in the idea of empowerment.

Our research team conducted monthly focus-group discussions which charted the flow of hope. We could see a gradual increase that seemed aligned with our campaign. A nationwide survey firm, Pulse Asia, provided bi-annual reports. By the end of the year-long campaign, we could measure its impact. The Pulse Asia survey released July 2010 said Filipinos hit their highest level of optimism nationwide since their surveys began in 1999: 53% of Filipinos are optimistic, while 11% were pessimistic, the lowest level measured since the surveys began.

---

[28] J. Lehrer, *The Decisive Moment: How the Brain Makes Up Its Mind*, (New York: Canongate, 2009), loc 327 of 5379, Kindle edition.

So if we accept that emotions and behavior spread through physical and virtual social networks, it's time to look at the volatile cocktail of intense emotions that lead to terrorism — anger, fear, hatred, religious fervor, among them. Technology now allows researchers to map these networks. Like the spread of emotions and behavior, we need to study the whole group, not just isolated individuals, because the group may show emergent properties not clear to — and in — the individuals. Mapping the social networks of al-Qaeda[29] and Jemaah Islamiyah (JI)[30] allows us to show the spread of an explosive mix of ideology and emotions we can call the jihadi virus.

\*\*\*

It's important to trace and define exactly what the jihadi virus is and where it came from. What networks did it travel through? How did it evolve? What is it exactly? In determining what we call this virus, what's the difference between jihad and jihadi? That one additional letter makes a world of difference. I've attended numerous conferences globally where Muslims argue passionately about how the West doesn't understand jihad, but many Muslims themselves aren't aware of distinctions that differentiate the religion from political systems. It's important to note that Osama bin Laden only used religion as an emotional motivator, a means to get power with the goal of changing political systems.

The term *jihad* comes from the Arabic root word *jahada* which means "to strive." In Islam, jihad means to do your best — "to strive with our utmost energies and to the best of our abilities in carrying out God's commands, be it to perform righteous deeds or to refrain from evil deeds with the overall objective of safeguarding the well-being of all creations."[31] Jihad takes many forms, including "verbal jihad, which means to offer advice to those who need it or jihad with the hand, as in performing community service for the less fortunate."[32] The best known interpretation of jihad

---

[29] V. Krebs, "Mapping Networks of Terrorist Cells," *Connections*, 24 (2002). Available at http://www.sfu.ca/~insna/Connections-Web/Volume24-3/Valdis.Krebs.web.pdf
[30] S. Koschade, "A Social Network Analysis of Jemaah Islamiyah: The Applications to Counterterrorism and Intelligence," *Studies in Conflict & Terrorism*, 29 (2006).
[31] Interview with Ustaz Muhammad Haniff Bin Hassan, International Centre for Political Violence & Terrorism Research, October 21, 2011.
[32] Ibid.

after 9/11, however, has been armed jihad — physically fighting and taking up arms to defend the religion.

The term *jihadi* refers to an ideology that aims to use armed jihad — violence — to establish an all-encompassing Islamic state that creates a political, cultural and religious system aligned with a certain strict interpretation of the Koran. This is about using arms to seize the mantle of governance — of power. With these distinctions, we can see that "jihad" is universal in the Muslim world, and "jihadi" is a very small subset of Muslims dedicated to violence to change existing political systems.[33]

The ideologies calling for global jihadi terrorism find their roots back to Sayyid Qutb, an Egyptian fundamentalist scholar whose work legitimizes violent Muslim resistance to regimes that claim to be Muslim, but whose implementation of Islamic precepts is flawed. He developed a distaste and distrust for the United States after going to school there in 1948 and decided that his salvation lay in an unswerving devotion to Islam. His body of work after he returned to Egypt made him the "forefather of Islamist terrorism."[34] His main disciple, Muhammad Abdel Salam Faraj, argued that "jihad was the neglected duty of each Muslim." Faraj's pamphlet published in the late 70's popularized the debate about targeting "the near enemy" — the local government — versus "the far enemy" — originally the Israeli state but later evolved to the West and specifically, the United States. By the mid-1990's, no Muslim government had yet been overthrown by jihad. Some argued it was because "the far enemy" was propping up "the near enemy." A very, very small faction, that would later be led by al-Qaeda, would switch strategies and target "the far enemy" in order to win their jihad against their governments. It's important to remember that al-Qaeda's main target is actually bin Laden's home government, Saudi Arabia.

People mistakenly believe there is one unified al-Qaeda ideology. Nothing is further from the truth. Like in the groups it inspired and hijacked, there is considerable infighting about the limits and types of operations they can carry out. What unites them is an overall strategic goal, but the tactics are often determined by whoever's in charge of a particular operation so doctrines can change depending on its members. (Like its associate group in

---

[33] For more on jihadism, see M. Habeck, *Knowing the Enemy: Jihadist Ideology and the War on Terror*, (London: Yale University Press, 2004).

[34] M. Sageman, *Leaderless Jihad*, (Philadelphia: University of Pennsylvania Press, 2008), p. 37.

Southeast Asia, Jemaah Islamiyah, the debate which centers on the killing of civilians continues until today.)

Sayyid Qutb's brother, Muhammad, taught Osama bin Laden and his deputy, Ayman al-Zawahiri. According to Mohammed Jamal Khalifa, who was bin Laden's best friend while in university and would later become his brother-in-law, he and bin Laden both "read Sayyid Qutb. He was the one who most affected our generation."[35]

The first mention of "Qaeda" was not by bin Laden but by his mentor, Sheikh Abdullah Azzam, also a friend of the Qutb family. By tracing the men and the evolution of the ideology, we can trace the jihadi virus. Azzam organized the Maktab al-Khadimat, the Services Bureau, in Afghanistan, drawing Muslim militants from all over the world to join the first modern jihad against the Soviet invaders in the 1980's. Azzam's message was radical — that it is a Muslim's duty and obligation to join the jihad. Both the Muslim world and the West lauded the young Muslim men who came to help fight the Soviets. Afghanistan became a model for future struggles, ultimately evolving to the objective of establishing a Muslim Caliphate over Muslim lands and eventually the world.[36] Azzam first mentioned "the vanguard" which "constitutes the Solid Base [*Qaeda* in Arabic] for the hoped for society. We shall continue the jihad no matter how long the way, until the last breath and the last beat of the pulse — or until we see the Islamic State established."[37]

Many of bin Laden's public messages drew heavily on Azzam's ideas, but they differed on major points: Azzam frowned on Muslims fighting Muslims, and he did not advocate franchising the tactics they taught in Afghan training camps to the militants' home countries as advocated by Qutb, Faraj and bin Laden. Between August 1988[38] and late 1989,[39] bin Laden broke away from Azzam, took the most extremist of the militants and formed al-Qaeda. On November 24, 1989, Azzam and his two sons were assassinated by a car

[35] L. Wright, *The Looming Tower: Al-Qaeda and the Road to 9/11*, (New York: Alfred A. Knopf, 2006), p. 79.

[36] Abdullah bin Omar, *The Striving Sheik: Abdullah Azzam*, Nida'ul Islam, 14th issue, July–September 1996.

[37] A. Azzam, "*Al-Qa'idah al-Sulbah*" *The Solid Base,* Al-Jihad, No. 41, April 1988, p. 46. Translation available in Supplement 1 here http://www.satp.org/satporgtp/publication/books/global/paz.htm#4

[38] P. Bergen, *The Osama bin Laden I Know: An Oral History of al-Qaeda's Leader*, (New York: Free Press, 2006), p. 75.

[39] *United States vs Usama Bin Laden, et al.*, Testimony of Jamal Ahmed Mohamed al-Fadl, United States District Court for the Southern District of New York, February 6, 2001.

bomb. No one took responsibility for his murder, but many suspect it was the work of bin Laden and his men.[40]

The Afghan training camps were the crucible which inculcated the ideology mentally and physically through its curriculum to thousands of young Muslim men. It bonded them and fused their social networks, infecting them with the jihadi virus, which they then brought back to their countries. This contagion effect is clear when you look at the Bali bombings in 2002, planned and carried out by Indonesian Afghan war veterans.

Both al-Qaeda and Jemaah Islamiyah (JI), its arm in Southeast Asia, operated the same way. They hijacked disparate groups, trained, funded and infected them with the jihadi virus that targeted both the "near enemy" and the "far enemy." Al-Qaeda co-opted JI to extend its reach into Southeast Asia. JI, in turn, acted like an umbrella organization for terrorist attacks. In Indonesia, it coopted groups like Kompak, Laskar Jundullah and other Darul Islam offshoots. Jemaah Islamiyah effectively transformed the Darul Islam social network and hijacked it for a global agenda. In Malaysia, it coopted Kumpulan Mujahidin Malaysia (KMM), and in the Philippines, it worked with the Moro Islamic Liberation Front (MILF), the Abu Sayyaf (ASG) and the Rajah Solaiman Movement (RSM).

At the time of each group's greatest strength, both al-Qaeda and JI used a top-down centralized command as well as bottom-up initiative to spread the virus and carry out attacks. While both started with a core central group, they quickly co-opted other groups with their own agendas into the global jihad that created a social movement,[41] connecting and mobilizing these groups for terrorist operations. Participants' zeal came from tightly knit and hard-to-penetrate social networks — evolving networks of family at 20% and friends at 70%.[42] The strength and resilience of the social network that carried out the attacks are often forged by blood and tightly-interwoven group dynamics.

A closer look at two key men highlight some of these principles and show the important role Southeast Asia and Jemaah Islamiyah played in the evolution of al-Qaeda and its most spectacular plots, especially 9/11. In a

---

[40] E. Blanche, "The Egyptians Around bin Laden," *Jane's Intelligence Review*, December 2001, p. 20. Also cited in R. Gunaratna, *Inside al-Qaeda: Global Network of Terror*, (New York: Columbia University Press, 2002), p. 24.

[41] M. Sageman, *Understanding Terror Networks*, (Philadelphia: University of Pennsylvania Press, 2004), p. 137.

[42] S. Atran & J. Stern, "Small groups find fatal purpose through the web," *Nature, Vol 437*, September 29, 2005.

social network, people are called nodes. The more connected nodes are known as hubs. Both of these men are hubs in their networks: one in al-Qaeda, the other in JI; they form key intersections of both groups. A few, highly connected hubs dominate the architecture of terrorist networks. Because of their numerous links, hubs play a key role in noticing and using the experience of innovators.

Khalid Shaikh Mohammed (KSM) conceived and carried out the 9/11 attacks — which he proudly admitted in a clandestine interview in 2002.[43] Much of what he said then has been verified by classified U.S. documents released by Wikileaks.[44] 9/11's architect and "al-Qaeda Chief of External Military Operations,"[45] KSM had six nephews in al-Qaeda as well as a brother who died fighting the Soviets in Afghanistan and another who "helped establish the Muslim Brotherhood in Kuwait."[46] He and his nephew, Ramzi Yousef, tried — but failed — to bring down the World Trade Center in 1993.

The genesis of the 9/11 plot shows how hubs recognize innovation from more isolated nodes, spread through the network and incorporate them into actionable plans. Yousef introduced his high school classmate, Abdul Hakim Murad, to his uncle in 1993. Murad, the first commercial pilot recruited by al-Qaeda, trained as a pilot in the Philippines, the UAE, Pakistan, and at four different flight schools in the United States. KSM, Yousef and Murad converged in the Philippines at the end of 1994 with numerous plots that would remain in al-Qaeda's tool kit, among them: a plot to assassinate U.S. President Bill Clinton on his visit to the Philippines; attacks on nuclear facilities in the United States; at least three plots using airplanes. The first was the most immediate: to use a crop-duster plane to assassinate Pope John Paul II during his visit to Manila — discarded once police announced a no-fly zone in the capital.[47] The second involved a light plane loaded with explosives, which would be used to ram into the CIA

---

[43] Y. Fouda, 'We Left Out Nuclear Targets, For Now,' *The Guardian*, (March 4, 2003). For a fuller treatment of Khalid Shaikh Mohammed's activities, see M. Ressa, *Seeds of Terror: An Eyewitness Account of al-Qaeda's Newest Center of Operations in Southeast Asia*.

[44] On April 25, 2011, news outlets began releasing classified U.S. Department of Defense assessments of Guantanamo Bay prisoners. Wikileaks published nearly a decade's worth of intelligence in the form of individual JTF-GTMO (Joint Task Force Guantanamo) Detainee Assessments.

[45] JTF-GTMO Detainee Assessment, *Khalid Shaykh Muhammad*, December 8, 2006, p. 13. Available at http://projects.nytimes.com/guantanamo/detainees/10024-khalid-shaikh-mohammed

[46] Ibid., p. 2 & 14.

[47] Ibid., p. 32.

headquarters in Langley, Virginia.[48] The third plot, which became the blue-print for 9/11, was to "board any American commercial aircraft pretending to be an ordinary passenger. Then ... hijack said aircraft, control its cockpit and dive it at the CIA Headquarters. There will be no bomb or any explosive ... in its execution."[49]

In 1996, KSM pitched this plot to Osama bin Laden, who replied: "why do you use an ax when you can use a bulldozer?"[50] Instead of a single plane filled with explosives targeting the CIA, bin Laden suggested the "bulldozer" approach of hijacking several passenger jets and crashing them into buildings as flying bombs. KSM expanded his plan to hijack a dozen aircraft simultaneously on both coasts and even target nuclear power plants[51] before it was trimmed down to the final four planes used in 9/11.

The other hub is KSM's Jemaah Islamiyah counterpart and "representative in Southeast Asia" — 47-year-old Indonesian Riduan Isomuddin, better known as Hambali.[52] The family connections continue: his brother worked for both JI and al-Qaeda,[53] and his wife was with him when he was arrested in 2003. Hambali and KSM met in Afghanistan in the late 80's, according to the documents, and "the joining of al-Qaeda and JI"[54] happened because of their friendship. A CNN investigation I led was the first to link them together in the mid-90's in the Philippines in a foiled plot known as Bojinka, which aimed to destroy U.S. airplanes flying from Southeast Asia in massive mid-air explosions that would have resulted in more deaths than 9/11.[55] They were the only two members of that terrorist

---

[48] Classified Philippine intelligence document, "After Debriefing Report," March 9, 1995.

[49] Classified Philippine intelligence document, "Debriefing Report," January 20, 1995.

[50] G. Mascolo & H. Starck. "Operation Holy Tuesday," *The New York Times* (October 27, 2003).

[51] Y. Fouda & N. Fielding, *"Masterminds of Terror: The Truth Behind the Most Devastating Attack the World Has Ever Seen*, (London: Arcade Publishing, 2003), p. 114.

[52] JTF-GTMO Detainee Assessment, *Riduan Isomuddin*, October 30, 2008, p. 1. Available at http://projects.nytimes.com/guantanamo/detainees/10019-hambali-riduan-isamuddin-

[53] JTF-GTMO Detainee Assessment, *Bashir Lap*, October 13, 2008, p. 7. Available at http://wikileaks.ch/gitmo/prisoner/10022.html

[54] JTF-GTMO Detainee Assessment, *Khalid Shaykh Muhammad*, December 8, 2006, p. 9.

[55] M. Ressa, "Investigators think Sept 11 & 1995 Plot Related, *CNN,* February 25, 2002. Available at http://edition.cnn.com/2002/WORLD/asiapcf/southeast/02/25/Philippines.Sept11/index.html?iref=allsearch.

More extensive treatment in M. Ressa, *Seeds of Terror: An Eyewitness Account of Al-Qaeda's Newest Center of Operations in Southeast Asia*, p. 21.

cell to evade arrest in 1995 so while authorities thought they had busted a terrorist cell, the two burrowed deeper and quietly built al-Qaeda's multi-layered network.

These men form large hubs in their jihadi networks, showing the inordinate influence they had, recruiting family and friends for the terror cells and plots they created. KSM crisscrossed the globe planning attacks, but he knew Southeast Asia well because of his friendship with Hambali. KSM's power in al-Qaeda rubbed off on Hambali. According to another senior al-Qaeda operative, Hambali had "elevated status in the al-Qaeda organization due to his relationship"[56] with KSM. That relationship also gave JI inordinate importance in the global terror network. We can see this in at least three of al-Qaeda's major initiatives: a parallel 9/11 plot, another 9/11 style attack, and a rejuvenated chem-bio program.

KSM told his interrogators of a "Manila portion" of the 9/11 attacks which was "a smaller version of the Bojinka plot" in the Philippines in 1995. KSM said he "split the September 11 operation into two parts to have a greater effect."[57] Yemeni and Saudi suicide bombers would hijack U.S. planes flying from Southeast Asian cities and detonate their explosives mid-air.[58] According to several of his leaders, Osama bin Laden cancelled that part of the plan mid-2000 "due to the difficulty in synchronizing the attacks."[59]

KSM also planned a second 9/11 style attack originally set to happen a year after 9/11. Former U.S. President George Bush said KSM began planning the attack a month after the collapse of the World Trade Center towers and planned to use members of Jemaah Islamiyah.

"Rather than use Arab hijackers, Khalid Shaikh Mohammed sought out young men from Southeast Asia whom he believed would not arouse as much suspicion," Bush said.[60]

The "West Coast Airliners Plot" was to be carried out by al-Qaeda operative Zacarias Moussoui and at least four Malaysian suicide bombers

---

[56] JTF-GTMO Detainee Assessment, *Riduan Isomuddin*, October 30, 2008, p. 5.

[57] JTF-GTMO Detainee Assessment, *Khalid Shaykh Muhammed*, December 8, 2006, p. 10. Corroborated by JTF-GTMO Detainee Assessment, *Riduan Isomuddin*, October 30, 2008, p. 8.

[58] JTF-GTMO Detainee Assessment, *Walid Muhammad Salih Bin Attash*, December 8, 2006, p. 6. Available on http://wikileaks.ch/gitmo/pdf/ym/us9ym-010014dp.pdf.

[59] JTF-GTMO Detainee Assessment, *Riduan Isomuddin*, October 30, 2008, p. 8.

[60] *Bush Details Foiled 2002 al-Qaeda Attack on LA*, CNN, February 9, 2006.

who were told to hijack planes "using two separate shoe bombs" with one plane to be "flown into the 'tallest building in California.'"[61]

Finally, when al-Qaeda wanted to formalize its chemical/biological weapons program, it turned to JI and Hambali, who recommended U.S.-educated, Malaysian JI member, Yazid Sufaat, to set up and head al-Qaeda's chem-bio lab. Hambali said he "originally discussed starting an anthrax program with Muhammad Atif,"[62] al-Qaeda's former military operations chief. Soon after, Sufaat stayed at KSM's house and told him "he was developing anthrax for al-Qaeda and was training two students"[63] — members of al-Qaeda.

KSM is one of 16 high-value detainees in Guantanamo, and a critical driver of al-Qaeda's most fantastic plots, many of which he first hatched with Yousef and Murad in Manila in the mid-90's. He recognized three innovators: Yousef for bomb-making; Murad for the use of planes in terrorist attacks; and, Hambali for organizing and motivating jihad. KSM used his connections to magnify and amplify their ideas, behaving exactly as hubs do in the spread of information. He drove al-Qaeda to become a learning organization, resuscitating and deriving lessons from failed plots in order to perfect them and turn them into lethal attacks. Some examples of multiple attempted plots trying to perfect an idea include the shoe-bombers (1994 and 2003), mid-air aircraft explosions (1995 and 2002), liquid bomb explosives (1994 and 2006), and the two attacks on the World Trade Center (1993 and 2001).

Terror networks are far from static. They evolve over time, particularly if they are under constant siege. After 9/11 triggered a fierce reaction from law enforcement agencies around the world, both al-Qaeda and JI were affected the same way: their centralized command structures collapsed and their operational capabilities were degraded. Enough hubs, like KSM and Hambali, had been captured damaging the network's ability to carry out sophisticated, large-scale operations. This means that law enforcement may have taken out as many as 15% of all hubs at once, preventing new hubs from restoring the network's ability to function.[64]

---

[61] JTF-GTMO Detainee Assessment, *Khalid Shaykh Muhammed*, December 8, 2006, p. 11. Corroborated by JTF-GTMO Detainee Assessment, *Bashir Lap*, October 13, 2008, p. 6; and JTF-GTMO Detainee Assessment, *Mohd Farik Bin Amin*, September 23, 2008, p. 2.

[62] JTF-GTMO Detainee Assessment, *Riduan Isomuddin*, October 30, 2008, p. 10.

[63] Ibid., p. 10.

[64] M. Sageman, *Understanding Terror Networks*, (University of Pennsylvania Press, 2004), p. 140.

Still, the nodes from the old networks remain and continue to spread the jihadi virus, adding more isolated nodes, growing the network in a more haphazard pattern. Smaller, more ad-hoc and less professional cells (made up of connected nodes) carry out attacks without central coordination. While the network is weaker, it's harder for law enforcement to predict when and where the next attacks will occur. Often, the smaller, disparate attacks happen more frequently. There is a constant danger that these isolated nodes may spontaneously regenerate some form of a network around them to carry out operations. That's precisely what happened with Jemaah Islamiyah shortly before — and after — the death of Osama bin Laden in 2011.

*\*\*\**

Wearing his traditional flowing white robes and white cap, 73-year-old Indonesian cleric Abu Bakar Ba'asyir has long been at the top of Indonesia's terror networks. On Thursday, June 16, 2011, he walked into a Jakarta court surrounded by police. Days before, bomb threats against 36 locations had been sent on text and Twitter so police were on high alert. Today was judgment day.

This was the third time since the 2002 Bali bombings that the bespectacled cleric would be judged by an Indonesian court. Police said he was a terrorist and was behind JI's deadliest attacks in the region. Although that was widely accepted outside Indonesia, public opinion in the country with the world's largest Muslim population was not so clear partly because of the government's own actions.

In 2002, an Indonesian court cleared Ba'asyir of leading Jemaah Islamiyah. He was, however, convicted of violating immigration law as well as the more serious charge of trying to topple the government to establish an Islamic state through terrorism. Less than half a year later, that decision was overturned by Indonesia's Supreme Court, which cleared Ba'asyir of any involvement with terrorism, leaving only the immigration charges. Ba'asyir was vindicated.

It didn't end there. On April 30, 2004, after serving one and a half years in prison, Ba'asyir was about to be released when authorities detained him again — this time for his alleged role in Bali and the JW Marriott attack in 2003 (strange because he was in prison in 2003, immediately pointed out by his lawyers). To his supporters, he was persecuted by an unjust government appeasing Western powers. A year later, he was sentenced to 30 months jail for conspiracy charges in Bali.

On June 14, 2006, he walked out of prison (with some time cut off for good behavior). Through the years, he remained constant — denying any involvement with terrorism, maintaining that Jemaah Islamiyah does not exist, saying the real terrorists are the U.S. and Israel.

"I do not accept the charges," Ba'asyir said in his first court appearance in 2003 after prosecutors read out a 25-page indictment. "These are lies from America."[65] He did not deviate from that position. His supporters believed him, and nine years later as he was about to receive another court's verdict, more than 200 of them chanted outside the courthouse for his release. He stopped imperceptibly and waved to them before he was ushered forward by his escorts.

This time, state prosecutors seemed to have an airtight case, with some of Ba'asyir's most trusted lieutenants testifying against him. When the presiding judge read the verdict of 15 years in prison, boos and jeers came from the crowd although it is far lighter than the life imprisonment prosecutors asked for.

"Ba'asyir planned and encouraged other people intentionally to use violence or threats of violence to create terror and fear among the people and cause massive [numbers of] victims," said the presiding judge.[66]

Ba'asyir replied in typical fashion: "I will not accept this proceeding as it is made by infidels. It is haram [prohibited under Islam] to comply with the rulings."[67] It was the same defiance that marked him as a hero when he stood up to the dictator Suharto decades before.

There are three waves of evolution for Islamist terrorism in Indonesia, and Abu Bakar Ba'asyir played a role in all three: first, the nationalist movement for an Islamic state — the Darul Islam movement from 1948 to 1992; second, the global jihad — when Jemaah Islamiyah (JI) was infected with the jihadi virus from al-Qaeda and, in turn, infected regional groups, acting as an umbrella organization for regional terrorist attacks from 1993 to 2005; third, the JI social movement, with the jihadi virus transforming the old

---

[65] M. Ressa, Seeds of *Terror: An Eyewitness Account of Al-Qaeda's Newest Center of Operations in Southeast Asia*, p. 63.

[66] "Indonesian radical cleric sentenced to 15 years for terrorism," *The Jakarta Post*, June 16, 2011.

[67] R. Witular & H. Widiarto, "Aides, protégés help Ba'asyir's conviction," *The Jakarta Post*, June 17, 2011.

Darul Islam movement completely.[68] Capable of self-regeneration, it rebuilt itself and set plots in motion again in 2009, led by Ba'asyir and key JI leaders, two of whom returned from the southern Philippines. While authorities were able to prevent most of the attacks from happening, it's clear the threat remains and continues to evolve.

These three waves represented cycles of regeneration of the same social network. In the first wave, Abu Bakar Ba'asyir fought against a dictator for his principles and religion. In the second, he was one of JI's founders and *emir*, leading JI through its deadliest attacks. Finally, in the third, he put a new face on JI, forming Jemaah Ansharut Tauhid or JAT in 2008.

The terror networks in Indonesia are much older than al-Qaeda and Osama bin Laden — overlays on militant networks that were formed to fight for independence, Islamic *sharia* law, and — under Suharto's repressive rule — democracy. Jemaah Islamiyah[69] traces its roots to Darul Islam, an Islamic militia network formed during Indonesia's fight for independence in 1948. After secular forces gained independence a year later, Darul Islam would fight another 13 years to try to establish an Islamic state. The history of the movement shows the existing forces which continue to mold the evolution of the JI network today, including the murky, behind-the-scenes footprint of Indonesia's covert military operations, which tried to exploit Islam for political ends to disastrous results.

Darul Islam (DI) was suppressed and forced to operate underground during the mid-60's and was ultimately defeated by the Indonesian military in 1965. That was when an attempted coup involving left-wing military officers and members of the Indonesian Communist Party (PKI) catapulted then General Suharto into power. Many DI members were fiercely anti-communist, and in the 70's, when Suharto was planning the first election, he mistakenly rekindled Muslim extremism when the head of his military covert operations rallied old Darul Islam members into a new group that was

---

[68] For more on the Darul Islam movement, see "Recycling Militants in Indonesia: Darul Islam and the Australian Embassy Bombings," *International Crisis Group*, February 22, 2005. Available online at http://www.crisisgroup.org/en/regions/asia/south-east-asia/indonesia/092-recycling-militants-in-indonesia-darul-islam-and-the-australian-embassy-bombing.aspx.

[69] Although Ba'asyir still disputes the existence of JI, hundreds of JI members across Southeast Asia testify to its existence and plots. They named Ba'asyir as JI's leader, succeeding Sungkar in 1999. See N. Abas, *Membongkar Jamaah Islamiyah: Pengakuan Mantan Anggota JI*, (Grafindo, 2005), p. 115 and *The 9/11 Commission Report*, (Authorized Edition), p. 152.

basically the military's creation, the Komando Jihad.[70] The group was set up to take a fall: Suharto created them in order to crush them and siphon votes away from the one recognized Muslim political party, the PPP. As government repression increased and Suharto policies were perceived as anti-Islam, more and more joined the fight against the government. In the election year of 1977, the government arrested 185 people it accused of trying to set up an Islamic state in Indonesia.[71]

A year later, Darul Islam members and Muslim clerics Abu Bakar Ba'asyir and Abdullah Sungkar were arrested. Both of Yemeni descent, the two founded an Islamic boarding school, or pesantren, in 1971 that would become the nexus for the ideology of radical Islam. Al Mukmin school in Pondok Ngruki, Central Java, would teach many of the men who would later be arrested and linked to Jemaah Islamiyah and al-Qaeda. This is one of the key ways hubs in the social network spread the virus, and as we'll see later, the probability of carrying out terrorist attacks increases by more than 23% if you attend one of three JI schools.

Ba'asyir and Sungkar were soon be released but the threat of another arrest pushed them to flee to Malaysia in 1985. That was pivotal because that move connected them with the global jihad and Osama bin Laden. By the late 80's, the two had established a *jemaah islamiyah* (a Muslim community) under Darul Islam. Their recruits were sent to Afghanistan, after being funneled through *Makhtab al-Khadamat lil Mujahideen al-Arab* (Afghan Services Bureau) to Camp Saddah, where they trained in weapons, tactics and explosives training and imbibed a strict *salafi* ideology[72] that lay the groundwork for their alliance with al-Qaeda. Afghanistan was the crucible which became a transformative experience for the men who went. As a psychologist who studied terror networks put it: "Friendships cultivated in the jihad, just as those forged in combat in general, seem more intense and are endowed with special significance."[73]

---

[70] M. Ressa, *Seeds of Terror: An Eyewitness Account of Al-Qaeda's Newest Center of Operations in Southeast Asia*, p. 48. Also in K. Conboy, *The Second Front: Inside Asia's Most Dangerous Terrorist Network*, (Jakarta: Equinox Publishing, 2006), p. 15.

[71] Author interview with former director of Indonesia's National Intelligence Agency (Badan Intelijen Negara) A. M. Hendroprioyono, Jakarta, Indonesia, September 14, 2002.

[72] *Jemaah Islmamiyah in South East Asia: Damaged but Still Dangerous* (Jakarta: International Crisis Group, 2003), p. 1–5.

[73] Sageman, *Understanding Terror Networks*, p. 155.

This sacred purpose of jihad and intense group dynamics was transmitted through its social network and molded the members of Jemaah Islamiyah (with capital letters). After a disagreement with another senior Darul Islam leader, JI leader Sungkar, with Ba'asyir as his deputy, formally established JI as a separate organization from Darul Islam on January 1, 1993,[74] beginning the second wave of global jihad in Indonesia.

One of the first things JI did was to write its manifesto — the General Guide for the Struggle of Al-Jama'ah Al-Islamiyah (*Pedoman Umum Perjuangan Al-Jama'ah Al-Islamiyah)*, more commonly known by its Indonesian acronym, PUPJI. Written in a combination of Bahasa Indonesia and Arabic, it was given only to its senior leaders. PUPJI is a first in Southeast Asia: it is an organizational charter, an operational handbook, and a religious-strategic program in one. In order to understand JI's terror network and its evolution, we must understand PUPJI.

Much has been written about JI's organizational structure, portraying it as largely a top-down, rigid hierarchical command in the years following the discovery of JI. However, a closer reading of PUPJI shows us that isn't true because JI resembles al-Qaeda in both ideology and structure far more than it does any other group in Southeast Asia. PUPJI itself resembles the founding charters and operational handbooks of other radical Islamist militant groups — knowledge and expertise that the writers imported from Afghanistan, previously unavailable to other Southeast Asian militant groups.[75]

PUPJI gives a phased approach for its overarching goal of establishing a Pan-Islamic state in Southeast Asia. In order to accomplish that, it aims to recruit and indoctrinate devout Muslims, small communities or study groups who also go through paramilitary training. The ideology pushes social transformation that leads to armed conflict in order to dislodge non-Muslim governments and install Islamic *sharia* law. PUPJI outlines a separate group in charge of its paramilitary activities as well as a technical and a territorial component in JI's administrative hierarchy. This is not one single hierarchy but "multiple loci of authority and hierarchies of

---

[74] Testimony of Achmad Roihan in the Indonesian trial of Abu Rusdan, August, 2003. Also in presentation to Jakarta International Defense Dialogue by General Muhammad Tito Karnavian, *Terrorism and Countering Terrorism in Indonesia*, (slide 3), March, 2011.

[75] E. Pavlova, "From Counter-Society to Counter-State: Jemaah Islamiyah According to PUPJI," *Institute of Defence and Strategic Studies*, November 14, 2006, p. 7.

command."[76] JI's interconnected links and networks seem to drive change from within — to create "an organization in intentional structural flux" using "core and periphery relationships, top-down and bottom-up approaches, and horizontal and vertical alignments."[77]

This is partly what gives the JI network its resilience: it is — like al-Qaeda and other successful terrorist groups — a starfish organization, able to self-regenerate under the right circumstances[78] (if you cut off a starfish's arm, both parts will regenerate and create two organisms). Unlike a traditional spider structure with a rigid hierarchy and top-down leadership (which dies if its leader is killed), JI is a hybrid organization — with two branches which are further subdivided — administrative (day-to-day operations and *dakwah*) and operational (paramilitary training and terrorist operations) giving JI "a parallel emphasis on a gradual, bottom-up, evolutionary approach and a rapid, top-down paradigm for revolutionary change."[79]

JI functioned as an umbrella organization that — like al-Qaeda — co-opted other home-grown groups in the region for its strategic and tactical goals, including carrying out terrorist attacks. Like most revolutionary groups, it had both overt and covert arms: overt groups like Majelis Mujahidin Indonesia (MMI) campaigned and lobbied openly for Islamic *sharia* law while covert groups carried out terrorist attacks. Like al-Qaeda, one of JI's main principles was secrecy (*Tandzim Sirri* [*Secret Organization*]) "to insulate the open organization — with its mass membership and public interactions — from the illegal activities of a small contingent of its cadres — usually deliberately and covertly trained for the purpose of violence."[80] This was part of the reason it's difficult to understand JI from what individual members claim. We must look at its collective actions, tactics, ideology, documents like PUPJI, and the source of its ideology — al-Qaeda.

Much has also been made of the internal split within JI on the use of violence against Muslims, but that only mirrored the same split in al-Qaeda and the global jihadi community. Even the core, hierarchical group, al-Qaeda, had internal discord. As the group evolved into a diversified movement, these

---

[76] Ibid., p. 26.
[77] Ibid., p. 27.
[78] O. Brafman & R. Beckstrom, *The Starfish and the Spider: The Unstoppable Power of Leaderless Organizations*, Portfolio, 2006.
[79] E. Pavlova, "From Counter-Society to Counter-State: Jemaah Islamiyah According to PUPJI," *Institute of Defence and Strategic Studies*, November 14, 2006, p. 35.
[80] Ibid., p. 16.

disagreements increased. Some cells or groups fell by the wayside, but the groups' shared goal "of purifying Islam through violent action helps them see past their differences."[81] JI's experiences mirrored al-Qaeda's. For both groups, much of the evolution was a necessary response to the intense pressure of law enforcement. In the end, the JI factions shared the same ideology of hatred and intolerance. They only differed on their timetables and tactical targets. From its structure outlined in the PUPJI, JI was set up to sort out these internal questions, in the process, helping the jihadi virus mutate.

That virus spread through three main ways in the network: kinship, schools and religious study groups and/or military training. These bonds that led to increasingly violent actions were developed through camaraderie and friendship as well as discipleship: the Afghan veterans were radicalized by their experiences; those who trained in the Philippines also retained a certain solidarity.

Although less than 1% of Indonesia's schools or pesantrens preached extremist views,[82] the ones that did, particularly the schools set up by JI, seemed to make its students more prone to terrorism based on religious motivations. For example, 16 out of 26 Bali attackers and planners either attended or were associated with one of three JI-linked pesantrens: Al-Mukmin in Pondok Ngruki, Lukmanul Hakim in Malaysia, and Al-Islam in East Java. Association with Lukmanul Hakim "increases the probability by more than 23% that a jihadi will play a major role in an attack."[83]

Finally, a closer look at one jihadi family shows us the dense interconnected ties of kin and intermarriage that hold this network together through time and geography. Malaysian Nasir Abas set up the first JI training camp in the Philippines. He later became the leader of JI's Mantiqi 3, which covered the Philippines, Brunei, the east Malaysian states of Sarawak and Sabah, and Sulawesi and Kalimantan in Indonesia. His brother, Hashim, was a member of JI in Singapore (his voice is on the target survey tape sent to Al-Qaeda in Afghanistan), while his three sisters married JI leaders. One sister, Faridah, married Mukhlas, former head of Lukmanul Hakim school in Malaysia and later a key Bali planner. One family spanned and united JI's terrorist operations in Indonesia, Singapore, Malaysia and the Philippines,

---

[81] R. Nelson & T. Sanderson, "A Threat Transformed: Al-Qaeda and Associated Movements in 2011," *Center for Strategic & International Studies*, February 2011, p. 13.

[82] Author interview with Sidney Jones of International Crisis Group, March 23, 2011.

[83] J. Magouirk and S. Atran, "Jemaah Islamiyah's Radical Madrassah Network," *Dynamics of Asymmetric Warfare*, 2008, p. 1.

giving it both formal and informal ties that created a dense and trusted communication structure for ideas and operational plans for attacks.

One other factor makes this network unique: kinship ties span generations. Many of the Darul Islam leaders arrested during the government crackdown in the 70's and 80's had sons who became JI leaders 20 years later. Many of their daughters also became wives of JI leaders in the 1990's.[84]

JI was formed in 1993, but it took seven years before it carried out its first terrorist attacks — the Medan church bombing and the bombing of the Philippine Ambassador's house in 2000. The same network that carried out those attacks learned their lessons, experimented with tactics and, two years later in 2002, carried out the Bali bombings which announced JI's existence to the world. Those attacks were the first suicide bombers in, and from, Southeast Asia — concrete actions spread by the jihadi virus. Al-Qaeda helped fund and took responsibility for Bali, which triggered a regional dragnet and added JI to the list of global jihadi groups targeted by law enforcement.

In a November 2002 speech, Osama bin Laden included Bali in a list of attacks against Western targets carried out by "the zealous sons of Islam in defence of their religion and in response to the order of their God and prophet."[85] Like al-Qaeda and 9/11, the Bali attacks marked JI's peak of power and influence as an organized core group.

For three more years, the JI network carried out near-annual attacks: the JW Marriott bombing in 2003; the Australian embassy in 2004; and the second Bali bombings in 2005. By then, law enforcement successes continued degrading the network, effectively cutting down the size of the bombs and the number of victims.

For nearly four years, there were no major attacks, but that ended on July 17, 2009 when suicide bombers hit two hotels in the heart of Jakarta: the JW Marriott, first bombed by JI in 2003, and its sister hotel, the Ritz-Carlton. A key JI leader and Bali bomb-maker, Noordin Top, carried out those attacks. This time the attacks seemed to herald the regeneration of the JI network, the beginning of the third wave. Like al-Qaeda, it was now a decentralized social movement.

Two powerful JI leaders had been sidelined in the Philippines since 2003, Bali bombers Dulmatin and his brother-in-law, Umar Patek. There

---

[84] S. Jones, "Darul Islam's Ongoing Appeal," *Tempo Magazine*, August 18, 2010.

[85] "Full Text: 'Bin Laden's Message," *BBC News World Edition*, November 12, 2002. Available at http://news.bbc.co.uk/2/hi/middle_east/2455845.stm

was a regional dragnet for Dulmatin, who had a US$10 million reward set by the U.S. "Rewards for Justice" program which also set a US$1 million reward for Umar Patek. Both men trained in Afghanistan and were part of Hambali's core team. They were explosives experts who gained further combat experience after Bali in the Philippines — first with the Moro Islamic Liberation Front (MILF) then the Abu Sayyaf.

What did they do in the Philippines? What social networks did they belong to and how did they affect the development of its home-grown groups?

\*\*\*

Some answers came inside was a nondescript room in November, 2005 in the police headquarters, Camp Crame. Ces and her camera crew had just arrived. Boying Palileo and Armand Sol, my old CNN team who transferred to ABS-CBN with me, were busy setting up our lights and cameras. I had just finished doing a two-hour documentary on the Philippines' connections to global terrorism, and I was taking everything I had learned and looking at them through Filipino lenses.

It had taken a little work to get the interview with Dulmatin's wife, Istiada Omar Sovie, who was arrested in Patikul, Sulu on October 3, 2006. Few seemed to sense the importance of her arrest. After all, Dulmatin was JI's top leader in the Philippines and carried a US$10 million bounty. I wanted to learn more about him, and I wanted Ces to report on this beat so I asked her to do the interview with me.

When she came in, I briefed her on Sovie and the role women played in JI's networks. I told her about Mira Agustina, the Indonesian wife of al-Qaeda's most senior operative based in Indonesia and the Philippines, Omar al-Faruq. Like many marriages in the network, these ties serve to bind operatives — not just with ideology but with blood.

A veteran of the Afghan war, al-Faruq was sent by al-Qaeda's top leaders, "to the Philippines in 1995 along with Al Gaza'tri, an al-Qaeda camp commander."[86] They were supposed to set up training camps inside Camp Abubakar. Al-Faruq became the liaison between "the Arabs" and the MILF chief Hashim Salamat.[87] He also wanted to get commercial flight training in the Philippines[88] but never did.

---

[86] Classified U.S. intelligence document, September 9, 2002.
[87] Ibid.
[88] Classified Indonesian intelligence report, "Umar Faruq," June 2002.

In Indonesia, he took the name Mahmud bin Ahmad Assegaf and married 24-year-old Mira Agustina. "I received his proposals," said the shy woman who was covered from head to toe in a burka. She had not yet even met him. "I was still in school so I didn't reply seriously. Mahmud proposed three times, but I didn't respond. In July 1999, I went home during a school holiday, and I was introduced to him. I prayed and asked for Allah's protection, and that very same day, we were married."[89] He proposed, she said, through her father, Haris Fadillah, a commander in Ambon who was was part of JI's Darul Islam network. Omar Al-Faruq told his interrogators his wife kept the books for al-Qaeda money funneled through the Saudi charity Al-Haramain. Al-Faruq also said his wife was present at a meeting in May 1999 attended by her father, at which a plot to kill Megawati Sukarnoputri, then Indonesia's Vice President was discussed. Money for the assassination changed hands,[90] but the weapons never arrived. Her husband said Mira took notes from the meeting and translated them into Arabic. "I am deeply hurt and shocked" by her husband's claims, Mira said. "I feel like the most violated person on earth. If they were true, automatically, it means that I have been lied to all of this time, but I cannot be sure now that they are true, and that my husband is responsible for all that." He was actually responsible for much more. After he was arrested, information from him, corroborated by other al-Qaeda operatives in U.S. custody, showed he and Hambali planned "large-scale attacks against U.S. interests in Indonesia, Malaysia, Philippines, Singapore, Thailand, Taiwan, Vietnam and Cambodia."[91] He was killed in Iraq in 2006 after escaping from prison more than a year earlier.

I told this and other stories to Ces so she could get a sense of how the women of JI worked and their relationships with their men. She listened intently and took copious notes. We waited nearly an hour. When Sovie walked in with her child, we saw a petite, self-contained woman. We introduced ourselves. I noticed she carried a paperback copy of the Koran. I asked to see it and saw it was in Arabic with English translations. I opened it to the page bookmarked by a piece of paper with a list of names. I looked more closely and from what I could guess, it seemed like there

---

[89] CNN interview, Jakarta, Indonesia, Nov. 7, 2002.

[90] Others who attended the meeting, according to a CIA document, were Yasin from Malaysia, Al-Bukhari from Singapore and Abdul Azis al-Kahar from Sulawesi. Al-Bukhari handed money to Yasin, who was tasked to buy the weapons.

[91] Classified U.S. intelligence document, September 9, 2002.

handwritten meticulously were dozens of different names for God. Ces and Sovie established an immediate bond — motherhood. Her child, Edar, was reading a copy of the Koran in Arabic and, at some point, was writing in Arabic on a piece of paper. During her interview with Ces, Sovie started to cry. She was arrested with two of her children, but she was worried because she was forced to leave her four youngest children behind: Adiba, nine years old; Osama, seven years old; Adija, five years old; and Musaiba, two years old. She said she immediately began to fast and pray for her children. I noticed her lips were pale, and at times, her hands were shaking.

Other details during the interview painted a picture of a woman I could see Ces beginning to admire: a medical doctor who gave up her career to follow her husband, courageous in the face of danger, focused on keeping her family together. She and Dulmatin are actually cousins so she knew him well. They grew up together in Pemalang: Sovie's father is the elder brother of Dulmatin's father.[92] Sovie was 26 years old when she married Dulmatin, and they seemed to have a good relationship. She also shared her husband's religious zeal. After all, they named one of their sons Osama.

Dulmatin is a good-looking man with intense eyes and a thin mustache — an Afghan war veteran who joined JI's hard-core military group. A teacher in JI's Lukmanul Hakim school in Johor Bahru, Malaysia, he had religious credentials. He was a key player in the Bali bombings and recruited many to join the global jihad, including Umar Patek. He is considered an electronics specialist and master bomb-maker. Some accounts say Patek was his brother-in-law.[93] After mixing the bomb explosives, Patek would wait for Dulmatin to place the detonation triggers. They worked together to make 38 bombs for the Christmas 2000 church bombings and for the massive Bali bomb, perhaps the most sophisticated one detonated in Southeast Asia. After most of the leadership of JI were either killed or arrested, Dulmatin was widely regarded as second only to Noordin Top, who carried out the 2004 Marriott attack, the second Bali bombings in 2005 and the second hotel bombings in 2009. After Top was killed in 2009, Dulmatin became Asia's most wanted even as his reputation within the jihadi community soared, particularly after at least two announcements from the Philippines that he had been killed

---

[92] Classified Armed Forces of the Philippines document: "Istiada Bte Hja Omar Sovie," report from RO-0/ACTIC-9 and Ro-12/SACTIC-12, Camp Navarro, Zamboanga City, November 7–10, 2006.

[93] Z. Abuza, "Umar Patek: Indonesia's Most Wanted," *Jamestown Foundation*, Vol. 1, Issue 4, April 30, 2010.

(both wrong). He continued to notch up combat experience after he and Umar Patek fled to the Philippines when the crackdown in Indonesia began. Sovie said she and her children joined them as well — although in staggered trips. He was also experienced in creating alliances that bind. Abdullah Sunata from Kompak was a key ally, extending JI's umbrella organization over groups that were also under attack, especially after 2002. Sunata helped Dulmatin and his family flee to Mindanao in April 2003. His brother-in-law, Hari Kuncoro better known as Bahar, and his wife also joined them.

When Sunata arrived in the Philippines, he allied first with the MILF. He strengthened ties with groups under the JI umbrella: Malaysian Zulkifli bin Hir is the leader of Kumpulan Mujahidin Malaysia and a member of JI's central command.[94] Known in the Philippines as Marwan, he comes from a family of jihadists. I met one brother in Jakarta in 2001 after he lost his leg trying to bomb the Atrium mall. Another brother was arrested and indicted by the FBI in San Jose, California for his work with JI. Marwan is married to a Filipina convert to Islam.[95] A Singaporean JI member, Muawiyah, whose real name is Mohammed Abdullah Ali, works closely with Marwan.

In 2005, after continued pressure from the Philippine government, these JI members, along with RSM and the Abu Sayyaf, were forced out of MILF camps. Dulmatin and Umar Patek continued to find sanctuary with individual commanders like Umra Kato, Commander Bravo and Abu Badrin (who fought with Patek in Afghanistan), but the MILF took a position that forced JI to move out of central Mindanao and work with the Abu Sayyaf in Jolo. The continued crackdown as well as the presence of U.S. troops made life harder for the JI operatives. In addition, Noordin Top had ambitious plans in Jakarta, and he needed help. At the beginning of 2006, Dulmatin began to make plans to return to Indonesia, but before he could move, his wife and two eldest children were arrested in a raid meant for him. They were soon deported by the Philippines back to Indonesia.

After several attempts, Dulmatin made it back to Jakarta safely, along with two others, including a Filipino. JI member Ridwan was originally a Kompak activist, but he acted as Dulmatin's bodyguard since he accompanied him to Mindanao in 2003.[96] Another example of the ties that bind:

---

[94] Rewards for Justice Program, "Zulkifli bin Hir," $5 million reward, Department of Justice. Available at http://www.rewardsforjustice.net/index.cfm?page=zulkifli&language=english

[95] Interviews with Filipino and U.S. intelligence officials from 2005–2012.

[96] "Indonesia: Jihadi Surprise in Aceh," *International Crisis Group*, Asia Report No. 189, April 20, 2010, p. 4.

Dulmatin took Ridwan's sister as his second wife soon after they returned to Indonesia, cementing ties between two different groups in the JI network. The second man who travelled with Dulmatin is an Abu Sayyaf member named Hasan Noor, better known by his alias, Blackberry.

Dulmatin picked up the leadership reins of the JI network, showing how easy it is to regenerate a social network if the right people with the right training and connections appeared. Almost as soon as he returned, he became a magnet for JI members, many of whom had just been released from prison. He also acted as a bridge between JI leader Abu Bakar Ba'asyir and Noordin Top, whom many thought had formed a splinter group. The reality though is that both men were embedded in the same social network that carried out the Bali attacks and continued to grow, although without central leadership. Much has been made about a greater majority of JI who didn't want violence. That's true, but it has always been true that only a minority was enough to define the character of JI and extend its reach across Southeast Asia to plot and carry out the region's worst attacks. That social network, the old Darul Islam social movement, remained, and Dulmatin had the gravitas, experience and connections to regenerate the social network, using weak links to build bridges with nearly every Indonesian jihadi group.

On September 17, 2008, Abu Bakar Ba'asyir launched Jemaah Ansharut Tauhid (JAT). He essentially took his supporters from JI and gutted most of MMI, its overt arm lobbying for Islamic *sharia* law in Indonesia. JAT reunites Noordin Top's group with Dulmatin, who was now working with Ba'asyir to set up a secure base, the *quoidah amina*. The regeneration of the JI social network was complete. The cells which remained had grown in different ways, but now a central leadership was ready to provide religious leadership and guidance and a military operations arm could begin to unite the disparate cells. JAT, according to counterterrorism officials, was JI's self-regeneration.

"JAT is the new camouflage of JI," said Ansyaad M'bai, the chief of Indonesia's National Counter-Terrorism Agency (BNPT). "It has the same leader, Abu Bakar Ba'asyir, and most of the key figures of JAT are also JI. So I call this the new jacket of JI."[97]

Sovie gave authorities another example of the social ties that make this network so robust: Zakiyah Daradjad, the wife of Bali field commander

---

[97] Author interview with General Ansyaad Mbai, Jakarta, Indonesia, June 24, 2011.

Imam Samudra, was her classmate in medical school.[98] Her children were picked up by Filipino authorities more than seven months later on May 11, 2007 in Tawi-Tawi. The children were relatively fluent in Tagalog and Tausug and told them about their uncle and aunt, Bahar and Tika. Dulmatin's brother-in-law, Bahar, is Umar Patek's bodyguard and stayed behind. They also spoke about another woman who came to take care of them, one who spoke Bahasa Indonesia. Bekto Suprapto from Indonesia's Densus 88 came to the Philippines to speak with them and showed them pictures asking them to identify their *ama*. They pointed to the picture of a woman Suprapto identified as Munfiatun als Fitri, the wife of Noordin Top. Densus 88 would later check and find their records showed she had never been to Manila so they chalked it up to children under stress.[99]

After the interview when we were riding back to the station, Ces was so bothered that Sovie had been separated from her children. She seemed impressed with her ability to handle the lifestyle she chose with her husband and asked questions about exactly how much she may have known about what her husband has done. I told her it's hard to gauge how much the women know. Sometimes, it's clear they're part of the jihad their husband has chosen. Other times, they may deny knowledge but may know all too well and may even be helping actively. The other JI leaders in the Philippines — Umar Patek, Marwan and Muawiyah — all have Filipino wives, and from the intelligence reports I've read, it's clear they — as well as their social networks — are helping their husbands actively.

Dulmatin and his family were back in Indonesia by the time Ces, Jimmy and Angel were kidnapped on June 8, 2008. Three and a half months earlier, Umar Patek and Bahar, Dulmatin's brother-in-law, were with the group of Radullan Sahiron in Sitio Tubig Bato, moving towards Patikul, Sulu. A little more than two weeks before the kidnapping, Patek, Marwan and Muawiyah moved to the camp of Isnilon Hapilon and Albader Parad in nearby Mount Timahu, Indanan, Sulu — the same areas where Sahiron's men would hold our team hostage.

---

[98] Classified Armed Forces of the Philippines document: "Istiada Bte Hja Omar Sovie," report from RO-0/ACTIC-9 and Ro-12/SACTIC-12, Camp Navarro, Zamboanga City, November 7–10, 2006, p. 9.

[99] Email interview with Brig. General Tito Karnavian, February 16, 2012.

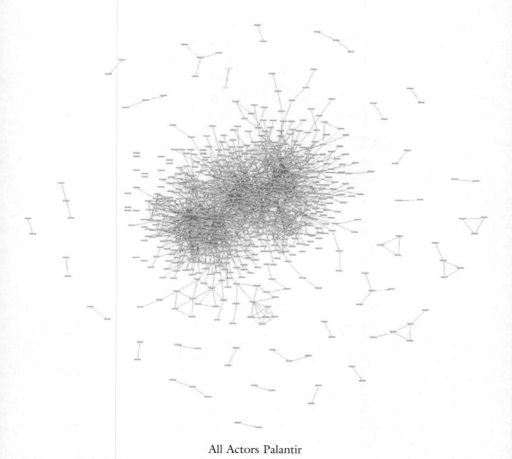

All Actors Palantir

This sociogram shows all the actors in the entire book: 648 entities, of which 387 are people, 39 are terrorist organizations, 35 are commercial groups. The book describes a total of 179 events, including 34 bombings, 32 meetings, 24 armed assaults (including kidnappings) and 17 plots. 1,790 links among entities and events appear in the data.

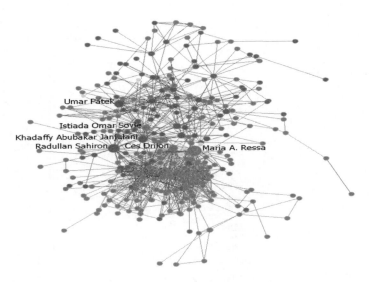

Table 1. All Top 10 ORA Key Nodes

This table shows the top scoring nodes side by side for measures.

| Rank | Betweeness centrality | Closeness centrality | Eigenvector centrality | Total degree centrality |
|---|---|---|---|---|
| 1 | Maria A. Ressa | Maria A. Ressa | Frank Oreña | Maria A. Ressa |
| 2 | Radullan Sahiron | Radullan Sahiron | Wed Iglesia | Ces Drilon |
| 3 | Umar Patek | Umar Patek | Grace Oreña | Frank Oreña |
| 4 | Khadaffy Abubakar Janjalani | Ronaldo Puno | Maria A. Ressa | Wed Iglesia |
| 5 | Ces Drilon | Mohammed | Col. Winnie Quidato | Grace Oreña |
| 6 | Istiada Omar Sovie | Istiada Omar Sovie | Ces Drilon | Col. Winnie Quidato |
| 7 | Ahmad Santos | Col. Winnie Quidato | Libby Pascual | Jimmy Encarnacion |
| 8 | Mohammed | Ces Drilon | Glenda Gloria | Libby Pascual |
| 9 | Ronaldo Puno | Khadaffy Abubakar Janjalani | Richard | Angelo Valderama |
| 10 | Eugenio "Gabby" Lopez III | Wed Iglesia | Jimmy Encarnacion | Glenda Gloria |

## All Top 10 Organizational Risk Organizer (ORA)

This sociogram displays the entire book network in ORA, a social network analysis program used to measure complex network metrics. Using betweenness centrality — one of the four basic centrality measures — this graph adjusts node size by the level in which each node lies on the shortest path between all other nodes.

(*Continued*)

You can see there is significant overlap between the friendly network (those who fight terrorism) in *black* and the *gray* network made up of terrorists and their supporters. Note the metrics are calculated for an aggregated network consisting of all one-mode networks and the converted two-mode to one-mode "Event" network. In other words, anytime two actors participated in the same event, we assumed a relationship formed between them. See Table 1 for All top 10 ORA. See the section below on 'Measures of Centrality' for a description of the different centrality measures.

## Measures of Centrality

**Degree centrality** is the count of the number of an actor's ties (relations). It is the level of activity, exposure to the network and opportunity to directly influence others.

**Closeness centrality** measures how close (on average) each actor is to all other actors in a network. This is the accessibility within the network, indirect influence and point of rapid diffusion.

**Betweenness centrality** measures the extent to which each actor lies on the shortest path between all other actors in a network. This is the brokerage potential and informal power.

**Eigenvector centrality** assumes that ties to highly central actors are more important than ties to peripheral actors. An actor's eigenvector centrality is its summed connections to others, weighted by their centrality scores. This is "snobbishness" and its "not what you know but who you know."

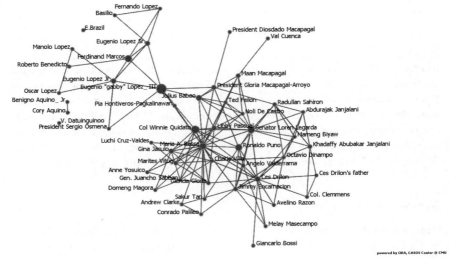

Chapter One: Betweenness Centrality Sociogram

This measures the extent to which each actor lies on the shortest path between all other actors in the network. This shows connections basically reflecting the formal power structures.

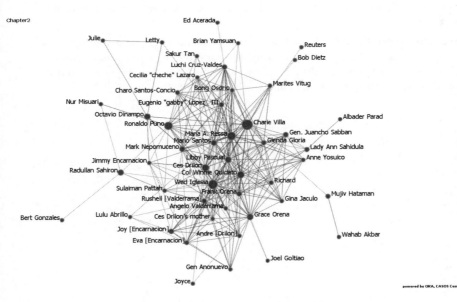

Chapter Two: Betweenness Centrality Sociogram

This measures the extent to which each actor in the chapter lies on the shortest path between all other actors in a network. High betweenness means actors may have the potential to act as brokers within the network or can be used as a measure of informal power.

## Table 2. Kidnapping ORA Key Nodes

This table shows the top scoring nodes side by side for selected measures.

| Rank | Betweeness centrality | Closeness centrality | Eigenvector centrality | Total degree centrality |
|------|----------------------|---------------------|------------------------|------------------------|
| 1 | Wed Iglesia | Wed Iglesia | Ces Drilon | Ces Drilon |
| 2 | Ces Drilon | Angelo Valderama | Jimmy Encarnacion | Wed Iglesia |
| 3 | Radullan Sahiron | Rock Drilon | Wed Iglesia | Maria A. Ressa |
| 4 | Angelo Valderama | Jimmy Encarnacion | Maria A. Ressa | Jimmy Encarnacion |
| 5 | Ronaldo Puno | Sulaiman Pattah | Angelo Valderama | Angelo Valderama |
| 6 | Sali Said | Ces Drillon | Grace Oreña | Grace Oreña |
| 7 | Jimmy Encarnacion | Col. Winnie Quidato | Sulaiman Pattah | Sulaiman Pattah |
| 8 | Maria A. Ressa | Sali Said | Alvarez Isnaji | Col. Winnie Quidato |
| 9 | Rock Drilon | Radullan Sahiron | Juri Isnaji | Rock Drilon |
| 10 | Sulaiman Pattah | Senator Loren Legarda | Col. Winnie Quindato | Radullan Sahiron |

## Chapter Two: Kidnapping ORA Centrality

The sociogram above depicts the June 9, 2008 kidnapping network while Table 2 lists the top 10 actors in terms of the four basic centrality measures. The node sizes in the sociogram are adjusted by betweenness centrality. Note the metrics are calculated for an aggregated network, meaning both direct person-to-person ties were used as well as ties between people who participated in the same event where participants have some communal relationship.

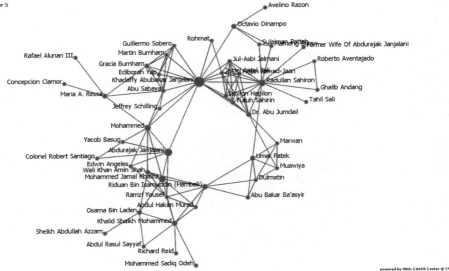

Chapter Three: Betweenness Centrality Sociogram

This graph shows the social network linking Osama bin Laden to the leadership of the Abu Sayyaf — from its founder, Abdurajak, his brother, Khadaffy, and on to Radullan Sahiron. Betweenness measures the extent to which each actor lies on the shortest path between all other actors in a network.

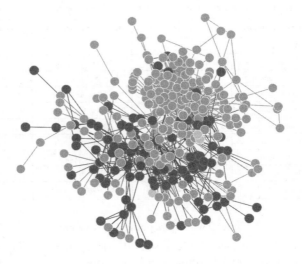

Chapter Three: All Actors

This sociogram in ORA represents the main component, which omits all disconnected smaller networks as well as isolates, of the entire coded book. The gray nodes highlight the non-terrorist affiliated actors — the friendly network. The black nodes are terrorists or insurgent-affiliated actors. The light gray nodes are unclear.

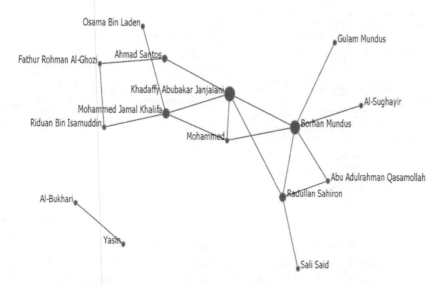

## Table 3. Financial Network Betweenness Centrality Key Nodes

This table shows the top scoring nodes side by side for selected measures.

| Rank | Between centrality | Closeness centrality | Eigenvector centrality | Total degree centrality |
|------|--------------------|-----------------------|------------------------|-------------------------|
| 1 | Khadaffy Abubakar Janjalani | Khadaffy Abubakar Janjalani | Borhan Mundus | Borhan Mundus |
| 2 | Borhan Mundus | Borhan Mundus | Khadaffy Abubakar Janjalani | Mohammed Jamal Khalifa |
| 3 | Mohammed Jamal Khalifa | Muhammed | Radullan Sahiron | Radullan Sahiron |
| 4 | Radullan Sahiron | Mohammed Jamal Khalifa | Mohammed | Khadaffy Abubakar Janjalani |
| 5 | Ahmad Santos | Radullan Sahiron | Mohammed Jamal Khalifa | Mohammed |
| 6 | Riduan bin Isamuddin | Ahmad Santos | Abu Adulrahman Qasamollah | Fathur Rahman al-Ghozi |
| 7 | Fathur Rahman al-Ghozi | Gulam Mundus | Al-Sughayir | Riduan bin Isomuddin |
| 8 | Gulam Mundus | Riduan bin Isomuddin | Sali Said | Abu Adulrahman Qasamollah |
| 9 | Muhammed | Fathur Rahman al-Ghozi | Osama bin Laden | Ahmad Santos |
| 10 | Al-Sughayir | Abu Abdulrahman Qasamollah | Ahmad Santos | Al-Sughayir |

## Chapter Four: Financial Network Betweenness Centrality Sociogram

This sociogram depicts all actors within the book that had financial ties to each other. Node size is adjusted by betweenness. See Table 3 for key nodes table.

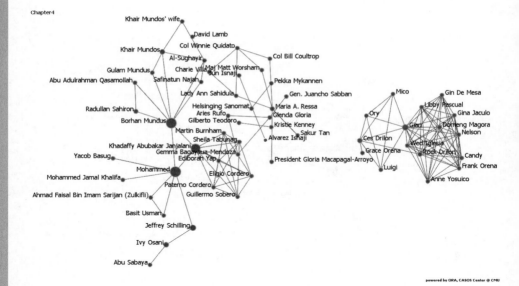

Chapter Four: Betweenness Centrality Sociogram

This sociogram shows the central role Mohammed played in the history of the Abu Sayyaf and its financial network. It also shows the betweenness centrality of some of the people in the crisis center. Betweenness measures the extent to which each actor in the chapter lies on the shortest path between all other actors in a network.

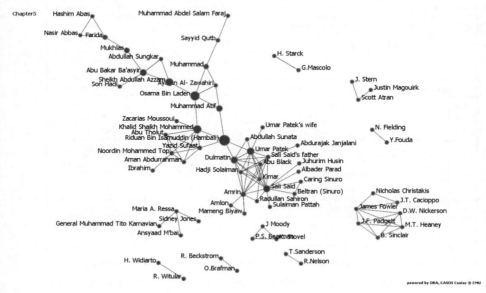

Chapter Five: Betweenness Centrality Sociogram

This shows the geographical spread of the social network from different countries from Afghanistan to Malaysia to Indonesia to the Philippines. High betweenness means actors may have the potential to act as brokers within the network or can be used as a measure of informal power.

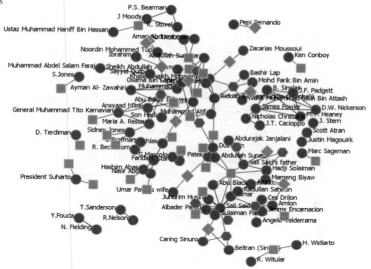

## Chapter Five: ORA Multi-Mode

This ORA graph of Chapter Five depicts all people (circles) connected to organizations, events, and locations (squares, diamonds, hexagons). Only people are labeled here.

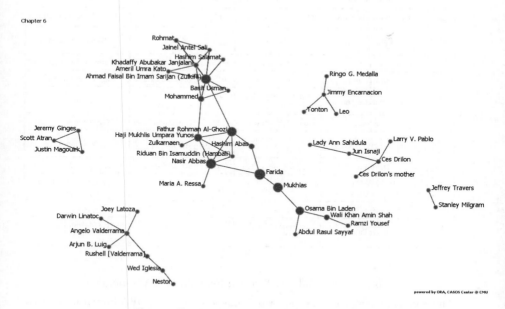

## Chapter Six: Betweenness Centrality Sociogram

From upper left to lower right, you can see the network and hubs. At the upper left, Indonesian Zulkifli is a hub in the southern Philippines. Fathur Rohman al-Ghozi connects the region. Hambali is a key hub, with the Indonesians linking the network to Osama bin Laden.

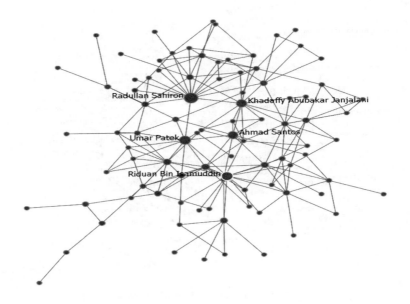

Table 4. Terrorist Centrality ORA Key Nodes

This table shows the top scoring nodes side by side for selected measures.

| Rank | Betweenees centrality | Closeness centrality | Eigenvector centrality | Total degree centrality |
|------|------------------------|----------------------|------------------------|--------------------------|
| 1 | Radullan Sahiron | Umar Patek | Fathur Rahman al-Ghozi | Radullan Sahiron |
| 2 | Riduan bin Isamuddin | Radullan Sahiron | Riduan bin Isamuddin | Khadaffy Abubakar Janjalani |
| 3 | Umar Patek | Ahmad Santos | Haji Mukhils Umpara Yunos | Riduan bin Isamuddin |
| 4 | Khadaffy Abubakar Janjalani | Khadaffy Abubakar Janjalani | Ahmad Faisal bin Iman Sarijan (Zulkilli) | Dulmatin |
| 5 | Ahmad Santos | Riduan bin Isamuddin | Khadaffy Abubakar Janjalani | Fathur Rahman al-Ghozi |
| 6 | Fathur Rahman al-Ghozi | Fathur Rahman al-Ghozi | Umar Patek | Mohammed |
| 7 | Dulmatin | Taufik Abdul Halim | Khahd Shaikh Mohammed | Khalid Shaikh Mohammed |
| 8 | Haji Mukhlis Umpara Yunos | Dulmatin | Dulmatin | Ahmad Faisal Bin Imam Sarijan (Zulkifli) |
| 9 | Omar Al-Faruq | Muawiyah | Mohammed | Umar Patek |
| 10 | Abu Bakar Ba'asyir | Haji Mukhils Umpara Yunos | Ahmad Santos | Haji Mukhils Umpara Yunos |

Chapters Five and Six: Terrorist Centrality ORA Sociogram

The sociogram above is the "Terrorist" network as seen in ORA but with the node sizes adjusted by betweenness centrality. The metrics shown in Table 4 are calculated against an aggregate network consisting of all one-mode relationships.

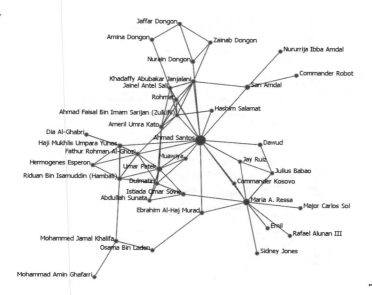

## Chapter Seven: Betweenness Centrality Sociogram

Again, you can see the betweenness centrality in this network. At its center is Ahmad Santos, the founder and former head of the Rajah Solaiman Movement (RSM). You can trace RSM's links to the Abu Sayyaf, Jemaah Islamiyah and MILF's Special Operations Group here.

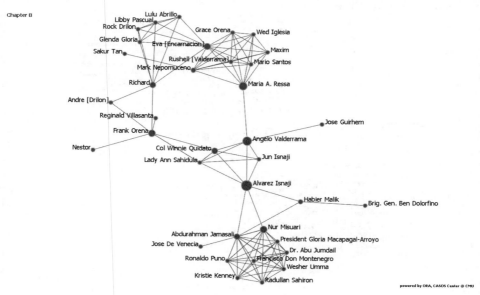

## Chapter Eight: Betweenness Centrality Sociogram

This diagram shows the links and subgroupings of the Abu Sayyaf and the MNLF and the network behind the failed surrender of senior Abu Sayyaf leaders. They're linked to the crisis group negotiating the release through Mayor Alvarez Isnaji.

## Chapter Nine: Betweenness Centrality Sociogram

This shows the social networks pulled together by two women, Istiada Omar Sovie, the wife of Indonesian JI leader Dulmatin, and Ces Drilon. Betweenness measures the extent to which each actor in the chapter lies on the shortest path between all other actors in a network. High betweenness means actors may have the potential to act as brokers within the network or can be used as a measure of informal power.

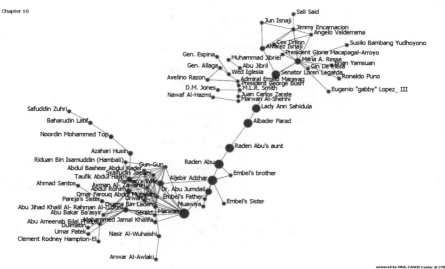

## Chapter Ten: Betweenness Centrality Sociogram

This is a visualization of the key role Marwan plays in connecting different networks. At the upper right, you can see Loren Legarda's bridging role. Betweenness measures the extent to which each actor in the chapter lies on the shortest path between all other actors in a network. High betweenness means actors may have the potential to act as brokers within the network or can be used as a measure of informal power.

# Deadline

Wednesday, June 11 — Day 4 of the kidnapping — reflected our collective mood in the crisis center: temperamental, dark and rainy. Few of us actually slept the night before. The phone calls with Ces started in the morning on logistics of communication between Lady Ann and Jun Isnaji. Ces continued giving veiled hints and directions regarding their location. Some were so creative, it was hard to understand like this one: "I have a resthouse which has 20 caretakers — 3,000 meters from a lone house facing the sunrise." The "resthouse" was their camp; the "caretakers" their kidnappers; and based on her other clues, their camp was facing Mt. Matanding. On one wall, Cusi, who was doing technical work for Iglesia, put up a topographical map, and we were now beginning to see their possible locations. The last location of her cellphone was near Panglima Estino. The police technical team was attempting to plot an estimated location from the inputs of intelligence groups and the phone companies.

At 11:15 a.m., Frank made a request: "The family of Jimmy and Angelo are here. Maybe you can ask permission so they can speak to them."

"Can the family of Jimmy and Angel speak to them?" Ces asked her kidnappers. "Okay. Here's Angel first then Jimmy." The sounds were muffled as she passed the phone. Then we heard the voice of Angel. Frank quickly stood up and gave his seat to Rushell, Angel's wife. She rushed forward.

"Hello, 'Chelle?" asked Angel. It was good to hear his voice sounding firm and strong.

"Hello, love," said Rushell.

"How are the kids?"

"They're okay. Just be careful, okay? Pray as much as you can. We'll all be fine." She started to cry although we could see her effort to hold back her tears.

155

Nestor Cusi mapping cellphone coordinates.

"Take care of the kids," said Angel. It felt strange to listen to Angel struggle to communicate with his wife, strange to see all of us around the table listening but trying to figure out how to give them a sense of privacy.

"Yes, don't worry."

"We're okay here." Angel tried to reassure his wife.

"Okay. Steel yourselves. Be brave, but just be careful." All of us around the table could feel her emotions. She wiped her eyes.

"Jimmy wants to talk," said Angel, handing the phone to Jimmy, whose brother, Leo, came closer to the table and took the seat next to Rushell. Jimmy's wife was picking up their children and, unfortunately, wasn't in the room for this call.

"Tol" — street slang for 'brother' — said Leo tentatively. Wearing a yellow shirt, he reminded me of yellow ribbons around an oak tree, of Cory Aquino in 1983. It was the color of hope.

"Hello, Tol," Jimmy voice was strong. "Don't worry too much about us. Please tell Mama ..."

"Yes, I spoke with Mama," interrupts Leo. "She was able to handle the news. I told her not to worry. We're doing everything here so you can come home. Ah, how are you there?"

"We're okay."

"Physically — you, Ma'am Ces and Angelo?"

"Yes, don't worry."

"The kids, Joy, Tonton, we're all praying for you. Don't worry. The family's doing everything."

"Okay, don't tell the media anything ..." started Jimmy.

"Yes, Tol. Just be careful. Be strong. Make sure you take care of yourselves and that you all stay together with Ma'am Ces."

"Can you also tell the wife of Angel not to give any information to anyone?" I thought if Jimmy was saying this then the kidnappers must have discussed it either with them or in front of them.

"Okay, Tol. God bless. Love you."

Ces came back on the line. Yesterday, she had asked her brother to contact the family of Dinampo and assure them he was safe. Frank updated her and asked how Dinampo was doing. Focusing on easy tasks like this gave all of us a sense of "normal" — that somehow we were in control. It was, of course, a fleeting illusion.

"Prof, do you have a message for your family?" Ces asked then turned back to relay his response. "Tell his wife not to worry." At this point, there were rumors circulating that Dinampo may have been part of the plot — allegations that were never proven. He has consistently denied any involvement in the kidnapping. Later, Angel, Jimmy and Ces did point out he received preferential treatment, but Ces and Jimmy added the kidnappers may have treated him that way because of his age.

The first sign of trouble came around 1 p.m. The kidnappers and Jun Isnaji had been having trouble calling Lady Ann, but this call showed the many layers of misunderstanding and cross-purposes of the people involved. It began to crystallize the brewing demands that would lead to a heart-wrenching ultimatum a few hours later.

"I talked to Jun Isnaji," said Ces. "He spoke with Lady Ann, and she said that she's waiting to hear from you, and that she will contact him when she has the money."

"Okay," said Frank. "What's their understanding? The Vice Governor hasn't started negotiating with them yet."

"They understand the money will be brought to them."

"We're not at that stage yet."

"That's the understanding of the people here — that once my safety is confirmed by Lady Ann she will get the money from you and give it to them. They will help if the money is in Jolo. They will get a police escort and deliver the money. That's their understanding."

"Isnaji is not relaying the right information. That's not where we are. We haven't started negotiating yet. Can you tell them the Vice Gov wants to speak with them so they know where we are and what we're thinking?"

"But she can't be reached so they're getting angry."

"Yeah, we're also trying to reach her and can't contact her.

About 45 minutes later, Ces called again. This time, her voice was strained.

"Frank, they're very angry. Lady Ann told them there's only ₱2 million. As far as they're concerned, it's ₱20 million. So they don't want to talk to her any more. They only want to talk to Mayor Isnaji. They said the ₱20 million is non-negotiable. They're very angry…"

"But you tell them that ABS is standing by its policy not to give ransom so the money is coming from us. We cannot raise the ₱20 million."

"Wait," Ces spoke to her kidnappers. "Wait, what's happening is that my family is having a hard time raising the money. It's not Lady Ann's fault. My family could only raise ₱2 million. ABS will not give any money."

Listening to these conversations was extremely frustrating. The night before, Frank and I spoke with Lady Ann, who asked us to stop communicating directly with Ces because she wanted all conversations to go through her. Iglesia agreed. I thought about the danger. Again, it was a matter of trust. If we gave up our line to Ces, we wouldn't have independent verification of what was happening and what people were saying or doing in the name of the families or ABS-CBN. At the same time, it was clear Ces was empowered, and the police said negotiations would go faster if she lost hope. It would be the first step for the kidnappers to begin to give up, see an end and accept a compromise. It's tricky logic: they pointed out that Ces could pick up the phone and call her contacts for money. Ces could make promises independent of us. She needed to stop actively helping her kidnappers, and the only way she would do that is if she lost hope. After they explained it to me, I discussed it with my team and agreed. Now I wanted the family to concur. Frank would be the point of contact, but everyone else would reject Ces'calls.

We were keeping track of the location of their cellphones, but we couldn't triangulate with any degree of accuracy. I began to realize that the authorities weren't really prepared for any kind of rescue mission, and, like the Burnhams, we would only put their lives at risk. The safest way to get them home was to pay the ransom.

\*\*\*

Nights in the jungle seemed endless. Ces woke up at midnight and thought it was near daybreak. She tried to go back to sleep but had a hard time so she began to pray. Her mind kept going back over events that happened the night before. She remembered her phone call with Grech, who asked to speak to Commander Putol Solaiman to explain it was her family who was raising the money, and all they could afford was ₱2 million. One of the kidnappers retorted, "Let's start digging their graves." It was the first time a threat seemed real. Ces knew she had to be prepared for anything, and she was resolved to face her kidnappers. For her, it was important she face them without losing her dignity, but she was scared. She told her sister, "Maybe we can borrow money from ABS-CBN."

She didn't know what was happening, but she knew she had to trust her network. The kids in the camp were taunting her, and she tried not to let it get to her. In their singsong, high-pitched voices, the taunts were like a nursery rhyme, *"kawawa naman si Ma'am, hindi nakikita ang mga anak niya, kawawa naman si Ma'am..."* (Poor Ma'am, she can't see her kids, poor Ma'am.") The singsong phrases reverberated in her head, and she started to cry.

The jungle air was heavy and oppressive. The sounds were magnified, startling her — making her realize self-pity would make her lose hope, something she thought she couldn't afford. Then she remembered her dad. He was a Lieutenant Colonel when he was assigned here. Today, June 11 was his birthday. He survived an ambush in these jungles. She thought about him until she convinced herself she could feel his presence and draw on the strength of his spirit. If he could escape, she could too. That comforting thought helped her, and she fell asleep. Soon after daybreak when her kidnappers gave the phone to her, she saw a text message from her mother: "Your release on your dad's birthday will be his most beautiful gift to us." It would turn out to be the most challenging day yet.

It was a day of phone calls. The kidnappers were trying to reach Mayor Isnaji and Lady Ann. It was good that Jimmy and Angel got to speak to their families as well. It began to turn ugly shortly after noon. She had a hard time finding Lady Ann, and when they finally spoke, the kidnappers didn't like her message: all her family could pay was ₱2 million.

Commander Putol grabbed the phone. Ces thought he would yell into it. He looked like a lunatic. Instead, he grabbed her, looked her in the eye and threatened to kill her.

*"Sanay naman kaming mabuhay sa gubat. Kaya naming mabuhay dito. Kayo mamamatay na lang kayo dito."* (tr. We're used to living in the jungle. We can live here. You will all just die here.)"[1]

There was an explosion of activity as the anger spread and was amplified through the group. Commander Putol yelled for someone to get ABS-CBN's video camera, threatening to set it on fire.

"That's enough," yelled Commander Putol. "We have nothing else to talk about. Don't call anymore." He was rabid, stood up and left Ces. Other armed men followed him. Ces walked back to her hammock next to Jimmy. He heard the yells and looked worried when he saw Ces walking towards him with the armed men following her.

"Ma'am, they're pointing their guns at us," Jimmy whispered to Ces. She didn't want to turn around and look. She sat down. "Ma'am, they took my camera. I shot more video this morning. What if they find it?"

"Let's just pray," said Ces, who began to pray the rosary, counting each Hail Mary on her fingers. After a short while, Jimmy reached for her hand, and the two prayed quietly together. After less than an hour, the men returned and encircled the team.

The mood turned ugly. Someone yelled, *"Pugat!"* which means behead. Ces felt her heart beat faster, the adrenalin rushed through her body as armed men surrounded them, pulled out their guns and aimed it at them. Several men picked up Jimmy and Angel. One man grabbed Jimmy and said, "We're used to eating bananas here. Two million pesos only and they'll still take a cut. We won't agree to that! We already told you not to get Lady Ann."[2]

Ces watched helplessly as the men pushed Jimmy and Angel down until they were kneeling on the mud. They positioned them back to back and began to tie their hands together. She couldn't let this happen and jumped up.

*"Sandali, sandali!* Hold on," she said loudly, trying to take control and be authoritative. "Let's call my family again."

---

[1] The following account is a composite picture taken from the sworn statements of Ces Drilon (given to SPO2 Larry V. Pablo at PNP Criminal Investigation and Detection Group (CIDG), Camp Crame, June 25, 2008 at 10 a.m.); Jimmy Encarnacion (given to PO1 Ringo G. Medalla at PNP CIDG, Camp Crame, June 27, 2008 at 11 a.m.); Angelo Valderrama (given to PCI Arjun B. Luig, PO2 Darwin Linatoc, Po2 Joey Latoza at PNP CIDG, Camp Crame, June 27, 2008 at 10:30 a.m.). Some details also come from articles written by Ces Drilon.

[2] In Filipino: *"Sanay kaming kumain ng saging ditto. Dalawang milyon lang may bawas pa. Hindi kami papaya. Sinabi na namin sa inyo huwag ng kukunin si Lady Ann."*

"We need to give an ultimatum," said Commander Putol. Jimmy noticed Dinampo wasn't tied. "If the money doesn't arrive by 2 p.m. tomorrow, that's it. The full amount needs to be with Mayor Isnaji or else Jimmy, you'll shoot the beheading of Angel, live!"

"We will behead Angel," a kidnapper told Jimmy while he was tying his hands. "You will shoot the video and then" — he turned to face Jimmy — "you'll be next!" Then the kidnapper turned to Ces. "You keep putting on make-up. Make sure you do a good job with your make-up so when we ship your head to ABS-CBN, you'll look pretty!"[3] Some of the men chortled. By this time, Jimmy and Angel were hogtied.

Among the kidnappers, Sali Said turned and walked away from the men seemingly feasting on Jimmy and Angel. The 5'9" youth spent all his time with Jimmy. They had become friends, and he didn't want to see this. He knew this was necessary because it meant they would get the money faster.

Ces surprised herself because she was calm. She had no choice. It was nearing sunset, and she looked around. The beauty of the jungle struck her again. The irony was that none of the men around her seemed to see it. She couldn't do anything to comfort Jimmy and Angel so she offered them a drink of water from a plastic gallon. She wanted to cry. Instead, she got up and spoke to Commander Putol. It was time to speak with her family again.

\*\*\*

Her call came at 5:32 p.m. on the fourth day, June 11. We had been sitting around the table trying to go over all the loose strands: their location, which was being mapped with three sources of information; the push and pull between negotiators Lady Ann and Jun Isnaji; the fact that Charie, who had been going through her own personal turmoil, asked to leave Jolo, leaving only Quidato and Lady Ann to work for our concerns. There were a million and one details, and the greatest challenge was dealing with hyper-emotion, cutting down to the basics, the core essentials, which needed to be addressed step by step. Now I could sense we had hit an impasse. The kidnappers were calling our bluff. Over the past two days, I could sense it was going to come to this and knew it was only a matter of time, but living through it is a different matter. I looked outside the window and despite the rainy weather, could

---

[3] In Filipino: "*Makeup ka ng makeup, mag makeup ka ng mabuti, para pag na-LBC ang ulo mo sa ABS-CBN, maganda ka!*"

see the sun, which had just broken through the clouds, just beginning to set. Ces' voice was strained when she spoke. She was also breathing heavier.

"Frank, they're tying Jimmy and Angel!"[4]

"Okay," said Frank, who maintained low and even tones even as we heard the noise behind Ces' voice.

"If the money is not here by ..." Ces voice gets fainter. I could picture her turning to her kidnappers and questioning them: "What time do you want it?" Then she turned back to the phone and said, "Two o'clock tomorrow, they will behead Angel, and Jimmy will take video of Angel being beheaded."

"Tell them not to do that," Frank says calmly. "We're still doing our best to raise the money."

"Frank, they're very, very serious."

"Yes, we know that."

"They want you to talk to Jun or the Mayor of Indanan," says Ces. Then her voice began to rise. "They tied them in front of me, Frank! They're already tied, and they're going to make Jimmy shoot the video of Angel when they behead him tomorrow."

"Okay," says Frank. I marvelled at his composure. Everyone at the table was quiet. This was beyond the realm of experience for most of the people in the room. You could see shock and dismay. I've lived through similar threats in the past, but they didn't affect the lives of people I knew. My heart was pumping fast.

"They want the money — ₱20 million — tomorrow by 2 p.m." I wrote "Lady Ann" and passed the paper to Frank.

"But the Vice Governor has already spoken to them, right?" asked Frank.

"They don't want to talk to her. They are so angry."

"No," Frank interrupted, "the two of them are together — the Vice Governor and the Mayor." Frank found an opening. We could feel something change in Ces. She had something new, and she confronted her kidnappers with it.

"They said the Vice Governor and Mayor are together, Commander," Ces said to her kidnappers. We overheard her conversation. Her voice gained strength — somewhere between bravado and real courage. "Yes, they're together," she answered Commander Putol. "Please don't do that to our people. They — the Vice Gov and Mayor — are together now. Please, let my friends go. Don't tie them like that. They won't do anything. I'm asking you

---

[4] Philippine Police Anti-Crime Emergency Response (PACER) transcripts of June 11, 2008 phone conversation between Ces Drilon and Frank Orena, which began at 5:32 p.m.

please."⁵ We hear mumbled voices in the background. "Frank, just talk to the Mayor, not Lady Ann. They are serious, Frank. They are very serious. Their guns are now pointed at us."

"Yes, yes," Frank stumbled, "but Lady Ann has to be part of it. We don't know Isnaji."

"Frank, Frank, Frank!" Ces' voice broke.

"Yes ..."

"Talk to the Mayor. Two o'clock tomorrow. That's their deadline."

The phone line dies.

\*\*\*

Networks shape and define how the world works. Take any group or organization: the shop around the corner, the United Nations, the Abu Sayyaf, your favorite charity, your college alumni group, Facebook, the company you work for. They are all networks with their own rules, many unwritten and operating below our consciousness. Two key ideas are important to understand the impact of any network: the "small world" theory; and the strength of weak ties.

As the world becomes more densely populated and technology evolves, the connections between people are expanding in more intricate ways. Social scientists say this means we live in "a small world" that's grown increasingly smaller. Stanley Milgram defined the "Six Degrees of Separation" theory in the early 1960's — that between you and any other person around the world, there's an average of six social circles or six hops. Milgram and a collaborator said: "The phrase 'small world' suggests that social networks are in some sense tightly woven, full of unexpected strands linking individuals far removed from one another in physical or social space."⁶

For perspective, let's go through history. Let's start from the time of the cavemen when the only information available came from your tribe, and it took a lot of time before information travelled from tribe to tribe. With modern transportation and the printing press, that accelerated tremendously. Today with new technology — starting with trains, planes, phones to the Internet, email, Skype, IM, Facebook — many of the barriers of geography

---

⁵ Transcript of phone conversation that began 5:15 p.m. on June 8, 2008. Original Filipino quote by Ces: "*Magkasama na daw si Mayor at si Vice Gov. Huwag niyo naman yan gawin sa mga tauhan namin, please. Magkasama na daw sila ngayon. Please pakawalan niyo na. Huwag niyo nang gapusin. Wala naman silang gagawin. Nakikiusap ako sa inyo.*"

⁶ J. Travers and S. Milgram, "An Experimental Study of the Small World Problem," *Sociometry, 32,* (December, 1969), p. 425–426.

and tribe are coming down, replaced by a world of instantaneous connections. Interestingly, Milgram's experiments have been repeated by many more researchers over the years. One of the most recent used 30 million Microsoft instant-message communications between 180 million people starting in June, 2006. These study results reiterated Milgram's original findings, revolving around the magic number: 6 — suggesting a social connectivity constant for humanity.

It doesn't stop there because *more* connections turns out to be less important than the *right* connections. Which leads us to the power of weak ties. It was first articulated by Mark Granovetter, a Princeton history graduate while working on his PhD in sociology at Harvard University — its title: "The Strength of Weak Ties." The idea almost seemed counterintuitive: that weak ties between acquaintances or strangers are actually more important to society than the strong ties of close friends and family. He says that close friends and family tend to be similar to us: we move in the same social circles; we think the same way. As a result, we can mirror ideas and may stay parochial in thinking unless we have an infusion of ideas from different networks and worlds. New ideas are necessarily introduced into our networks through people we barely know, who belong to other social networks. These necessarily "weak" links can act as *bridges*, not just links between two different people but between two different worlds. As Granovetter wrote: "This means that whatever is to be diffused can reach a larger number of people, and traverse greater social distance, when passed through weak ties rather than strong."[7]

Of course, he wrote this before the age of social media. Imagine how information and emotions spread through the much weaker links we create on Facebook and Twitter today. A study on Facebook using 721 million members at the time of the experiment — about 10% of the global population — show there are on average less than four degrees of separation between any one Facebook user and another.[8] Or as the authors put it: "When considering another person in the world, a friend of your friend knows a friend of their friend." Still, I digress — although social media now plays a role in the spread of terrorism today.

---

[7] M. S. Granovetter, "The Strength of Weak Ties," *American Journal of Sociology,* 78, (May, 1973), p. 1366.
[8] Facebook users average 3.74 degrees of separation, BBC, November 23, 2011. Available at http://www.bbc.co.uk/news/technology-15844230.

Why are weak links important when studying terrorism in Southeast Asia and the Philippines in particular?

Here's how. Earlier, I wrote about how the Afghan war became a crucible of terror. Now let's show specifically how it spread from Afghanistan to the Philippines through the eyes of one Filipino man, Muklis Yunos, so you can see how the jihadi virus spread through many men from different countries, men who may have shared the same religious zeal but may never have met if not for Afghanistan. Their experiences there changed them because they became the intersection — the weak ties connecting different social networks, allowing the contagion to spread globally.

Muklis was born in Sawer, Masiu in Lanao del Sur. At 5'3" and 60 kilograms, he's a Maranao (an ethnic group). Born July 7, 1966, he went to high school in Marawi City, and with the help of the brother of an MILF member, he got a passport and travelled to Pakistan to study at the International Islamic University in November, 1986. There, he was recruited to join the Afghan jihad.[9]

A little more than a month after he arrived, he was at Camp Saddah near the border of Afghanistan. The camp is run by Abdul Rasul Sayyaf, for whom the Abu Sayyaf is named — a mujahideen commander with the closest ties to Osama bin Laden and to Saudi Arabia. Muklis was one of 100 new recruits for a three-year training program. The group was divided into three, and he was assigned to the artillery division. This was a pivotal time for both the Afghan war and the Southeast Asians who came to fight. Muklis met and was trained by Zulkarnaen, an Indonesian who became JI's military leader.[10] Another key Indonesian figure arrived in Muklis' class: Riduan Isamuddin better known as Hambali, who would become the mastermind and planner of all of JI's terrorist attacks until he was arrested in 2003. He also met Malaysian Nasir Abbas, who later created and headed JI's training camps in Mindanao. There are conflicting reports about whether Muklis overlapped with Indonesian Fathur Rohman al-Ghozi, with whom he would later carry

---

[9] Details from classified Philippine intelligence reports: *Debriefing Report: Haji Mukhlis Umpara Yunos aka Saifulla Yunos,* FILO-D00330-MUY-002, June 17, 2003. Also FILO-D00324-SMY-001, May 27, 2003; FILO-D00325-MUY-002, May 30, 2003; FILO-D00324-MUY-003, July 4, 2003.

[10] I cross-verified names mentioned by Muklis as quoted in Philippine intelligence debriefing reports with "Jemaah Islamiyah in Southeast Asia: Damaged but Still Dangerous," *International Crisis Group Report #63,* Jakarta, August 26, 2003, p. 7–8.

out the Rizal Day bombings in Manila on December 30, 2000 — 14 years after they reportedly met in Afghanistan.[11]

While in Saddah, Muklis met many of the key leaders of the 2002 Bali bombings. Indonesian Ali Gufron alias Mukhlas, who later became the field director of the Bali bombings for which he recruited his two brothers, said this was where he met Osama bin Laden.[12] Singaporean Mohammad Aslam bin Yar Ali Khan, arrived in the camps shortly before Muklis arrived. He's another pivotal figure because his detention by the Northern Alliance in 2001 began the unraveling of the once secret JI organization. Details from his arrest provided Singaporean authorities with information they needed to warn neighboring countries Malaysia, Indonesia and the Philippines. Only one nation took the information seriously: Malaysia began a crackdown soon after. It would take a year and the Bali bombings before Indonesia and the Philippines began to admit they were the targets — and sanctuary — of this clandestine group carrying the jihadi virus spreading through home-grown networks.

Muklis said he fought against the Russians in Afghanistan, saying he was involved in "the actual bombardment of Russian tent camps and soldiers position in the provinces of Kush"[13] and Joji. From his descriptions, it seemed he was at the turning point of the Afghan war, the battle of Joji, near Khost (sometimes grandly referred to as the legendary Battle of the Lion's Den) in April, 1987 that was said to last 22 days. This was the battle that made Osama bin Laden a legend and stopped the Soviet advance. It brought together many familiar names: bin Laden himself said he fought alongside Afghan Wali Khan Amin Shah, who would later work with Ramzi Yousef to train Abu Sayyaf members in the Philippines. Khalid Shaikh Mohammed was also at that battle. He was then Sayyaf's secretary and "the shadow that never

---

[11] There are conflicting reports about whether Muklis Yunos and Fathur Rohman al-Ghozi actually overlapped in Camp Saddah. One report says they overlapped. Another just lists them as having attended the camp, with a list of those who were there. Al-Ghozi's name appears. International Crisis Group says they missed each other by six months. "Southern Philippines Backgrounder: Terrorism and the Peace Talks," *International Crisis Group #80,* Singapore, July 13, 2004, p. 18.

[12] Berkas Perkara No. Pol. BP/06/II/2003 Dit Reskrim Ali Gufron alias Muklas, Interrogation deposition of Ali Gufron alias Muklas, December 13, 2002.

[13] Classified Philippine intelligence report: *Debriefing Report: Haji Mukhlis Umpara Yunos,* FILO-D00330-MUY-002, June 17, 2003.

left his side."[14] He would go on to mastermind the 9/11 attacks as well as do practice runs for terrorist attacks and conduct training in the Philippines.

I've shown in more detail how al-Qaeda's virulent jihadi virus travelled from Afghanistan to Southeast Asia through hubs like Khalid Shaikh Mohammed, and his nephew, Ramzi Yousef — both now in U.S. custody.[15] They bridged worlds by forming weak ties with Filipinos who were members of home-grown groups. Information, ideas and emotions from one social network flowed into the other and vice-versa. Osama bin Laden's brother-in-law, Mohammed Jamal Khalifa, started as a weak tie, becoming a bridge between different social networks and breaking geographical boundaries. Khalifa then became a key hub in the Philippines because he actively tried to unite all the different groups — the MNLF, MILF and the Abu Sayyaf.

Khalifa was a funnel of both radical ideas and money from a more extremist interpretation of Islam to Filipinos like Mohammed, who helped form the Abu Sayyaf, documented its history and was involved in some of its most notorious acts. An Ustadz (or Muslim scholar), Mohammed said he met Muklis Yunos in 1989 during training in Camp Bushra for Darul Imam Shafi'ie, the school Khalifa set up to try to train members of the MNLF, MILF and Abu Sayyaf together.

Mohammed's actions in later years would bring the Abu Sayyaf and Jemaah Islamiyah or JI together in the Philippines. This is pivotal because it meant that JI would bring the Abu Sayyaf together with its primary ally: the MILF.

JI had primarily worked with the MILF to set up training camps in 1994, an alliance that found its roots in the Afghan war. The Rizal Day bombings in December, 2000 were a collaboration between JI, represented by Fathur Rohman al-Ghozi, and the MILF, represented by Muklis Yunos[16] and part of

---

[14] "What Sheikh Abdullah Azzam said about Khalid Ash-Shaeikh Muhammad," *Muslim News Online,* March 5, 2003.

[15] For a more detailed treatment of the period leading to and a little after the October, 2002 Bali bombing, see Maria Ressa, *Seeds of Terror: An Eyewitness Account of Al-Qaeda's Newest Center of Operations in Southeast Asia* (New York: Free Press, 2003); Zachary Abuza, "*Militant Islam in Southeast Asia: A Crucible of Terror* (Boulder: Lynne Rienner Publishing, 2003) and Sally Neighbour, *In the Shadow of Swords,* (Sydney: Harper-Collins, 2004).

[16] Classified Philippine intelligence report: *Debriefing Report: Hajji Mukhlis Umpara Yunos aka Saiffula Yunos,* FILO-D00324-SMY-001, May 27, 2003, p. 4. The MILF has repeatedly denied any institutional links with JI, and according to Muklis, the group placed him on "floating status" after his name was linked to the bombings.

a larger, regional plot including the Christmas bombings in Indonesia. While there had been smaller attacks in Indonesia in 2000, December was the coming-out party of JI, and its plans included the Philippines.

JI's operations chief, Hambali, who trained with Muklis in Camp Saddah, came to Manila in December, 2000 to push for an attack on the U.S. embassy, but it was a difficult target. According to intelligence documents, Hambali gave al-Ghozi nearly US$50,000 to buy explosives in the Philippines. That was used for 20 bombs which exploded in churches in Indonesia on Christmas eve and five near-simultaneous explosions in Manila six days later on December 30. The largest was at the LRT (light-rail transit), killing 22 people. JI provided US$4,000 for the LRT bombing alone. The man JI worked with in the Philippines and who provided operatives for those attacks was Muklis.[17]

Al-Ghozi connected his interlocking social networks in the Philippines with JI and al-Qaeda in plots in Singapore, Indonesia and the Philippines.[18] After both al-Ghozi and Muklis were arrested, a new generation of leaders stepped up. This is where Mohammed played a critical role, carrying out Khalifa's dream.

In 2001, Mohammed became the bridge between Zulkifli, Jemaah Islamiyah's Indonesian leader, and Khadaffy Janjalani, the leader of the Abu Sayyaf. Zulkifli, in turn, acted as a bridge between the Abu Sayyaf and the MILF — which allowed the Abu Sayyaf to find sanctuary and set up camps in central Mindanao. This never happened in the past because the MILF called the Abu Sayyaf "bandits," and the Abu Sayyaf thought the MILF was only interested in money. That triangular relationship carried out many of the terrorist attacks from 2002–2006. Key to making all that happen was this quiet, unassuming teacher.

This was the fourth time Mohammed and I met. It was lunchtime. He had black army-type sunglasses in his right hand. He wore an orange and brown thin-striped shirt, blue jeans and brown shoes. I noticed a diver's watch on his wrist, the heavy kind that many soldiers like. In 2001, Mohammed found Zulkifli in a mosque in Cotabato, called Khadaffy Janjalani in Jolo on his cellphone and handed it to Zulkifli.[19] That was the

---

[17] Documents shown in television documentary, "9/11: The Philippine Connection," *ABS-CBN*, September, 2006.

[18] The actions of Fathur Rohman al-Ghozi are documented exhaustively in my first book, *Seeds of Terror.*

[19] These details came from a classified Philippine intelligence document: *Debriefing Report: Ahmad Faisal bin Imam Sarijan* (alias Zulkifli), September 9, 2005, p. 13.

first time the leaders of the Abu Sayyaf and Jemaah Islamiyah spoke to each other. They agreed to meet, and a few months later, Zulkifli boarded a ship in Zamboanga City. He carried a letter that was written by Mohammed verifying his identity.

"I made possible the connection between ASG and the JI with the letter that I sent to Khadaffy. Zulkifli was able to meet for the first time the ASG leader in Jolo," said Mohammed.[20]

When Zulkifli reached the seaport in Jolo, two Abu Sayyaf members picked him up. They rode "a single motorcycle and travelled for almost two hours" until they reached the house. Khadaffy was waiting for him inside. It didn't take long for them to start talking about future plans. Khadaffy asked if Zulkifli and JI could train members of the Abu Sayyaf. Zulkifli agreed. He noticed the Abu Sayyaf didn't ask for money. In fact, Khadaffy offered money to JI but then laughed loudly and said he knew JI had more money than his group.

Zulkifli's story is another example of how emotions and behavior spread through social networks. He attended and graduated from the ground zero of JI: the al-Mukmin or Pondok Ngruki school in Solo, Indonesia run by Abu Bakar Ba'asyir. Social scientists have shown that "attendance and other forms of association (teaching, socializing or attending lectures)"[21] with this and other JI schools is "correlated with both participation and role in JI terrorist attacks." Using aggregate level data on Indonesian education rates, researchers studied the social networks that carried out attacks and found that those who attended schools like this are 19 times more likely to carry out a terrorist attack than the highest estimated rates of the general population. Even the role played in a JI terrorist attack is influenced by social networks: attending Pondok Ngruki probably means you'll take a greater role or become one of the leaders of JI terrorist operations. One study showed that attending JI feeder schools — becoming immersed in the Ngruki social network — increases not only the probability that you will carry out terrorist attacks but also increases the probability you will play a major role in that attack by 16%![22]

Zulkifli was recruited while at school, and soon after, he received JI's manual, the PUPJI, a copy of which was found in his safehouse in the

---

[20] Author interview with Mohammed, Manila, Philippines, February 2011.

[21] S. Atran, J. Magouirk and J. Ginges, "Radical Madrasas in Southeast Asia," *CTC Sentinel*, Vol. 1, Issue 3, February, 2008.

[22] J. Magouirk, "Connecting a Thousand Points of Hatred, *Studies in Conflict and Terrorism* 31: 4 (2008).

Philippines after he was arrested in 2003. JI sent him to the Philippines in 1998 for training in Camp Hudaibyah[23] inside MILF territory. The man who first set it up, by his own admission, was Malaysian Nasir Abas. Another veteran of the Afghan war, Nasir became the head of JI Mantiqi 3, which covers the southern Philippines and parts of Indonesia.

"I think this is my chance to help the Muslims in the Philippines after helping the Muslims in Afghanistan," Nasir told me with a smile. He is a good-looking, soft-spoken man, not at all the stereotype of a terrorist. He had wire-frame glasses, a thin mustache and wore a striped shirt. Look at his social network: his brother, Hashim, was the JI leader in Singapore who helped plan the truck bombing attacks and whose voice narrated a surveillance tape found in Afghanistan in the bombed-out ruins of al-Qaeda's hide-out. Their sister, Farida, is married to Mukhlas, the operations chief of the Bali bombings. Nasir spoke in halting English for our camera. "I go only to help Muslims in southern Philippines by training them because I have an expertise to train."[24]

In 1996, Nasir handed the leadership of Camp Hudaibyah to an Indonesian, Umar Patek, one of the Bali bombers who would later return to find sanctuary and train Filipinos in Mindanao. Between 1996–1998, one JI member said "over 1000 Indonesian *mujahideen* were trained at Camp Hudeibia [sic][25]" but the numbers were probably far less. Nasir would go back to Hudaibyah two more times, once for two months in 1999 and again for three weeks in 2000. While he was there, JI's leader, Abu Bakar Ba'asyir, visited the MILF camps.[26]

Fathur Rohman al-Ghozi appeared again: he helped Nasir set up Camp Hudaibyah. In 1998, al-Ghozi was a senior JI member — an instructor for Zulkifli's class. While teaching, Al-Ghozi was already travelling extensively in the region, expanding his social network, ready to pull operatives together for the terrorist attacks which began in 2000 in Indonesia. Zulkifli said he had no idea what al-Ghozi was working on outside of the classes he taught.

---

[23] Note on spelling: when I wrote *Seeds of Terror* in 2003, the only spelling available was from Philippine documents. That was why I used "Hodeibia." Since then, the camp has been written about more extensively and the most commonly-used spelling is what I am using now — "Hudaibyah."

[24] Interview with author, Jakarta, Indonesia, August, 2005.

[25] Classified Philippine intelligence document, "Debriefing Report: Faiz bin Abu Bakar Bafana," March 31, 2002.

[26] Classified Indonesian intelligence report, "Interrogation of Mohammad Nasir bin Abbas," April 18, 2003.

Zulkifli's group graduated mid-2000, shortly after Philippine President Joseph Estrada ordered the bombing of the MILF's main headquarters in Camp Abubakar. From March 16 to June 12, 2000, the military's 4th Division captured 15 major MILF camps, 49 satellite camps, a training base and control tower. It was "all-out war."

Zulkifli said he and his Indonesian classmates fought alongside the MILF during the siege and defense of Abubakar: they "became actively involved in the defense of the camp"[27] and "involved in the conduct of ambushes against military troopers." He said "JI's main contribution during the war was the planting of land mines along the enemy routes and around the camp perimeter." Zulkifli told authorities he "served as team leader of some eight MILF fighters in the final defense of Camp Abubakar."[28] His group was the last to pull out because they waited for the MILF to retrieve stored ammunition. They then helped set up a new military training camp they called "Muaskar Jabal Quba" in Mount Kararao.

That was when Zulkifli took over the leadership of Jemaah Islamiyah in the Philippines. In November, 2000 he was elected the "Qoid of Wakalah Hudaibiyah or WAHUD"[29] The "only senior JI leader" who attended was Nasir Abas, who was "the Qoid of Wakalah Sabah III at that time." Soon after, he "paid a courtesy call to the then MILF Chairman, Ustadz Hashim Salamat."[30] They had four points of agreement, which extended and enlarged their ongoing relationship. The MILF would "continue to give protection and safe haven to the JI." In exchange, JI would support the MILF "in terms of financial and logistical assistance" with a focus on "bomb-making/demolition." Two other points formalized an ongoing practice.[31] Salamat asked Zulkifli to strategically conceptualize operations against the military and police; and, more significant, Salamat gave Zulkifli and JI members "full authority to participate in the tactical operations of the MILF." Perhaps in recognition of JI's help, Salamat allowed Zulkifli to work directly with MILF field units. During this time, the MILF repeatedly denied any connections with JI.

---

[27] Statements from a classified Philippine intelligence document, "Ahmad Faisal Bin Imam Sarijan," September 9, 2005, p. 10.

[28] Classified Philippine intelligence document, "Summary of Information: Ahmad Faisal Bin Imam Sarijan," July, 2005.

[29] Classified Philippine intelligence document, "Ahmad Faisal Bin Imam Sarijan," September 9, 2005, p. 11.

[30] Ibid., p. 11.

[31] Ibid., p. 12.

In the meantime, Muklis and al-Ghozi were working closely together to avenge the MILF after the government took over Camp Abubakar. Al-Ghozi travelled to Indonesia, and on August 1, 2000, he carried out the first retaliatory attack planned with Hambali — a bomb planted at the gate of the Philippine embassy in Jakarta, just 10 minutes away from the CNN office. We felt the explosion in our office and rushed out the door with our camera. When we got there, body parts of two vendors were strewn on the sidewalk, and as we got closer to the Mercedes-Benz at the gate, I realized Philippine Ambassador Leonides Caday was still inside the car. The ambulance arrived as we were running towards him. I watched as the police pulled up behind and began to cordon off the area. About a week later, authorities published a sketch of the man who planted the bomb — a sketch I remembered when I came face-to-face with him in the Philippines two years later during the presentation of a suspected terrorist to media. The man was Fathur Rohman al-Ghozi.

When he was arrested in Quiapo, Manila on January 15, 2002, he was working on at least three other terror plots. Information from him led authorities to 1.2 tons of explosives hidden in General Santos City, slated for truck-bombing plots in Singapore (for which surveillance tapes had been sent to al-Qaeda by Hashim Abas, Nasir's brother). Authorities would later learn that he had shipped another two tons of explosives to Indonesia through Borneo to its final destination: Bali. At the time of his arrest, al-Ghozi knew about the plans for Bali, which would be carried out nine months later on October 12, 2002. They were the worst terrorist attacks since 9/11 — five near-simultaneous explosions in Bali, which killed 202 people.

It was a wake-up call for Southeast Asia, the first time anyone from the region would carry out a suicide bombing. Nearly all the men who carried out those attacks admitted they trained in the southern Philippines.

*\*\*\**

Zulkifli turned out to be a key figure in the evolution of the Abu Sayyaf and the MILF, training their members to create more effective and sophisticated bombs as well as pushing a more ideological approach to jihad. His influence on the Abu Sayyaf spurred its third cycle: a regeneration of its ideological terrorist foundation. His friendship with Mohammed sparked that development.

The first joint JI-MILF-ASG operation happened on April 21, 2002 at the Fitmart Mall in General Santos City. Zulkifli casually mentioned to Mohammed that JI was going to fund an attack being planned by Basit Usman for the MILF. During that time, Muklis Yunos, now hunted by authorities for the Rizal Day bombings in Manila, was being eased out as the company commander of the MILF's 3rd Field Division, Special Operations Group (SOG).[32] Abdul Basit Usman was his replacement.

Mohammed immediately offered to help fund the operation. Zulkifli set up a meeting in the JI safehouse in Cotabato City that lasted less than an hour. Mohammed made the offer to the MILF. Basit immediately accepted it. The three decided funds would be coursed through Zulkifli. A week before the attack, the Abu Sayyaf gave ₱8,000 to Zulkifli which he handed over to Basit.

Zulkifli was involved in the planning, funding and implementation of this joint effort. Using tactics they learned in Camp Saddah and were being taught in their military training in Mindanao, he set three bombs: the first exploded inside Fitmart, driving people outside where a second bomb exploded near the exit. The last one was set in the parking lot.

After the attack, Zulkifli immediately called Mohammed. Zulkifli said it seemed Mohammed and the Abu Sayyaf wanted to join the operations — even if it's just funding — to send a signal: the group is still a force, and "more importantly, the ASG wanted to divert the attention of the military"[33] from the Abu Sayyaf members in Jolo. This is consistent with what Mohammed admitted to authorities.

Zulkifli planned and funded some of the most devastating bombings in Mindanao from 2000 until his arrest in 2003. Aside from that, he trained the Abu Sayyaf and helped make their move from Jolo and Basilan to central Mindanao possible. By November, 2001, he sent two JI operatives to Khadaffy Janjalani in Jolo to begin training members of the Abu Sayyaf. The leader is a 25-year-old Indonesian named Rohmat, also known as Zaki, who was the top graduate of Camp Jabal Quba's second batch of cadets. He gave an idea of how closely JI and the Abu Sayyaf or ASG began to work together. "I'm JI. I was ordered to go to ASG. Now we're all together," said Rohmat.

---

[32] Classified Philippine intelligence report: *Debriefing Report, Haji Mukhlis Umpara Yunos aka Saiffula Yunos*, FILO-D00324-SMY-001, May 27, 2003.
[33] Classified Philippine intelligence document, "Ahmad Faisal Bin Imam Sarijan," September 9, 2005, p. 15.

"Now my life is ASG."[34] JI began to pass on bomb-making skills and technology. Such close quarters also helped re-ignite the Abu Sayyaf's ideological roots, pulling it back from its criminal tendencies.

As this was happening, U.S. special forces, working with the Philippine military, continued its pursuit operations. Janjalani's core group moved from Basilan to Jolo, drawing on kinship alliances with Radullan Sahiron in Patikul, Jolo. Rohmat trained about 90 Abu Sayyaf members, including its leaders from March to May, 2003.

Zulkifli said training was difficult because the military was in constant pursuit, forcing the group to stay mobile. Many times while speaking with Rohmat, Zulkifli said he could "hear the sound of heavy artillery"[35] in the background. Finally, he decided to call up Khadaffy, who told him he wanted to move his group to central Mindanao. His deputy, Abu Solaiman, was speaking with members of the MILF for sanctuary and training. Zulkifli offered to help "fast-track" talks. Working through Ameril Umra Kato, Zulkifli got the MILF's consent and "relayed the information" to Khadaffy, who "thanked him profusely." The Abu Sayyaf moved from Jolo to Palimbang in central Mindanao the last week of June, 2003. Zulkifli and JI helped fund their travel, food and accommodations.

"In the past, the Abu Sayyaf had no place in [central] Mindanao," said Rohmat. "They have to hide in the area of the MILF. Of course, while they're there, they help each other — with food, whatever else is necessary."[36]

That link between the JI, the MILF and the Abu Sayyaf led to several joint bombing operations in Kidapawan City, North Cotabato, South Cotabato, Koronada, Parang as well as the Cotabato Airport and Davao bombings in 2003.[37]

There is one more group, the Rajah Solaiman Movement, which would be brought into the terrorist fold in 2004. It alarmed authorities because its

---

[34] Interview with ABS-CBN, Manila, Philippines, July, 2006. Original quote is translated from Pilipino: "*Ako JI, tapos inutusan sa 'yan, ASG. Tapos, sama-sama na kami. Ako, yung buhay ko ngayon sa ASG na. Sama-sama kami.*"

[35] Classified Philippine intelligence document, "Ahmad Faisal Bin Imam Sarijan," September 9, 2005, p. 20.

[36] Interview with ABS-CBN, Manila, Philippines, July 2006. Translated from Pilipino: "*Pag sa Mindanao ito, walang lugar ang ASG. Wala silang miyembro, kaya yong pinagtataguan nila lugar ng MILF. Tapos, siyempre nagtutulong sila sa pagbili ng pagkain. Ganon, pag daan yong bang may kailangan.*"

[37] Bombings at Davao International Airport on March 4, 2003 and the Davao wharf at Sasa on April 2, 2003 were allegedly masterminded by Zulkifli.

members are former Christians who converted to Islam. It's leader is a charismatic man, who occasionally worked as a broadcaster. His brother would involve an ABS-CBN anchor, and unknown to me at the time, I would stumble onto part of a terrorist cell and its propaganda after I returned home to the Philippines in 2005. I got a first-hand taste of how security groups, competing for President Arroyo's interest, misrepresent and twist information. Soon after I took over as the head of ABS-CBN News, President Aquino accused our prime-time anchor, Julius Babao, of aiding terrorists. This shadowy group, the RSM — the Rajah Solaiman Movement, also sometimes referred to as the Rajah Solaiman Islamic Movement (RSIM) — would help extend the reach of the groups in Mindanao into the capital, Manila.

***

The heavy bolt on the gate slammed shut behind me, and I waited for the gate in front of me to open. I was carrying a microphone so the sensor wailed as I walked through. I was inside the Bicutan prison in Manila, where 22 inmates were brutally killed on March 15, 2005 during an alleged prison jailbreak led by Abu Sayyaf leader, Commander Kosovo. Most among the 129 Abu Sayyaf suspects held here, including many of the 22 killed, were waiting for trial. That sparked a flurry of activity for revenge, taking years before the whole story can be told. Abu Sayyaf's spokesman, Abu Solaiman, vowed to take the fight to Manila, and he did — with the help of JI, the MILF and the Rajah Solaiman Movement or RSM.

The man I was coming to meet was the founder and leader of the Rajah Solaiman Movement, Ahmad Santos. He was arrested in Zamboanga City on October 26, 2005. Police recovered a mini-arsenal as well as a treasure trove of documents and propaganda materials, saying he was simultaneously the head of the Abu Sayyaf's propaganda arm. To show you the ties that bind and the complex overlapping social networks, he was arrested in the house of PO3 San Amdal, a Muslim policeman who turned out to be a good friend of Khadaffy Janjalani.[38] At one point, San Amdal allegedly negotiated the release of a kidnap victim and received a cut of the ransom.[39] Social network

---

[38] Classified Philippine intelligence document: "Update on the Arrest of RSM Leader Hilarion Santos III," *Philippine National Police*, October 28, 2005, p. 2.

[39] Nururrija Ibba Amdal, the wife of PO3 Amdal, told authorities her husband was involved in the kidnapping of a Filipino-Chinese businesswoman by the Abu Sayyaf's Commander Robot. Her husband became the chief negotiator and negotiated a ransom of ₱1 million.

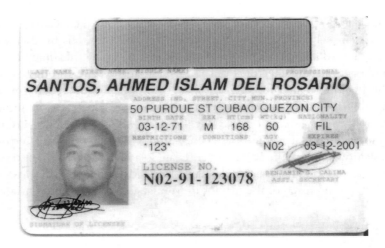

Driver's license of Ahmad Santos

ties go deep and connect the criminals with law enforcement in surprising ways that explain why the cycle of kidnapping continues. Anyway, let's focus on a key hub.

Born Hilarion del Rosario Santos III in 1971, he was Roman Catholic and married his first wife in a church. He converted to Islam in 1992 while working in Saudi Arabia. He then joined ISCAG, the Islamic Studies Call and Guidance — one of the groups linked to Osama bin Laden's brother-in-law, Mohammed Jamal Khalifa. Authorities say RSM was built up on Khalifa's network, which was largely left unscathed since 1995. Santos' three main funders are Jordanian nationals linked to the al-Qaeda network. Two of them were arrested in the Philippines and later deported.[40]

Like JI, the social network reveals the spread of the jihadi virus. Santos married into the top ranks of the Abu Sayyaf. In 1999, he took a second wife, Nurain Dongon. Her sister, Zainab, is married to the Abu Sayyaf's leader, Khadaffy Janjalani, while another sister, Amina, is married to Janjalani's

---

[40] Nedal al-Dhalain of Darul Hijra Foundation and Islamic Information Center is a significant link to the funding of the global jihad. He was arrested in Manila on May 10, 2002. Mohammad Amin Ghafarri is with the Islamic Wisdom Worldwide Mission (another Khalifa NGO with global links) and was arrested on October 7, 2002 in connection to the killing of a U.S. special forces soldier in the Malagutay bombing in Zamboanga two days earlier. The last man is Humoud Mohammad Abdulaziz of ISCAG. More details available at "Summary of Information: Hilarion del Rosario Santos III," Philippine National Police, undated.

second-in-command, Abu Solaiman.[41] Their brother, Jaffar Dongon, helped carry out one of the joint Abu Sayyaf-RSM-JI operations.[42]

The police allowed us to set up our cameras in a cell in the middle of the Bicutan prison. We were at the center of the structure, with the prison inmates held in cells overlooking the central, open area. Aside from the bars surrounding us, everyone on the floors above us could see us. I could see Ahmad Santos making his way to us from his cell, escorted by guards. His black hair cropped military-style, he walked leisurely. He wore a black t-shirt and jeans, gold-rimmed glasses and carried prayer beads he kept in his left hand during the interview. We sat across from each other over a small metal table. He had an intense look, matched by a charismatic personality, amplified when the cameras turned on. It was clear he knew how to sway people. He admitted his personal ties to the Abu Sayyaf, but he denied being a terrorist and emphatically argued he was being unjustly detained.

"There is no such thing as the Rajah Solaiman Movement," he told me.

"You say the RSM doesn't exist at all. It's not a terrorist group?" I reiterated.

"I'm telling you, there is no RSM. It really doesn't exist. If it exists at all, they created it. It came from them, not from us."

"Did you train with the MILF?" I asked.

"Train? No. I wanted to."

"Did you ever set a bomb?" He shook his head. "Did you do explosives training?"

"No," he said slowly. Then a steady rush. "No, no. *Hindi* [no]. Set up a bomb?" he asked quizzically. Then he shook his head again.

While I was listening to him, I thought about what authorities had told me and what intelligence documents showed. They said Santos and his two brothers travelled to Camp Abubakar in 1999 to meet with MILF leaders, including its leader, Hashim Salamat. In December, 2001, Santos received military and explosives training at another MILF camp in Lanao del Sur. Between March and May 2003, an eyewitness said Ahmad Santos taught Islam and martial arts to the Abu Sayyaf in Jolo along with two JI members (including Rohmat).[43]

---

[41] Abu Solaiman's real name is Jainel Antel Sali.

[42] Linked by authorities and Abu Sayyaf members to the Valentine's day bus bombing on February 14, 2005.

[43] "Philippines Terrorism: The Role of Militant Islamic Converts," *International Crisis Group #110*, Jakarta/Brussels, December 19, 2005, p. 11.

Santos did admit he set up an Islamic community in Anda, Pangasinan. Police raided what they called a training camp in May, 2002. Two men arrested then later admitted carrying out the two major attacks claimed by the Abu Sayyaf and JI: the *Superferry* bombing on February 27, 2004, one of the world's worst maritime terrorist attack, the second most lethal in Southeast Asia since Bali; and the Valentine's day bombings in 2005 — two near-simultaneous explosions in General Santos City and Davao City followed an hour later by an explosion on a bus in the financial capital, Makati.

These attacks showed the importance of the RSM, its close ties to the Abu Sayyaf, their Indonesian JI mentors and the MILF commanders who sheltered all three groups. "We're seeing a vehicle," says the International Crisis Group's Sidney Jones, "by which some of the terrorist activities that up till now had been confined to the south, having at least the potential for moving north."[44]

There's no doubt JI increased the sophistication of Filipino bombs, partly through the work of JI members like Zulkifli and expert bomb makers and leaders like Dulmatin and Umar Patek — who fled to Mindanao for sanctuary in 2003. Santos admitted working closely with JI leaders Umar Patek and Muawiyah. He also met and trained with Zulkifli, Muklis, al-Ghozi and Abu Sayyaf leaders Khadaffy Janjalani and Abu Solaiman. Among his papers were a picture with MILF Chairman Hashim Salamat and a letter from his successor, Al Haj Murad, authorizing Santos to collect money for the MILF.

In 2005, authorities found more sophisticated bombs injected into toothpaste tubes and shampoo bottles. Intelligence officials said these bombs were intended for planes. During that same year, numerous terrorist plots were foiled involving the alliance between JI, ASG and RSM — including "Madrid-style bombings," a plot to bomb the U.S. embassy, a plot to assassinate selected officials and several plots involving suicide bombers, all involving the MILF. The leadership continued to say there was no official relationship with JI but began acknowledging personal links between its members and JI. Behind the scenes, the government began to pressure the MILF to stop protecting and providing sanctuary to "criminals" and "terrorists."

Still, JI was working closely with the MILF, Abu Sayyaf and RSM. As Umar Patek was working with Santos and other Filipinos to source

---

[44] Author interview, Jakarta, Indonesia, May 21, 2006.

explosives and put together tactical details, Dulmatin was working on the Indonesian side with a man named Abdullah Sunata, the leader of Kompak, a group allied with JI.[45] The alliances were built during the fighting of Muslims and Christians in Ambon, Indonesia — where JI successfully fomented sectarian violence. Sunata used his network to help Dulmatin and Patek evade the manhunt in Indonesia and find sanctuary in the Philippines in 2003. He also told authorities that Umar Patek was leading the JI group in Pawas and moving separately from the more conservative main body of JI. Sunata funneled men and money to JI in the Philippines. Several of the Indonesian jihadists were arrested en route while Indonesian authorities arrested Sunata himself on July 20, 2005 for the 2004 Australian embassy bombing in Jakarta. He was later sentenced to seven years in prison.

All this rushed through my mind while I was sitting across from Santos. Despite the information I had, he was charming and had an intensity that powered his soft-spoken and direct manner. He railed against the United States and the injustice of Filipino authorities. I brought the conversation to the Superferry and February 14 bombings, and the two bombers Santos trained.

"These attacks happened and people were killed by men you know," I half-asked, half-stated.

"I can't answer that directly," said Santos. "In the first place, once they left our training, it's their life, right? This is all about religion. That's where everything returns. All these issues boil down to religion, the freedom of our religion. Islam is a complete code of life. It tells us to live the teachings of Islam. This is what we feel: Christianity as a whole will not allow us to live according to the laws of our religion. Is it jealousy? I'm saying that they need to give Muslims what we're asking for in Mindanao. If the government doesn't give it, then a lot more will happen. A lot more blood will flow. Many more people will die. But if they talk about it and say 'Okay, we'll allow this — go practice your faith' — this is only my opinion — because Muslims lack so much — education, poverty. I don't know. I know the government will be hurt by this but why doesn't it have an answer to poverty? Islam has an answer."

"What's that?"

He smiled and said, "Zakat — the payment of 2.5% of each Muslim's annual income that will go directly to the poor. Can I ask you a question — can government do that? Because we know the rich, it's hard for them to

---

[45] Briefing by Indonesian intelligence sources, April 25, 2005.

do that. They think 'I worked hard for this, and I'll just give it away?' They won't, but in Islam, we're taught by Islam to give to the poor."

"So for you as a whole way of life, Islam made more sense?" I asked while thinking that he sounded like Abu Bakar Ba'asyir and other JI members I had spoken to. Their words were reverberations of Osama bin Laden's global pronouncements.

"Of course. It helps people's morality grow. Islam is not only a religion *per se*. We're not talking about just spiritual belief. We're talking about a way of life, meaning you practice it every day — how we talk to people, how we deal with our businesses, how we sleep — in everything we do. Even in the way you sleep beside your wife — how you do that. This is a complete way of life."

"I think the clash happens when Muslims use that as a justification for terrorism. Like what do you think of Osama bin Laden?"

"He looks like my father," answered Santos. I started to laugh. "No, I'm not kidding."

"He preaches a very exclusive world." I said. "Abu Bakar Ba'asyir in Indonesia said, 'Between Us and Them there will forever be a river of hatred.'"

"I think they have a deeper understanding, a reason why. For example, look at me here. America's meddling in my case. They're calling me a terrorist. They want me in prison. What do I feel? Will I feel happy about that? Of course not. Since I was in high school, I admire America, but look at what they've done. Like in Iraq. You know, a Muslim, even if he doesn't speak or tell you, the Faith dictates how he feels and should behave."

"What does jihad mean?"

"First and foremost is to protect the Muslims," he started animatedly. "We're protecting the religion itself. Muslims, even if they don't speak to you, they know it. It's the Faith that tells us what we should feel. Among us, we have a saying — like us Filipinos: what affects one of us, affects all of us. That's what we're taught. You have to be more careful about those who don't speak."

His eyes were flashing when he finished. Police investigators said Santos is an experienced propagandist. When he was arrested in Zamboanga City, he was the "chief of the Abu Sayyaf's media bureau" — a charge he vehemently denied. Yet, according to a classified report, Santos told authorities that JI gave RSM ₱250,000 or about US$4,500 to be used in a truck bombing plot in Manila.[46] Santos was working closely with Bali bomber Umar Patek. The

---

[46]Tactical Interrogation Report, "Hilarion del Rosario Santos III @Ahmad Santos," October 28, 2005.

document states "Santos envisioned to stage a Bali-like bombing" using one ton of explosives to attack a nightspot "frequented by foreigners in Ermita," the old red-light district in old Manila. On March 28, 2005, authorities found 16 sacks of explosives in Santos' house in Quezon City, a Manila suburb. Santos would later admit he gathered 600 kilograms of explosives. Police also found circuitry diagrams and a list of potential targets for a series of attacks.

Seven months later, shortly after he was arrested, Santos admitted the Holy Week plot to our reporter Jay Ruiz. This was a different Santos from the one I would meet six months later. This Santos was flinty, hard-eyed, with an aggressive edge. His hair was longer giving him a more disheveled look. His words were cold and calculating. The military allowed the interview with Santos less than a week after his arrest, and he seemed to strike a conspiratorial air with the reporter, often using the term "pare" or friend. Despite the fact they were talking about jihad in terms I've heard from hardened JI and al-Qaeda leaders, their conversation was punctuated by camaraderie and laughter — some of it seemingly masking the reporter's discomfort. Santos seemed straight-forward and honest in his replies.

"We wanted to shake the government," said Santos. "Economic sabotage. That's the purpose of jihad — to attain that goal. In everything, war, everything."

"What's the plan of "big bang", asked Ruiz, referring to the code name for the Manila plot. "Can you go over the details? It's hard to understand from the way you tell the story."

"Two buildings will collapse," replied Santos. "The explosion's so strong it can easily send two buildings crashing simultaneously. With that bomb — even if it's a four-storey building. Put it in the middle and it will bring it down."[47]

"*Grabe naman kayo* [You guys are bad.]," interrupted Ruiz laughing. "*Pare, grabe naman.* [Friend, that's horrible.]

"That bomb can flatten two four-storey buildings."

"Why are you admitting this now?"

"I'm admitting it because it's the truth. At least everyone will know that there's really someone fighting — to the degree that we'd do everything to attain the goal. This is a fight. This is war."

---

[47] Interview with ABS-CBN's Jay Ruiz, November 1, 2005. The conversation was in Filipino, but I've translated it into English. Where difficult to capture the flavor of the complexity, I've maintained the Filipino and given direct translations next to it.

"So you're admitting it?"

"Yeah."

"You're admitting what?"

"That I'm involved."

"Where?"

"In keeping the bomb."

"The one-ton bomb?"

"No, six hundred."

"What's that?"

"Six hundred."

"Six hundred kilo of a bomb?"

"Uh huh."

"... that can do?"

"That can flatten two buildings."

"You're admitting this?"

"Yeah. So the government understands we're not joking. That our intentions are real. That our goal is real. That we will work for what we want — which is an Islamic state. That's all we want — to have an Islamic community."

I watched this interview several times when I was preparing for our Bicutan interview. His candor reminded me of the Bali bombers and Osama bin Laden. They logically explained reasons for their actions: that the "real terrorists" are the nations and societies who prevent Muslims from following the teachings of their faith. This is where religion meets politics: any semblance of injustice is used to justify violence and helps explain why the goal is power. Santos explicitly said he wanted an Islamic state. JI's founders envisioned a Muslim Caliphate stretching throughout much of Southeast Asia. To make that happen, they actively fomented Muslim-Christian violence in Indonesia, Malaysia, Singapore and the Philippines. Among the materials seized from Santos were tracts and propaganda materials justifying kidnap-for-ransom, the rape of women and the killing of civilians.[48] When I reminded him of the interview he did with Ruiz, he said he was under pressure.

"I was fucked-up then,"[49] he quickly answered. "First, they were building a case, and second during those times, we were with them — my wife,

---

[48] Interviews with arresting officers, intelligence sources and case agents, November, 2005.

[49] The literal phrase he used was "*Sabog ata ako 'nun.*"

my sister-in-law and five others in my family. They had us, so anything they want! We understand. What I'm afraid of is that they drag families in. If it was just me, anything they want me to admit, I'd admit it just so they don't drag our families in."

"Were you tortured?" I asked.

"Yeah. Can I say that?" He shook his head and lowered his voice in a conspiratorial whisper. "They'll really take it out on us. That's what I'm afraid of. Until now, they don't stop taking it out on my family." He was believable, particularly since I knew his wife connected him to the Abu Sayyaf, but it's also believable that he could be mistreated while in prison.

Charges of human rights violations complicate and muddle counterterrorism efforts globally. It's part of the reason it's difficult to tell the good guys from the bad guys. Intelligence can also be badly mishandled because of the rivalries between agencies and the struggle to get the attention of superiors. Without knowing it, I stepped right in the middle of one of these cases involving the Santos family.

Santos' brother, Dawud, also converted to Islam and travelled with him to the MILF camps in the late 90's. When their house was raided in March and the explosives discovered, Dawud was arrested. He cried discrimination and human rights groups flocked to help him. ABS-CBN anchor Julius Babao was reporting on his arrest and court appearances. He gave him a ride from court at some point. Somehow, that was misconstrued by the agents in the Intelligence Services of the Armed Forces of the Philippines (ISAFP). A few months after I officially took over as the head of the news group, President Arroyo announced that Julius Babao was aiding terrorists. He immediately took a leave while I investigated the charge. After two weeks, we published our findings: the "intelligence" whispered to President Arroyo was gossip given to her because agents said she was upset with the way ABS-CBN reported the news. To me, it seemed they wanted to please the President. During a lunch, I explained to her what we found, and it was disturbing for both of us. Military intelligence left a lot to be desired. It wasn't the last time I would see flagrantly wrong information passed off as verified intelligence.

So when Santos talked about charges being fabricated against him, it wasn't a far-fetched notion. During the time we spoke, some of his anecdotes showed the incompetence and sloppiness of law enforcement and the justice system. Combine that with charges of discrimination against Muslims and the lack of information about men like Santos and you have a public easily confused about the real state of affairs.

# Ultimatum

There was silence after the phone line dropped. We all could feel the quiet panic in Ces' voice. The ultimatum was set: money had to be delivered by 2 p.m. the next day, Thursday, June 12 — Day 5 of the kidnapping — or they would behead Angel. Mayor Isnaji was talking directly with the kidnappers, and we were talking to them through Lady Ann. Isnaji told the kidnappers the family promised ₱20 million. Lady Ann offered them ₱2 million, and that was partly why they got so angry. They thought Lady Ann was taking money away from them. Ces clarified with us that the Abu Sayyaf took her promise of the ransom money as her family's acceptance of terms. We were pushed against the wall. I looked at Glenda and then at Mark.

"Mark, can you please call Sakur Tan and see if he can do anything to control Isnaji? Can he ask him to backpedal?" I asked. Mark nodded. I looked around the table. Angel's wife, Rushell, pulled back to the edge of the couch where Eva, Jimmy's wife, was comforting her.

"Okay," I said, taking a deep breath. "Wed, can you guys find them from the cellphone signals? I can get new coordinates from the telcos. Do we have any other options? I'll also call the Americans and see what — if anything — they can do to help. Glenda, can you please see where the military is and what they plan to do?" Everyone nodded and started making calls. "Why don't we take a short break? Everyone take a deep breath. This is the time for us to really think this through. Everyone will be okay. Just remember, this is easier because we know that all they want is money. Okay?" I looked around and saw uncertainty and fear. "Then let's separate into two groups. The families, you can stay here — can you guys meet and give us suggestions on what you'd like to do? Richard, can we use the main bedroom — can I see Glenda, Mark, Mario, Maxim? Here are some of the questions we need to think about. Do we pay now? How much? If we pay now, what does that mean for our team? Are we giving the kidnappers more money to hold us hostage? If we don't pay, do we put our team at risk? There's really no right and wrong answer, but can we think out what may possibly happen? Okay? Let's do 10-minute break, do our break-outs and then come back together here in about 30 minutes."

I texted my sources for new information. I wanted to clear my head so I stood up, pulled Libby aside, and we walked out into the hallway. The rooms overlook an open atrium so just being able to step outside the room made me feel better. I spoke to Libby about handling the needs of the families. She was watching them closely, trying to anticipate their emotional barometer. She suggested we bring in someone they could speak with — a counselor and a priest. I agreed and asked her to come up with a plan and people we can trust to bring to our crisis center. We walked back through the living room and pulled our team into the master bedroom. We began to sort out the potential problems. What if we give the money, but it falls into the wrong hands? How do we define proof-of-life? Who will bring the money? What timetable do we use? How do we get them out safely? I explained what happened in past hostage-takings: the money going to the wrong people, the hostages being kidnapped again as they were being released. There were so many pitfalls.

After about half an hour, we gathered again around the dining room table. It became clear we were going to pay to meet the deadline. Word filtered back from Sakur Tan: the kidnappers agreed on an installment basis for the amount they demanded — ₱20 million. Five million must be delivered before 2 p.m. of June 12. That would give a 24-hour reprieve on the threat of beheading. The second tranche of ₱5 million should be delivered a day later on Friday, June 13. Once that's in their hands, they said they would release one of the three. Another ₱5 million on June 14 would mean another release, and the last installment on June 15 would end the ordeal. There was obvious confusion because we never agreed on their initial demand of ₱20 million. That was the message I sent back. I asked Frank if he could go to Jolo to deliver the money. Nestor Cusi, one of Iglesia's police operatives working with us in the crisis center, would travel with him to guide and protect him. Frank's family was justifiably nervous, but they supported his decision.

At 9 p.m., Frank called Lady Ann and turned on the speakerphone. The table was littered with plates and water bottles. Rock Drilon, Ces' artist ex-husband, sat with his head in his hands. Mark, head of corporate HR, and Mario, our news lawyer, sat on the other side of the table from Frank, who was hunched over the speakerphone. I was sitting next to Frank. Glenda was next to me. Rushell was sitting on a chair pulled further away from the table. Eva, Jimmy's wife and her brother-in-law, Leo, were standing near Rushell's chair. The HR girls, Libby and Lulu, were near them. Iglesia and his police team sat on the couch in the living room. Everyone was listening intently. Lady Ann complained that Mayor Isnaji told the kidnappers the family agreed to pay the ransom they demanded.[1]

"I need to ask you that," she said, "because now I'm being painted as the bad guy. They're saying they don't like me because I might take the ₱20 million. How did it only become ₱2 million, they said. I got angry! I'm only helping, and I'm being made to look bad. So what can you afford?"

"You, Ma'am," said Frank. "What would you suggest? We can't afford much. We're raising the money ourselves."

"Well, I told you earlier, ₱2 million. Add another ₱2 million. Let's see." The conversation continued, and she settled on ₱5 million. "We talked about a handover. I give the money — they asked that I show it to them first so they can make sure it's not fake. I'm supposed to show it to Isnaji's son. They're supposed to bring Ces so only when I see her will I give them the money." Listening to the conversation, it was confusing to follow what were actual conversations with the kidnappers. Lady Ann assured Frank that perhaps the money would be enough. She said it needed to be that way because they could just as easily lie. "That's going to be all we'll pay," she said.

"If that's possible, yes."

"The problem is if we give ₱5 million, we don't know whether they'll make it ₱50 million. Or they might just let Ces die."

"God forbid."

"What I'm getting is that they're trying to fool us so let me see what I can do now. I'll make some calls and try to finish it. I want it to be a straight hand-over — money, and then Ces," said Lady Ann.

Frank told her he would bring the money himself and meet her in Jolo. It was a long, meandering conversation which lasted nearly half an hour. We were looking for reassurance, but Lady Ann gave little — partly because she seemed volatile and angry that the Abu Sayyaf was questioning her motives. Through her, we got a small glimpse of what Jolo may really be like: full of distrust, anger, quick knee-jerk reactions. What gave me faith was that Quidato was with Lady Ann. I received running reports from him as well and

---

[1] Transcript of conversation that occurred 9:00 p.m. at Discovery Suites on June 11, 2008.

consulted him on our next moves. In the middle of the conversation with Lady Ann, I looked at Angel's wife, Rushell. She was wearing jeans and a baseball shirt that had a finger pointing at you. It said, "Hey you, get busy!" She was holding up her head with her right hand, a finger at her temple. I could sense her tension and didn't know how to help ease it.

Lady Ann called back about 15 minutes later. She didn't have good news: the kidnappers agreed on ₱5 million. If it was double the amount, they said they would release one of their hostages. She said she felt she could get more for less. We had to trust her. Strangely, the woman's voice on the other end of the phone did give me some comfort — if only because she seemed sure, and she was ready to act.

When the conversation ended, the family pulled away from the table and I sat down with the police and Frank to go over the route we would take. Libby, Mark and Mario were with us as we made plans and called people to implement them. We'd need cars in Manila, Zamboanga and Jolo — and permits for the plane to fly. We decided Frank would fly by private plane from Manila to Zamboanga then take a commercial SeaAir flight from Zamboanga to Jolo. Cusi, our second PNP officer, would accompany him, and Quidato would meet him in Jolo. Frank only would go as far as the Jolo airport where Lady Ann would meet him. Frank would give her the money and get back on the same plane for the return flight to Zamboanga. If all went according to plan, he should be back in Manila within 12 hours.

Our meeting ended at 1 a.m. Frank left Discovery Suites at 3 a.m. He wore a brown baseball cap and a blue jacket. He cleaned his glasses and adjusted them on his nose. I hugged him tight and hoped we were doing the right thing.

*** 

It's impossible to fully understand the social networks that bind Mindanao and its groups to global terrorism without taking a closer look at the Moro Islamic Liberation Front (MILF). We turned onto the dirt road leading into the MILF's Camp Darapanan, the stronghold of its leadership. The MILF is the latest in an insurgency that started fighting for an independent homeland in the southern Philippines 400 years ago, part of a historic Muslim resistance to non-Muslim rulers. Ostensibly founded in 1978, it received international funding from Libya and Malaysia in its early years. When that ended, the Afghan war connected it to groups it would later invite to the Philippines for training.

Our military escorts led by Major Carlos Sol turned us over to their MILF counterparts. A young man who introduced himself as Emil joined us in our car, and I asked him questions. He turned out to be a relatively new recruit, a young man looking for purpose, and he found it in the MILF. I looked around the sprawling Camp Darapanan. This is where members of the MILF's Central Committee live. It was also home for a time to Bali bomb-maker Dulmatin, his wife and children.[2]

We passed two checkpoints, small guardhouse posts with men in fatigues and after five minutes, we turned off into an even smaller road and stopped at the gate of a house surrounded by a large swathe of green.We waited in the car for a few minutes and watched a man leave and board his car. He looked familiar. Later, I'd find out he was one of the leaders of Indonesia's second largest Muslim group, the Muhammadiyah. The MILF is networked and con-nected to a global community and while that's a plus for a political group, it can create its own problems like the MILF has discovered.

There's no doubt that the MILF had a close working relationship with Muslims in the global diaspora who would later become notorious as ter-rorists — from al-Qaeda down to its affiliates, particularly Jemaah Islamiyah. Those relationships began before either of these groups were even formed — in the training camps in Afghanistan and Pakistan, where for a period of time, there was a special "Moro" subbrigade. How did they get there? MILF Chairman Hashim Salamat answered bin Laden's call for jihad — the first modern holy war.[3] Salamat started sending Filipinos in 1980, one year after the Soviet Union decided to invade Afghanistan. Present Chairman Ebrahim Al-Haj Murad said he met bin Laden.

"I met him personally in Afghanistan," said Murad. "We have our peo-ple in Afghanistan fighting side by side with the Afghan Mujahideen at that time becase we are all over the world — the Muslim countries contributed some people to join the fighting in Afghanistan."[4]

The group openly acknowledged funding from Mohammed Jamal Khalifa, bin Laden's brother-in-law, who created bin Laden's financial network in the Philippines. Rafael Alunan, former Interior Secretary, said Khalifa was respected in Filipino society. Only later would they find out what he was actu-ally doing. "Jamal Khalifa headed NGOs," said Alunan, "as well as businesses

---

[2] Author interview with Dulmatin's wife, Istima Omar Sovie, Manila, Philippines, November 15, 2006.
[3] M. Ressa, *Seeds of Terror*, p. 126.
[4] M. Ressa, "9/11: The Philippine Connection," ABS-CBN documentary aired on September 10, 2006.

that were used to funnel funds and to bring recruits from Mindanao for religious training abroad, mainly Pakistan — religious training first, then military training, then some on-the-job training across the border in Afghanistan."[5]

The MILF admits it received funding from bin Laden when he was working with the United States years before the 9/11 attacks. Its leader said the MNLF saw nothing wrong with the donations of his brother-in-law. "He has been coordinating with us his activities," said Chairman Murad. "He was helping the depressed communities. So we welcome this because it's in the name of the International Islamic Relief Organization." In 2006, the United States froze the funds of IIRO in Indonesia and the Philippines, saying it bankrolled the al-Qaeda network in Southeast Asia. The announcement identified Khalifa as a senior al-Qaeda member.

By the mid-90's the MILF had allowed al-Qaeda and its affiliate groups to train in its camps in the Philippines. That cemented the relationship that burgeoned in Afghanistan. Aside from JI and al-Qaeda, there were others: Iran's Hezbollah used the same networks as al-Qaeda to funnel money, create front organizations and recruit people for its plots. While I was reporting from India and Pakistan, I discovered the MILF's links to Harkat-ul-Unsar, which signed bin Laden's 1998 *fatwah* declaring war on Americans. This is the group which hijacked an Indian Airlines flight in 1999 in order to free Omar Sheikh, the man later convicted of murdering Wall Street Journal reporter Daniel Pearl in February 2002. Harkat-ul-Unsar said it sent *mujahideens* to train in the Philippines — a claim I verified in classified intelligence documents from the Philippines. After it was declared a terrorist group by the United States, it changed its name to Harkat-ul-Mujahideen then Jaish-e-Mohammed. Two years later, I'd report on Jaish-e-Mohammed's attack — along with another al-Qaeda affiliated group — on the Indian Parliament in New Delhi.

The MILF, because of its credibility as a legitimate political organization, is a magnet for Muslim groups around the world. The partnership with JI was a natural development, stemming from their Afghan experience. Travelling the region for CNN allowed me to put together documents and witnesses to see JI's reach before many of the authorities, particularly in Indonesia and the Philippines. It seemed the terrorists were more capable of working cross-borders than nation-states, which tended to hoard information and, often, lacked the understanding of conditions in other countries.

After the arrest of Singaporean Mohammed Aslam bin Yar Ali Khan at the Afghan border, Singapore went into overdrive and began putting the

---

[5] Author interview with former Department of Interior & Local Government Secretary Rafael Aluman III, Manila, Philippines, March 21, 2006.

Mohagher Iqbal with Maria Ressa at the MILF's Camp Darapanan June 3, 2011
(Photo by Beth Frondoso).

links together. It privately warned its neighbors, but only Malaysia acted quickly. In December, Singapore arrested 15 people, 13 of whom were members of Jemaah Islamiyah, for multiple bomb plots in Singapore against the U.S. embassy and other foreign targets. The explosives were coming from the Philippines, sourced by JI member Fathur Rohman al-Ghozi. Singapore released more information which substantiated that the MILF provided key training and other assistance to members of JI.[6] I had reported much of this information earlier based on intelligence reports from different countries. This was the first time any nation publicly pinpointed the training ground and theater of operations in Southeast Asia.

"Our situation is similar to the United States in Afghanistan," MILF chief negotiator Mohagher Iqbal told me. "The Americans and Osama bin Laden, they were friends. They were siding with each other when the Russians were invading Afghanistan. They were even sharing the same troops, see? In other words, sometimes you cannot choose your friends."[7]

---

[6]White Paper: "The Jemaah Islamiyah Arrests and the Threat of Terrorism," *Ministry of Home Affairs, Republic of Singapore,* January 7, 2003. Available at http://www.mha.gov.sg/publication_details.aspx?pageid=35&cid=354
[7]Author interview with Mohagher Iqbal, Camp Darapanan, outskirts of Cotabato City, Philippines, June 3, 2011.

We were in a large open field in Camp Darapanan. About a dozen MILF troops, in army fatigues like soldiers, were standing guard in an open wooden structure about 10 feet away from us. Some of them were sitting on the wooden bench underneath the *nipa* roof. Considered a leading ideologue of the MILF, Mohagher Iqbal was wearing a bright, solid aquamarine shirt and black pants. Of medium build, he has piercing eyes and a weary air. We were sitting across from each other in white plastic chairs. A soft wind was blowing in the morning light. He struck me as substantive, knowledgeable and pragmatic. Sixty-two years old, he "joined the revolutionary struggle" in 1972 after getting his masters degree on Mindanao. In the early 80's, he became the chairman of the MILF's Committee on Information. He said he had been involved in peace talks with the government for more than 14 years. We moved easily between topics — from questions about religion, philosophy, politics and security. It struck me that he never evaded a question — even though he warned me that I was perceived to be anti-MILF because I had done so much work about its links to terrorism.

"Sometimes you cannot choose your friends," he repeated. "After that, the Americans and Osama bin Laden were the bitterest of enemies. I am not saying that some elements of the Jemaah Islamiyah were not in Mindanao. What I'm saying here is that we have no organizational links with them. Maybe individual people in Mindanao, but as to official linkage with them, we don't have because we have nothing to gain. This is a home-grown sovereignty based conflict. The MILF antedated al-Qaeda for several decades."

"When I was based in Indonesia," I began. "We documented the MILF's Special Operations Group or SOG ..."

"That is highly exaggerated. You know, in every military organization, there is always a special operations group, but it's a small group. It's not company size. It's not battalion size. To say that the MILF has a very big special operations group is to exaggerate the issue. It's natural in military organizations that you have special operations group. Even in the AFP. Even in the PNP."

"They said it's in every base command."

"Maybe they're saying that about the guerrilla operation."

"The one I documented is Muklis Yunos, and ..."

"I cannot say whether that's correct or not because I've not seen the document."

"I can share them with you. Other books have been written after mine, and they say Muklis Yunos led the MILF-SOG working with JI's Fathur Rohman al-Ghozi."

"I'm not aware of that."

"Intelligence sources tell me the head of the special operations group now is Bedz."

"That is usually floated by the military."

"So you're saying that's military propaganda?"

"Well, I'm not saying it's military propaganda, but it's coming from the military. Because you know, it's really difficult to determine the name. For instance, in my case, I have at least four or five names so sometimes names floated in the media cannot be recognized because it's just an assumed name."

I was thankful these questions were finally being answered. One of my greatest frustrations beginning in 2000 was the constant denial from both the MILF and the Philippine government about the MILF's links to terrorism. I had first-hand knowledge — in August, 2000, I followed the investigation of the bomb at the Philippine ambassador's house closely. Working with multiple intelligence sources from three different countries, I was told the trigger of the bomb used then resembled bombs made by the MILF. Years later, it became clear why — the man who made the bomb had learned from and trained MILF operatives: Indonesian JI leader Fathur Rohman al-Ghozi.

At the beginning, I took the denials at face value, but when the evidence mounted and turned denials into lies, it had an impact on the credibility of the MILF and the Philippine government. It came to head after the Singapore government published its findings publicly documenting the links, and still, the denials continued. I wondered why they couldn't have just said what Iqbal told me in 2011. Later, I realized they had a lot to lose: at one point the United States was seriously considering putting the MILF on the list of terrorist organizations. Former President Gloria Arroyo said she personally lobbied against that.[8]

"The MILF is certainly not a terrorist organization," she said soon after her term of office ended. She then ran for — and won — a seat in Congress. She retained some of the power and personal ties. She asked former cabinet secretaries to join her for our interview. "There may have been rogue elements or they may have been some who were MILF at the same time they were also either related to or they were part of another group. There's no exclusivity here of membership. As you have seen for yourself, the MILF wants peace, and so we dealt with them and looked for peace with them. In

---

[8] Author interview with former President Gloria Macapagal-Arroyo, Quezon City, Philippines, June 8, 2011.

Author interview with former President Gloria Macapagal-Arroyo.

fact, as far as we are concerned, if we are able to have peace with the MILF then that would even isolate the terrorist groups."

2005 was a pivotal year. At that point, JI had helped regenerate the terrorist foundations of the Abu Sayyaf and helped broker an arrangement which brought the group to central Mindanao in MILF camps. JI also helped link Santos' Rajah Solaiman Movement with the Abu Sayyaf and the MILF, partly using the networks laid down in the mid-90's by al-Qaeda. The ceasefire with the MILF was holding, but the pressure was mounting about its terrorist links.

Soon after the foiled JI-Abu Sayyaf-RSM "big bang" plot in Manila, Santos, JI leaders Dulmatin and Umar Patek as well as the top leaders of the Abu Sayyaf were in the camp of the MIFL's 105th base command under Ameril Umra Kato. That was when the MILF made a decisive move: the leadership decided to cut its ties with all three groups — JI, Abu Sayyaf and RSM. Santos wrote in his diary dated June 27, 2005:[9] "It was around seven in the morning. A letter addressed to Al-Harakatul al-Islamiyah was handed over from Chief of Staff Sammy Al-Mansoor of MILF Central Committee. The Mujahideens were forced to immediately leave the place, and an ultimatum of three days was given." Santos' diary was a long account of how he felt betrayed by the MILF and the hard journey he, along with members of the Abu Sayyaf and JI, faced

---

[9] I obtained a copy of portions of Ahmad Santos' diary which was recovered by Philippine authorities during his arrest in Zamboanga, Philippines, October 26, 2005.

in finding their way back to Jolo. Little had been written about it publicly, partly because it's tricky: if the MILF says it kicked them out, they would have to admit they were there in the first place. I wanted to confirm it with Iqbal.

"Ahmad Santos said in his diary that the MILF kicked out JI, Abu Sayyaf and RSM members from its camp in 2005. Is that correct?" I asked Iqbal.

"The Ad Hoc Joint Action Group was in place, and we had the cease-fire," he answered quickly. "The military was very persistent in saying that there are JI and Abu Sayyaf militants here. So to comply with the require-ments of the AHJAG and the ceasefire, we made an arrangement through the International Monitoring Team that our entire combat forces in the area were withdrawn and then allowed the Armed Forces of the Philippines to come in and interdict and isolate or probably kill the Abu Sayyaf."

"So the MILF decided to push them out. Was it in response to the ceasefire?"

"That was in response to the ceasefire."

"When I spoke with the wife of Bali bomber Dulmatin, she said that their family actually lived here in Camp Darapanan. But you're saying they were all pushed out in 2005?"

"I can't say it like that — otherwise I'd be saying here that we have official contact with them, but definitely we don't have. Maybe only indi-vidual cases because we have thousands of members in Mindanao ..."

"Could you have, at some point, given sanctuary without realizing it?"

"I'm not aware of that. I'm supposed to know it because I'm in the central leadership of the MILF, but I'm not aware of that."

"And to your members, what do you tell them about groups like Jemaah Islamiyah?"

"Well, it's common news that the JI are labeled as a terrorist organiza-tion." Iqbal then went on to point out that the MILF actually had an "understanding" with the New People's Army. He said they chose that over the Abu Sayyaf. "The Abu Sayyaf," he adds, "has no political agenda. We have a political agenda, and we have to follow the rules of engagement of both international law and Islamic law."

For years, the MILF kept the JI card, its special operations group and links to the Abu Sayyaf as options — but far enough away for plausible deni-ability. Revolutionary groups and guerrilla armies around the world use tactics like this to level the playing field against larger and better armed forces of government. The problem, of course, is that the level of disclosure accel-erated in the region and globally after 9/11, and the tracks led to the legitimate revolutionary MILF. If the group wanted to stay legitimate, it needed to act — and it did in 2005.

There were other complications. The foreign jihadists brought in new bomb-making technology and tactics which changed the landscape of domestic conflicts. Also over time, the MILF found it wasn't so easy to impose discipline on some of its brigade commands including Ameril Umra Kato, the commander who sheltered JI members. In 2011, Kato and his men broke away from the MILF, and formed the Bangsamoro Islamic Freedom Movement (BIFM).

On October 7, 2012, the Philippine government and the MILF announced a historic framework agreement. Although "the devil is in the details," both sides say they hope to have a comprehensive deal hammered out by April, 2013. Peace will bring development and jobs, draining extremist groups of recruits and pushing them further to the edges.

***

Two key figures felt betrayed by the MILF, and their stories give us further insights. After three years in Afghanistan & Pakistan, Muklis Yunos returned home to the Philippines and joined the MILF rising to become the first head of its special operations group. He knew and worked closely with JI leaders Hambali and Fathur Rohman al-Ghozi. After the Rizal Day bombings, Muklis was identified early on, his pictures splashed in newspapers. The MILF "blatantly disowned" him after he was named a principal suspect. He was relieved of his command, but given his Afghan war experience, he remained a trainer.

The story of his arrest again shines the light on some of the tactics in the murky world of intelligence and counter-terrorism efforts.[10] Muklis said on May 9, 2003, he received a call from the father-in-law of MILF Chairman Hashim Salamat asking him to meet with two foreigners. One of them is an Egyptian named Dia al-Ghabri. Over the next two weeks, Muklis and al-Ghabri worked on several terrorist plots, including a suicide bombing attack on Malacanang. They worked on blueprints, and Muklis said he was bringing four men from the MILF's 3rd field division.

By this point, Muklis was afraid he might be recognized if he travelled to Manila by plane so he bought ferry tickets. Al-Ghabri, however,

---

[10] Details from classified Philippine intelligence report: *"Debriefing Report: Haji Mukhlis Umpara Yunos,"* FILO-D00325-MUY-002, May 30, 2003.

Muklis Yunos in "disguise" at Zamboanga airport.

convinced him to try one of the funniest and unwieldy disguises I had heard of: to travel in a full body plaster cast masquerading as a medical patient with the Egyptian as his doctor. When they got to the airport, Muklis was brought in on a stretcher, his face bandaged and his body in a cast. Al-Ghabri also convinced him to take a sleeping pill to "maintain his cover." It worked too well. Muklis was semi-conscious when he was arrested and the plaster sawed off from his body. When I tried to find out more details about al-Ghabri, I was told this was actually an intelligence "sting" operation by another nation to lure Muklis and his group out.

The other man who felt betrayed by the MILF was RSM leader Ahmad Santos, who said he had always wanted to join the MILF. For him, the ultimatum given to his group, the Abu Sayyaf and his JI mentors kicking them out of MILF camps cemented the JI-Abu Sayyaf-RSM alliance.

"The MILF Central Committee forced us to leave," he said. "I suppose it was part of their agreement with the government — that if they kick Al-Harakatul al-Islamiyah and the rest of the group out, then the government will give their independence." In all his conversations, Santos always referred to the Abu Sayyaf by its more ideologically rooted formal name, Al-Harakatul al-Islamiyah. "So it turned out the MILF's Central Committee traded us in so they can attain their goal. You see, their goal was to have an Islamic state, but what kind of Islamic teaching is that? That's one reason why I've lost any faith in the MILF. They sold us, and that's un-Islamic. You would sell your brothers, who are — in the first place — fighting for the Islamic cause."

Santos' arrest signaled the end of the Rajah Solaiman Movement. It was never again able to plan or carry out another attack, but RSM's next leader, Khalil Pareja, would take the battle to the virtual world and use the Internet and social networking site, Facebook, to reconnect with al-Qaeda.

***

The military's Operation Plan Ultimatum — "Oplan Ultimatum," was launched in August, 2006 and, according to officials, killed nine key leaders and at least 70 members of the Abu Sayyaf.[11] In September, 2006, Khadaffy Janjalani, the group's nominal leader and the brother of its founder, was killed — verified by DNA testing in January, 2007. That was the same month Filipino forces killed Abu Solaiman, the operations leader behind the group's latest string of terrorist plots and attacks, including the region's worst maritime attack, the SuperFerry bombing in 2004, which killed at least 116 people. The military was triumphant and released victorious statements. Then Armed Forces Chief General Hermogenes Esperon said he wanted "Ultimatum to be remembered as having been responsible for the neutralization of the #1 and #2 of the Abu Sayyaf."[12] Each man had a US$5 million bounty on his head.

The Abu Sayyaf is "disorganized and suffering from a major leadership vacuum," said military spokesman Lieutenant-Colonel Bartolome Bacarro. "We will keep up the tempo and take advantage of that. We're confident we can finally put an end to the menace of the Abu Sayyaf."[13] Of course, that didn't happen.

Ces and her team were in Mindanao reporting on the deaths of both Janjalani and Abu Solaiman. She heard Bacarro make his statement. That was when she asked former MNLF member and now Mindanao State University

---

[11] Office of the National Security Adviser, "Implementation of the Leaders' and Ministers' Statements," APEC-CTTF Meeting, Cairns, Australia, June 22–July 3, 2007. Document available on aimp.apec.org/Documents/2007/CTTF/CTTF3/07_cttf3_022.doc.

[12] R. de Jesus, "End of Oplan Ultimatum Doesn't Mean Soldiers Withdrawal in Sulu," ZamboTimes, June 6, 2007. Available at http://www.zambotimes.com/archives/5487-End-of-Oplan-Ultimatum-doesnt-mean-soldiers-withdrawal-in-Sulu.html

[13] K. McGeown, "Is this the End for the Abu Sayyaf?" *BBC,* January 23, 2007. Available at http://news.bbc.co.uk/2/hi/asia-pacific/6290805.stm

Professor Dinampo to "explore the possibility of an interview with Radullan Sahiron."[14]

A year and a half later, she was with his men, held for ransom in the jungles of Jolo.

\*\*\*

Frank and Cusi, his police escort, arrived in Zamboanga at about 6:30 in the morning on Thursday, June 12 — Day 5 of the kidnapping. Frank was nervous. At times, he balled his fists, his way of managing tension. Outwardly, he seemed composed and alert — even if he had gotten little sleep. He just kept thinking of Ces and pushed forward.

At about 8 a.m., police senior superintendent Reginald Villasanta, the head of case operation "Island Deep," as well as other police officers left Zamboanga on a chartered plane for Jolo to set up the intelligence and operations unit. One of the men who would later join them — both as an invaluable resource and another operative — was a former Abu Sayyaf founder you know as Mohammed. This was the first time Mohammed would return to Jolo since his arrest.

Frank took an 11:20 a.m. SeaAir flight to Jolo. Although Cusi was supposed to travel with him, the flight was full so Frank travelled alone. That worried me because I thought Zamboanga safer than Jolo, but Quidato told me he and his team would take care of Frank once he landed. The plane arrived at the airport at 12:20. Frank carried a black duffel with ₱5 million in cash. As instructed, he waited on the plane until Quidato came to get him. They walked off and headed towards a car parked at the airport road. Quidato opened the right car door and Frank got inside. It was a tight squeeze. Quidato closed the door quickly and got in the front seat. Lady Ann was in the back seat along with her bodyguard. She was wearing a white long-sleeve zippered shirt, tight blue jeans, white shoes and a white cap over her long, black hair. Her bright red lipstick stood out. Frank remembered some of the stories from the safehouse: Lady Ann, lady leader in the Wild, Wild West was a singer who recently produced her own album.

She asked to see the money. Frank put the bag in the middle on the lap of her guard. They opened the bag, and she pulled out a wad of ₱500 bills

---

[14] C. Drilon, "Days of Captivity in the Depths of Sulu," *abs-cbnnews.com*, July 11, 2008. Available at http://rp3.abs-cbnnews.com/special-report/07/11/08/kidnap-days-captivity-depths-sulu

held together with a rubberband. She quickly put it back in the bag. They talked for a little bit: Lady Ann described Ces in their last conversation and how she was dealing with Isnaji. Then she did something that surprised Frank: she asked to pray over the money. She held out both her hands and reached for his, and they prayed over the bag. Lady Ann cared what people thought about her, and she wanted Frank to know she wasn't going to get any part of the money — or at least that's what she said. When they finished, Frank got out of the car and Quidato walked him back to the plane, which was getting ready for its return flight. It was 12:44 p.m.

I was getting updates in Manila on each leg of the trip. I always felt better every time Frank was in the air. He landed in Zamboanga at 1:30 p.m. He transferred to the private plane which was waiting for him on the runway, and he was back in Manila at 3:45 p.m. When he walked through the door of our crisis center, I hugged him again and felt a collective sigh of relief from everyone in the room. He was safe, and it was time for the next step.

# Double-Cross

**8**

After Frank got out of the car, Lady Ann drove to Mayor Isnaji's house in Indanan. She asked to speak privately with the mayor, but he asked her and her party, which included Quidato, to go to the house of his son, Khan, about 50 meters away from his house. Quidato had decided to work undercover to stay as close as he could to Mayor Isnaji.

The negotiator chosen by the Abu Sayyaf, Alvarez Isnaji, was a former MNLF leader once loyal to its founder, Nur Misuari. In 2002, he formed one of the three factions which broke away from the MNLF leader. The second faction was led by former Cotabato City Mayor Muslimim "Mus" Sema. The factions were reunited a year later. Isnaji ran for Indanan mayor in 2007. A few months before the ABS-CBN team's kidnapping, Isnaji recognized Mus Sema as Misuari's replacement.

On the fifth day of the kidnapping, Isnaji was wearing blue jeans with a yellow polo under a tan vest. His son, Jun, was with him. Lady Ann walked into the house followed by Quidato.

"Good afternoon, Mayor," Quidato said to Alvarez Isnaji in Filipino. He established his cover without deviating too far from the truth. "I'm from the Department of Interior & Local Government. I'm an aide of the Secretary" — referring to Ronaldo Puno. "He wants to make sure you have all the help you need." Quidato stepped aside for Lady Ann.

"Good, good," said Isnaji. "This is my son, Jun. Now what do you have?"

"I have the ₱5 million from the family," said Lady Ann. "It will lift the ultimatum."[1]

---

[1] There are conflicting accounts of exactly what was said and what happened at Khan Isnaji's house. This is a composite picture from author conversations with Quidato, Lady Ann and the Isnajis' *Joint Counter-Affidavit*, IS No. 2008–617, Quezon City, July 7, 2008.

Lady Ann's car in Jolo. Winnie Quidato is at the right front of the car talking to
Lady Ann. He is in front of Frank Orena. The bag of money is on the lap of
Lady Ann's aide.

Isnaji nodded and gestured for everyone to go inside. They sat down on
the black sofa and chairs in the living room. A soldier stood guard behind
them while Lady Ann's bodyguard helped them open the bag with money.
Another of her aides took pictures as they counted the money. While that
was happening, the elder Isnaji was on the phone in alternating conversations with police officials in Manila and the kidnappers.

*\*\*\**

The camp was quiet the morning of Thursday, June 12 — Day 5 of their
captivity. Angel woke up while it was still dark and shivered. Ces opened her
eyes, saw the orange glow and began to pray. It made her feel better. As the
sun rose, there was a sense of expectation in the air. Ces was meticulously
keeping a journal, partly because it gave her something to do. Yesterday, she
couldn't write what was weighing on everyone's mind: the ultimatum. She

took out her notebook and began to write: "I prayed the rosary again as the sun rose. It eases the soul and calms me. There is an ultimatum issued by the group that if ₱5 million is not received by the mayor of Indanan at 2 p.m. today, Angel will be beheaded. I could not write that yesterday as it was difficult."[2] She stopped to think why she couldn't write this yesterday, and she had to admit it to herself first. She wasn't prepared to think about dying. That was what she struggled with all night, and she resolved that if that was going to happen, she would have to learn to accept it with dignity. She thought again of all the many things she wished she could've done differently. Then she shook it off and wrote her last lines before closing her notebook: "I took the news as calmly as I could. And the possibility that I too may die here."

Somehow, the sounds of the jungle seemed louder as the 2 p.m. deadline approached. News of any movement from Manila and Zamboanga rippled through people and would ultimately reach Ces, Jimmy and Angel. All three noticed that Dinampo was neither tied nor threatened. Ces remembered that they came because Dinampo told her Sahiron wanted to surrender. The irony, of course, is that although they were in Sahiron's camp, they would never actually meet him. He approved negotiations and refused to go below ₱20 million. His nephew was one of the first three to bring in the ABS team and would stay with them throughout.

Angel was quietly going through different scenarios in his head.[3] He whispered to Jimmy that if anything happened to him, Jimmy should ask ABS-CBN to take care of his family. He felt such anguish thinking about Rushell and his family, wondering what they would do if something happened to him. He decided that if they were going to kill him, he would take some of them with him. He planned it in his head, down to whose gun he would grab and the men he would shoot. While he was imagining this, he thought about what would happen to Ces and Jimmy if he did what he was planning, and he was thrown into confusion. Still, he was determined to die fighting.

Commander Putol was on the phone periodically. At one point, he left the camp for several hours. Angel saw him carrying his laundry and thought he must be going to town.[4] Around 1 p.m., one of Angel's guards came up to him and joked, "So no beheading today. You're lucky. How hard did you

---

[2] From the diary that Ces Drilon wrote in captivity, June 8–18, 2008.

[3] Author interview with Angelo Valderrama, series of conversations in July 2008. Also mentioned by Valderrama in ABS-CBN documentary, *Kidnap*, aired July 13, 2008.

[4] Classified Philippine intelligence document: "*Debriefing Report: Angelo Valderrama*," IG-6-13-08-RIO-9, June 13, 2008.

pray for it?" Angel didn't know how to respond. He looked up and saw Dinampo with the other kidnappers across the field. Dinampo smiled at Angel and flashed a a thumbs-up.

Angel didn't know how to feel. All he knew was that today, he wasn't going to die. He let out a steady stream of air and breathed in deeply.

Soon after, Commander Putol called a meeting and the kidnappers clustered in a group while Angel, Jimmy and Ces waited. Ces again berated herself for believing the story that Sahiron and Doc Abu, senior leaders of the Abu Sayyaf, wanted to surrender. What she didn't know was it was actually true.

*\*\*\**

It was a daring plan that aimed to break the seemingly endless cycle of violence. What everyone who's truly worked on terrorism in Mindanao knows is a story they will never willingly tell the public: the social networks create the system. With lack of governance and effective law enforcement, the communities create their own systems and priorities. I've heard it many times from men and women on both sides — the villagers, the military and police: they know where the "high-value targets" are — the terrorists who carry large rewards from both the Philippine government and the U.S. Rewards for Justice Program. "I couldn't understand why they couldn't get these guys," a senior official told me. "Everybody knew where they were."

This is like the cycle of kidnapping. JI leaders like Dulmatin, Umar Patek, Marwan and Muawiyah lived in communities and moved freely through society much of the time they were in the southern Philippines. "There's this whole civilian population that's surrounding them, and it's just impossible to get in and get out," said former Interior Secretary Puno.[5] "You can get in, but you can't get out." It's a concept of *pintakasi* — when the community turns on you if you attack someone they're protecting, when you become the common enemy of the different groups. It's something experienced soldiers are all too aware of. Those who don't understand this suffer unnecessary casualties.[6]

---

[5] Author interview with former DILG Secretary Ronaldo Puno, Manila, Philippines, March 12, 2011.

[6] A recent *pintakasi* happened on October 18, 2011. 19 soldiers were killed and the community fought alongside MILF members and alleged Abu Sayyaf members in Al-Barka, Basilan. More details at http://www.rappler.com/thought-leaders/159-fiasco-in-basilan

There are built-in safe areas and sanctuaries where soldiers are forbidden entry: the MNLF camps under the 1996 peace agreement and the MILF's designated "safe zones" called ATS, the Area of Temporary Stay, under the ongoing peace talks. When the military pursues members of the Abu Sayyaf, they make it a point to flee to these areas and ask for help, dragging other groups into open conflict.

In 2006, the MNLF began to splinter further. It actually begun five years earlier after Misuari led an uprising against the government after saying it failed to implement the 1996 peace agreement. Misuari fled to Malaysia, where he was arrested. Deported to the Philippines, he waited for trial on rebellion charges. This split the MNLF, and authorities began referring to an MNLF Misuari Breakaway Group (MNLF-MBG). By February 2, 2007, MNLF Commander Habier Malik actually held hostage Brigadier General Ben Dolorfino and 20 others, including the head of the government's peace panel, for two days. By April, Malik was considered a rogue MNLF commander, and the government offered a ₱1 million reward for him.

MNLF Vice Chairman Abdurahman Jamasali, a nephew of Misuari, was a key backroom negotiator during this time period, often acting as a bridge for House Speaker Jose de Venecia, Jr. and Secretary Puno with the MNLF or the Abu Sayyaf. This was ironic at times because Jamasali also acted as Misuari's spokesman and openly attacked the government. Jamasali served as a local government undersecretary while Misuari was the Governor of the Autonomous Region in Muslim Mindanao (ARMM). He was also one of the negotiators during the 2000 Sipadan kidnappings. In May, 2007, he ran for a seat in Congress for the 1st district of Sulu and lost, but he became a key player in an extraordinary government proposal that could've changed the cycles of violence.

Shortly after the killing of the Abu Sayyaf's Khadaffy Janjalani and Abu Solaiman at the end of 2006, Puno asked Misuari, his classmate at the University of the Philippines, and Misuari's cousin, Jamasali, to contact the Abu Sayyaf's two senior leaders — Radullan Sahiron and Umbra Jumdail better known as Doc Abu.

"Nur," Puno told Misuari, "You're not benefitting from these guys being there. You're looking irrelevant."

"What do you mean?" answered Misuari.

"Why don't you allow us to work on something?"

"What did you have in mind?"

"I don't know what Cong Jamasali is doing, but he has relatives who can get our offer to Radullan and Doc Abu. They're the ones controlling

Dulmatin, Umar Patek and Marwan. I have an unusual proposal. Why don't they turn them in and get the reward?" The U.S. Rewards for Justice Program was offering US$1 million for Umar Patek, US$5 million for Marwan and US$10 million for Dulmatin. "They can turn them in and then surrender to us. We will now deputize them. We're obligated to hire 2,000 more policemen so we can hire them as policemen and assign them there."

It's a controversial idea full of possible pitfalls, but Misuari agreed to let the proposal happen. Jamasali became the emissary, and in a short time, he returned. Both Abu Sayyaf leaders agreed to the offer. Sahiron and Doc Abu were tired and getting older. Puno discussed his plan with the CIA in Manila. He then spoke with then U.S. Ambassador Kristie Kenney. Both agreed to take the plan to Washington. During a classified meeting with then President Arroyo and a select group, Puno said, "This is very unusual. All of them have a price on their heads, you know, and then they will surrender. And then we will give them the reward and they will end up working for us."

"How did they take it?" asked President Arroyo.

"Well, I said, tell your legal guys to figure something out because, you know, they might be witnesses for us." Puno received a legal briefing paper and met with Kenney twice.[7] The proposal was in the early stages, but all involved agreed to move forward. It went as far as the implementation stage: the Abu Sayyaf leaders actually left their camps while Puno and his top leaders waited in Zamboanga. Their plan was simple. Sahiron would come down from Patikul and would be joined by Doc Abu and his men coming from Indanan. They would meet in a nearby beach area. The police dispatched its Special Action Forces (SAF) to "pick up" the JI leaders. The whole group would be met by the police's provincial mobile group who had easily identifiable police t-shirts. They would give the t-shirts to the Abu Sayyaf members, who would put them on immediately for protection and identification. All this had been planned and scheduled. Everything was set. Then inter-agency rivalry stepped in.

"On the day we were going there," said one of the men involved, "the marines came and arrested two people in one house, and then when Sahiron started coming down, they ambushed him. Doc Abu was in Indanan near us when the marines also ran after him. Of course, we knew their escape routes and we shared that with the marines in the past. What a mistake! The marines blocked their escape routes. They got a beating, and then they ran into the MNLF area."

---

[7] Confirmed by high-level sources in the DILG and U.S. State Department.

"So it looked like a set-up," I said.

"Yeah, when they ran into the MNLF area, the marines began bombing them. The MNLF started fighting back. So that's where the fighting with the MNLF began."

"Oh God."

"Because they were hiding Doc Abu. When the marines came, the MNLF attacked them so they also suffered casualties." While all this was happening, the top leadership, including Puno, were in Zamboanga receiving reports, watching a potential game-changing idea fall apart. "You know, the marines are very jealous about anybody being able to do anything. It's true in every kidnapping. We're the ones on the ground. Why is it that when we're capturing someone, they want to be there? Instead of us bringing these people down the way we wanted to, they wanted to capture them. Even if they're not capable of doing that. That's the sad part. They can't do it! If only they could. Then never mind if they did that and they were able to capture Sahiron and Doc Abu. But they couldn't!"

The rivalry between the police and military on the ground is fierce. The police are homegrown and understand the social networks because they're part of them. They're from the community. This is sometimes used against them: they're perceived as less professional, more accommodating, more corrupt. Local policemen were implicated in several kidnappings allegedly working with the Abu Sayyaf. The marines, on the other hand, are foreigners to the community. The charges of corruption though are just as strong: extortion from existing businesses or syndicates. One officer was recently moved because of suspicions he was using an Abu Sayyaf leader for his own purposes, in the process, protecting him. This is what goes on behind the scenes, and since the charges are rarely addressed head-on, the problem festers.

"The military wants all the credit. They knew that our people were there negotiating so they focused on Jamasali. The whole thing just collapsed! And then it got worse because now the MNLF was dragged into a full-blown war. So the MNLF wasn't involved before — but because Doc Abu went inside their restricted area — the MNLF fought back. Now they're part of the war. The military forced them into the fight."

Jamasali, the negotiator, bore the full impact of the failed attempt. The MNLF was angry with him because they blamed him for bringing the war to them. The Abu Sayyaf thought the entire plan was a double cross, and Jamasali was knowingly part of the deception. "The Muslims blamed Jamasali," a Muslim elder told me. Another high-level official said, "they thought from the beginning that was the plan." Puno tried to speak with town mayors, but he didn't think they were listening. Misuari denied any knowledge of the plan.

A few months later, Doc Abu sent word he wanted to try again. "The fact of the matter is Sahiron and Doc Abu both wanted to surrender," said a top official. "Abu's tired. So many of his relatives have already died. Sahiron's old. He's sick. They're both tired. They really don't want to fight anymore." They asked to meet in a school in barangay Buanza in Indanan, the same place they had met before. Again, there was top level approval. Francisco Don Montenegro of the Criminal Investigation & Detection Group (CIDG) was involved in the operation, and he spoke to Puno about its details.[8]

"We have to bring a little money as a sign of good faith," Montenegro told Puno.

"How much?" Puno responded after hearing the plans.

"₱100,000."

"Okay, you bring it."

"So we'll go up to Indanan? We were going to let Cong and his group go ahead. I will bring a small group behind him, maybe about four people. There will be five of us so people don't doubt us. We'll be behind Cong so we can also monitor everything."

"Who is Cong going with?"

"It'll be him, his cousin and two other guys." Jamasali was bringing his nephew, Wesher Umma.

"Okay." Puno paused. "Something doesn't sound right. This seems fishy. Don, if you go, there would only be five of you. You can't help if something goes wrong. Don't go. Just wait for them."

On October 19, 2007, Jamasali and his nephew, Wesher Umma, were walking near a school in barangay Buansa in Indanan around six in the morning. According to Joel Goltiao, the police chief of the Autonomous Region of Muslim Mindanao (ARMM), the two men stopped to talk to two others, who pulled out their guns and shot them "at a foot's distance."[9] Witnesses said that happened at 6:40 a.m. Eight empty shells from an M16 Armalite rifle were recovered "from the crime scene." Goltiao said Jamasali

---

[8] Author interview with source involved in operations, Manila, Philippines, March 11, 2011.
[9] "Abus behind Misuari aide slay?" ZamboTimes, October 22, 2007. Available at http://www.zamboangatimes.net/archives/7213-Abus-behind-Misuari-aide-slay.html

was hit in the face and hands which "also indicated that he tried to cover his face."

Benjamin Dolorfino, the commandant of the Philippine Marine Corps, said Jamasali's death "is a big loss in our effort to have peace in Sulu."[10] He said Misuari told Jamasali not to go to Indanan "because of many [sic] information he will be killed."

\*\*\*

Alvarez Isnaji was sitting on the sofa talking on his cellphone. The bag of money had been emptied on the low coffee table in front of him. His son, Jun, was counting the money with Lady Ann's bodyguard.[11] They were unwrapping the bundles of cash, removing the rubber bands holding them together and counting the bills. After the money in each bundle was counted, Jun Isnaji put back the rubber band and returned the bundle to the bag. Quidato watched and listened as he sat on the couch next to Isnaji, while Lady Ann stood over the table watching, directing, negotiating.

The question they were trying to answer was what will the kidnappers give in return? The ultimatum was dropped as the kidnappers quickly agreed Angel would not be beheaded. Lady Ann pushed for more as she promised Frank: she wanted the three released. The kidnappers immediately said no. They countered: "If you give ₱2 million more, we'll release one of them." Lady Ann said, "Be serious — there's not enough time to come up with that money. The family's done all it can. They're not rich. This is all they can give." A long discussion followed. At one point, Mayor Isnaji got irritated and said if they "didn't release the victims, he would back out and resign as negotiator." At that point, Jun grabbed the cellphone and reminded the kidnappers the money was there. "If you're really sincere and in good faith," said Jun, "You should not only lift the ultimatum. You should release at least one of the hostages if not all."[12]

---

[10] "Abu Sayyaf killed MNLF leaders," ZamboTimes, January 8, 2008. Available at http://www.zambotimes.com/archives/8404-Abu-Sayyaf-killed-MNLF-leaders.html

[11] In a sworn affidavit, Jun Isnaji would deny counting the money although pictures I obtained show him handling the money.

[12] Composite picture from descriptions of Lady Ann and the Isnajis' *Joint Counter-Affidavit*, IS No. 2008–617, Quezon City, July 7, 2008.

Isnaji's house in Indanan, Sulu. From left to right: Lady Ann's aide, Jun Isnaji, Lady Ann, Alvarez Isnaji, Winnie Quidato.

Finally, they reached a decision: the kidnappers said they would release one person, and they would choose who it would be.

Lady Ann left Isnaji's house at 4:40 p.m. on Thursday, June 12.

\*\*\*

"You're lucky you're safe," Sali Said told Angel. He was followed by Commander Putol, who triumphantly pulled Ces, Jimmy and Angel to a corner and told them, "Mayor asked us to release one of you as a sign of good faith. We decided it would be Angelo." Angelo's adrenalin surged, but not for long. He began to worry about Ces and Jimmy.

The camp began to bustle with activity as some of the kidnappers prepared to leave. Said gave Angel an army camouflage shirt to wear over his clothes. He also asked him to carry loaded magazines — ammunition for M203 and M16. Around 3 p.m., Said and about nine other Abu Sayyaf members led by Commander Putol walked Angel out of the camp.[13] He hugged Jimmy and Ces, looked behind him as he walked away from them. They stopped to rest a few times, and when they passed one group of homes, they asked for water. They also bought bread at a store. Angel noticed they had to ask for directions a few times. About three hours later, they arrived at Sitio Danasih, Patikul, near the boundary of Talipao. The group stopped when it hit a feeder road and settled in an abandoned hut nearby. Angel noticed two more armed men joined the group. They stopped to pray. Immediately after, Commander Putol called Sali Said and Sahiron's nephew, Kimar, and told them to get Jun. They changed out of their military camouflage and left their big guns.

Said and Kimar returned after about an hour. They led the group to a parked car nearby. When they got there, one of the kidnappers gave Angel a bottle of Coke. Jun Isnaji came to him, shook his hand and introduced himself. Angel looked around and saw the kidnappers shaking hands with the policemen with Jun. He noticed they knew each other and greeted each other as friends. The police bundled Angel and Jun into the car, and they drove to the Isnaji home where they were greeted by Alvarez Isnaji. They only stayed a short while before transferring to another house where they were joined by Lady Ann and where Angel would stay the night. Quidato shadowed Jun and stayed with Angel every step of the way. We had hurdled one danger point: Angel made it out of the jungle and was now back in civilization.

By this time, Angel was physically and emotionally exhausted. He ate dinner, but he couldn't stop thinking about Jimmy and Ces.

* * *

Social network theory gives us a framework for examining terrorist networks and anticipating how they behave. As I've shown, some of Ces' kidnappers are linked to the Indonesians and Arabs who carried out the worst attacks in the region and the world. To see how the networks evolved over the past decade, we can look closer at Jemaah Islamiyah's bomb-makers — crucial

---

[13] Classified Philippine intelligence document: "Debriefing Report: Angelo Valderrama," IG-6-13-08-RIO-9, June 13, 2008, p. 8. Also details from the deposition given by Angelo Valderrama to SPO1 Jose Guirhem at Camp Crame on June 27, 2008. Combined with author interview with Sali Said, undisclosed location, Manila, Philippines, July 2011.

members of their attacks whose accessibility is an indication of the stability of their network. Over time, we quickly see the attrition caused by the efforts of the Indonesian police because the quality of JI's bombs decreased as its better bomb-makers were arrested or killed.

JI's most skilled bomb-maker was Western-educated university lecturer Dr. Azahari Husin. Trained in Afghanistan and the southern Philippines, he designed JI's lethal bombs for Bali in 2002 and 2005, the Marriott Hotel in 2003 and the Australian Embassy in 2004. One of his university students, Noordin Top, was meticulously taught by Azahari and became his second-in-command. The Bali 2002 bombs, JI's most sophisticated, were designed by Azahari and built by Indonesians Dulmatin and Umar Patek. The Marriott bomb in 2003 was built by Azahari and Noordin.

Some analysts have written that starting in 2003, Azahari and Noordin began to splinter away from JI and form a breakaway group, saying they "had some communication with the JI leadership but not its endorsement."[14] If we look at the social networks behind the bombings from the beginning, we can see this isn't true. The larger JI group has never given its endorsement for any of the bombings, which were carried out by a small minority — its key leaders. JI always had an overt and covert operation, and not all its members knew the plans. In fact, only key members received its manual, the PUPJI. JI was a loose umbrella organization harnessing groups in the Darul Islam social movement and anchoring them to al-Qaeda. That JI network was headed by Abdullah Sungkar and Abu Bakar Ba'asyir. Over the years, the vision of leadership and training evolved with the death of Sungkar and the arrests of Ba'asyir and Hambali (in Thailand in 2003). Take them away though, and their men — the cells — remain. They continued working as they always have, carrying out operations largely kept secret from the larger JI group, and recruiting new members to the same cause with the same methods.

After a long manhunt, Azahari was finally cornered by Indonesian police in an East Java home on November 8, 2005. Instead of surrendering, he blew himself up. Noordin Top picked up where Azahari left off, harnessing the social networks the two men built together around the region. It took Noordin several years to recruit enough people to regenerate the network to carry out an attack, but once he did, he was ready with multiple plots. On July 17, 2009, four years after the second Bali bombings, suicide bombers attacked two hotels in Jakarta's business district: the Ritz-Carlton and the familiar Marriott Hotel.

---

[14] "Indonesia: The Hotel Bombings," *International Crisis Group*, Asia Briefing No. 94, July 24, 2009, p. 2.

Palace interview with President Bambang Yudhoyono. Photo by Beth Frondoso.

"They work underground even though we hit them hard," said Indonesia's President Susilo Bambang Yudhoyono.[15] We were in one of the smaller rooms in Istana and his security officials were sitting to his right. It's interesting to see how Yudhoyono has changed in the last 15 years as he rose to the presidency. I had reported on him when he was in the military and followed him during his campaign and election. Now in his second term, he seemed steadier, more in control of forces which pummeled Indonesia. He switched in and out of Bahasa Indonesia, but at a certain point settled into English. "They have the capability to consolidate, to reorganize and try to find the opportunity to strike us again. There are many smaller organizations. There are many branches that developed, but actually the mainstream remains. Al-Qaeda is the big brother. That is my view."

To our left sat three of his security officials, and when I looked, they were nodding their heads. The head of Indonesia's anti-terrorism council was specific: "This is the terrorist network that has had experience operating throughout Indonesia, Philippines and Southeast Asia," Said Ansyaad

---

[15] Author interview with Indonesian President Susilo Bambang Yudhoyono, Istana, Jakarta, Indonesia, June 24, 2011.

Mbai.[16] "It's the same group known by different names. We can see this in the nature of the bombs, the style of assembly of explosives, the nature of the explosives. This is the same group."

The planning showed foresight, long-term goal-setting and dogged persistence. One of the men applied to work in the flower shop at the Ritz-Carlton in 2005, leaving a higher-paying job in another hotel. He is one of four members in ONE family involved in the hotel bombings. Mapping the social network tapped by Noordin for this attack unveiled numerous connections to JI's hard-core operations group long carrying out terrorist attacks — family ties that held it all together and weak ties that cemented different groups acting under the new umbrella group. It showed us that terrorist networks are constantly shifting and evolving, especially with sustained pressure from law enforcement across Southeast Asia, but the underlying foundation and pool of new recruits is the Darul Islam social movement — there long before al-Qaeda ever existed.

JI itself was unraveling. In 2008, Ba'asyir took the majority of its members, led by the network which helped in terrorist attacks, and gave the group a new name — JAT, Jemaah Ansharut Tauhid. Several old JI members, now part of JAT, had been imprisoned and released. They rebuilt their lives but kept their ideology — providing a larger support network. Urwah is a typical example of this group. After spending three years in prison, he took a wife in an arranged marriage set up by Abu Bakar Ba'asyir. Shortly after, he started a company which produced al-Qaeda videotapes with Bahasa Indonesian subtitles and became part of the network which carried out the hotel bombings.

Intense family connections continued to hold the network together. Noordin married into a family in Cilacap, Indonesia that gave him access to two schools for fresh recruits. His father-in-law, Baharudin Latif, founded an Islamic school. Authorities later found a cache of explosives in Baharudin's backyard. Baharudin's nephew was an Afghan war veteran and JI member who spread the jihadi virus further by providing bomb-making training and supplies to anyone interested.[17]

Noordin roped in another family, key for operations and funding, some of whom later helped authorities uncover a plot to assassinate

---

[16] Author interview with Ansyaad Mbai, Jakarta, Indonesia, June 24, 2011.

[17] Safuddin Zuhri, also known as Sabit, was a well known JI member. His uncle is Baharudin Latif.

Indonesian President Yudhoyono. It revolved around Syaifudin Jaelani, a religious teacher who recruited many youths — including the suicide bombers for the two hotels — and was believed to have contact with al-Qaeda. He studied in Yemen from about 1995 to 2000 and was in contact with the leaders of JI's next generation known as al-Ghuraba. Sent to Karachi, Pakistan by Hambali, the group's leader is Abu Bakar Ba'asyir's son, Abdul Rohim, and included Hambali's younger brother, Gun-gun. At one point, group members acted as direct conduits to al-Qaeda and trained with Lashkar-e-Taiba in Kashmir, a Pakistani-based group which carried out the 2008 Mumbai attacks.

Syaifudin's brother was a Garuda technician who acted as a weak tie bridging other networks. Syaifudin's brother-in-law quit his higher-paying job in another hotel to work as a florist in the Ritz-Carlton in 2005. Another brother-in-law booked the room where the suicide bomber stayed and led police to the discovery of the plot against Yudhoyono barely a month after the twin hotel bombings.

Noordin's network, according to Indonesian officials, was less than a month away from carrying out a double-pronged assassination attempt against Yudhoyono. The operation which recovered 500 kilograms of explosives at a house in Bekasi, just outside Jakarta, happened on August 8, 2009. Police found the vehicle and explosives as well as the suicide bomber for the operation. The plot to assassinate Yudhoyono was set for September, 2009, Tito Karnavian told me at a late lunch in Jakarta.

"The safe house is near the President's residence in Cikeas," said Tito. "This is like our Malacanang.[18] They prepared the bombing materials. They just needed to assemble the components. Then the car was already there. The suicide bomber, Ibrahim, was already there and ready to die!"[19]

Tito punched the air with his fork. He was animated, passionate about what he was saying. He described an elaborate, well-planned assassination plot using two suicide bombers. One car was supposed to block the presidential convoy while President Yudhoyono's car crossed another vehicle loaded with two suitcases of explosives and three gas tubes as boosters. At that point, the suicide bomber inside the vehicle would ignite the explosives, but it didn't stop there. "Just in case the President survives," said Tito, "there's another suicide bomber on a motorcycle wearing a vest bomb.

[18] Malacanang is the official residence of the President of the Philippines.
[19] Author interview with Brigadier General Tito Karnavian, Jakarta, Indonesia, March 24, 2011.

If President Yudhoyono survived, the motorcycle would make sure their task was accomplished."

When he was told about it, Yudhoyono immediately told his family and ordered the police to continue its aggressive campaign to break up the terrorist networks. This wasn't the first time authorities found evidence he was a target: in 2003, his picture was used as target practice in a shooting range inside a makeshift camp. "I know the risks, and I know the consequences," said Yudhoyono. "I have to be tough. I will never stop fighting terrorism because this is the way I save my people."

Tracking this evolving network with its present-day cells led police to other plots. "We are quite surprised with the resilience of this movement," said Tito. "Based on our investigations and findings," he added, "they had another plan after the President — to attack the American Embassy. It was found in the laptop of Noordin M. Top." The plans included detailed surveillance as well as timetables.

Noordin was killed by government forces on September 17, 2009. That was a blow to the ongoing plots, but less than six months later, police dealt crippling blows to the network's regeneration. A series of police operations in February, March and April of 2010 arrested and killed members who were setting up a secure base in Aceh, a training camp much like Mindanao — the evolution, perhaps, of what the network had tried to set up earlier in Ambon and Poso. The social network of the jihadists, now in its third regeneration as JAT, again came under intense attack, but its composition shows how the jihadi virus spread. The training camp included "men of virtually every known jihadi organization"[20] in Indonesia.

More than 100 people were arrested at the beginning of 2010. Authorities said they were training Muslim fighters for Mumbai-style commando attacks. The arrests led police to other cells and high-profile leaders, including Kompak's Abdullah Sonata (who worked closely with Dulmatin and Umar Patek), master recruiter Aman Abdurrahman, JI leaders Dulmatin, Abu Tholut and Abu Bakar Ba'asyir himself.

"The organizational structure of these terrorists," said Ansyaad Mbai, the chief of Indonesia's National Counter-Terrorism Agency (known by its Indonesian acronym, BNPT), "originally formed from the core members of JI, which broke into smaller units. Now there's a reunification. They're bound by the same ideology." Since the crackdown began after the Bali

---

[20] "Indonesia: Jihadi Surprise in Aceh," *International Crisis Group*, April 20, 2010, p. 1.

bombings in 2002, Mbai said police arrested more than 600 members of JI and its affiliate groups. About 500 have been tried and sentenced. What's alarming is that many of those who were released from prison were found working at the Aceh camp or with the reinvigorated JI network. "JI has morphed because of the severe pressure from the security forces; new organizations have emerged, and existing organizations have been infected by JI," said Rohan Gunaratna, author of *Inside al-Qaeda* and the head of Singapore's International Centre for Political Violence and Terrorism Research. "JI mutants have become more active."

Dulmatin, who led the network's resurgence, was killed on March 9, 2010, among more than two dozen killed after the Aceh arrests. His move from the southern Philippines to Indonesia showed how easily the degraded network can rebuild once skilled leaders emerge. With his killing, the Aceh arrests, and Ba'asyir's imprisonment, the network's leadership was again degraded, but the networks remain.

As always happens, the disparate cells left behind by its top and middle-rank leaders continued to evolve. Without central leadership again, each cell was left to fend for itself: with each cell trying to do what it could to live up to its ideology. Some randomly killed police officers, like Yuli Harsono, a former soldier, who galvanized highly educated young men together. They began with what they knew. Angry with the Aceh arrests and killings, Yuli walked into a police station and shot the officer on duty. His group repeated this a few times. Some of the members were chemical engineers who were making bombs.[21] Other cells were doing the same thing: the damaged network robbed banks, carried out book bombings and suicide attacks in police mosques, which killed only the bombers themselves.

Much has been written about a switch in tactics — from bombings to targeted attacks and assassinations. These were driven by necessity: this was all each cell — and the network — could do without central training and coordination. While the physical network has been severely damaged, the existing cells continue to recruit and grow in haphazard ways.

In 2011, there were more, smaller attacks. In March, new recruits sent "book bombs" to moderate Muslims — showing an evolution in targets: a switch from Western targets to government and law enforcement authorities and now to moderate Muslims who campaign against terrorists.[22] In April, a

---

[21] Author interview with Ansyaad Mbai in Jakarta, Indonesia on March 22, 2011.

[22] Quote from terrorism analyst Ken Conboy in "JI blamed for Indonesian mail bombs," *The Straits Times*, March 17, 2011.

suicide bomber detonated the bomb he carried inside a police mosque. A week later, police arrested about 20 people after they found a 150-kilogram bomb buried under a gas pipeline about 100 meters from a church. It was set to go off during Good Friday mass during the busy Easter weekend. Police said the terrorists planned to film the explosion and the devastation it caused. By that point, the police had started unraveling the network behind all these attacks.[23] Other plots were discovered, including one to poison drinking water and another Bali attack in 2012.

In February, 2012, the United States designated JAT a foreign terrorist organization. Its spokesman, Son Hadi, denied any terrorist links, calling it a Western ploy to undermine the JAT, which is working to establish an Islamic state through peaceful means. "It says it is peaceful," said Gunaratna, "but it is the most violent terrorist group in Southeast Asia. It is a terrorist organization that at times masquerades as a political and religious organization."

Intelligence and security agencies around the world have been very successful at tracking the old structured organizations which had assets to track and large-scale plots which leave a footprint. Now as these networks evolve into disparate cells, several things are happening. First, there are just more of them and the connections don't seem apparent at first glance. That's part of the confusion analysts face today — one that can be made clearer by looking at their social networks and the ideas and emotions they spread. Second, they are more ad hoc and have less training, meaning they are less skilled. So there are more cells with decreased capabilities of carrying out successful attacks. This leads to a situation where authorities now have to reassess their tactics so they can anticipate the spread of the ideology. Otherwise, the unpredictable potential increase in numbers alone means stretching limited resources.

Still, the connections to al-Qaeda remain. In June, 2009, Indonesian Umar Patek, embedded initially with the MILF and later the Abu Sayyaf, left the Philippines and arrived in Indonesia. Intelligence reports say he stayed in Jakarta with Dulmatin, who helped arrange his trip to Pakistan in August, 2010. Indonesian authorities say he and his Filipino wife wanted an audience with Osama bin Laden. They were arrested by the Pakistanis on January 25, 2011 in Abbottabad, Pakistan, the same town where bin Laden would be killed by U.S. commandos a little more than three months later.

---

[23] Many reports and analysts say the leader of the group, Pepi Fernando, was not connected to any known radical group. That, according to Ansyaad Mbai and Tito Karnavian is not true.

One thing is clear globally: while al-Qaeda in its heyday pulled attention to "the Far Enemy" — the United States and the West, now more than a decade later, the associated groups are focusing the target on "the Near Enemy" — their own governments. The degradation of capability and the breakdown of al-Qaeda's central command means domestic groups are bringing their targets back home.

*** 

Thursday, June 12 — Day 5 — was another very long, tension-filled day at the crisis center. Except this time, there was some relief, no matter how short-lived. After a little more than 12 hours, Frank was back. He was still wearing his white shirt and blue jacket. I looked around the room and realized none of us had changed our clothes from yesterday. Mark chose to deal with the constant stress by escaping to the gym for a short time. He was still wearing his shorts and had thrown a jacket over his shirt so he could watch developments with us. We were monitoring television, radio and the internet, but I realized our actions were about six hours or so ahead of what would be reported, oftentimes at that point, wrong because the information was distorted when relayed to reporters. Lady Ann updated us as she moved through the day, and Quidato, as often as he could, texted me what was happening and what actions he would take.

Around 9 p.m., he finally called with Angel next to him. He was safe.

"Are you going to send a plane to get him?" asked Quidato.

"No, not with Ces and Jimmy still held hostage."

"Can we debrief Angelo — get whatever information he has to see if it can help us."

"Yes, absolutely. Do you know what he wants to do?"

"No, do you want to speak with him?"

"Yes, please," I answered. Quidato handed the phone to Angel.

"Angel, how are you?"

"I'm okay, Ma'am," he answered in Filipino. I felt a sense of relief when I heard his voice.

"How are Jimmy and Ces?"

"They're okay."

"Can you go to Zamboanga and tell the police what you know?"

"Yes, Ma'am. I'll tell them everything. I don't want to go to Manila without them. I'll help the police every way I can."

"You can come home earlier once you tell the police."

"No, Ma'am, it doesn't seem right. I'll stay with the police and tell them everything I know."

"Are you sure? Rushell and your daughter are here."

"Yes, Ma'am. She'll understand. It's not right I go home while they're still here." At that point, I had a lump in my throat. I didn't know Angel well but his courage and his tenacity affected me deeply. I thanked him and told him Quidato would give him a cellphone so he could call his family. Quidato took the phone again.

"He doesn't want to go home without them," I told Quidato.

"That's good. I'll take care of him."

"Please, Winnie, make sure he's okay. Do you need anything else from us?"

"Were you able to find the video of your last visit to the Abu Sayyaf?"

"Yes, I've asked for a dub and it's been sent to you."

"Okay, we can use that video to see if any of them are familiar to Angel." We talked more about details and the kidnappers' demands. They requested Angel's release be kept secret — something I agreed with immediately because that would also help Ces and Jimmy.

When we hung up, I looked up. I was at one end of the long table. The chairs had been pushed back from the long table, and everyone was milling around the room. It felt like a pressure cooker that was just beginning to release air. To my left was Frank. Next to him was Iglesia. Across the table was Grech's partner, Richard. Next to him was Ces' youngest son, Andre. Next to him and to my right was Grech. Other chairs had been pulled back. And I could sense a lot of movement. Mario called everyone's attention, and I updated them: Angel would stay in Jolo overnight then go to Zamboanga to work with police investigators to try to identify the kidnappers. My voice choked slightly when I told them Angel didn't want to go home without Ces and Jimmy.

Rushell was standing in the living room listening to it all, and when someone asked her how she felt, she joked that now she'd have to go home and clean. We started to laugh. Grech got up from the table and hugged her, and when she did, Rushell started crying and wouldn't let go of Grech. The room became quiet. It was a moment emblazoned in my heart: Rushell happy her husband was safe, shortly after the threat of beheading less then 24 hours earlier. But that relief was also tempered with fear — a fear we all felt but couldn't verbalize. Ces and Jimmy were still in the jungle. For Rushell, there was also a sense of guilt — the same emotion I felt from Angel. Grech rubbed Rushell's back, and I thought about the incredible generosity of spirit in the room. Ces' family didn't have Ces. but they didn't blame Rushell because Angel was now safe. It seems odd to write these words, but it's something I could verbalize only much later. There's a point where it's a fight for survival. It becomes every man for himself. Except this group just didn't go there.

Frank hugged Rushell awkwardly after Grech, who quickly turned away and wiped her tears. I remembered Angel would need help and held a short chat with Mario, Mark and Maxim Uy, our corporate lawyer. I asked Maxim to fly to Zamboanga to be with Angel while he was helping the police. My assistants made arrangements for him to take the morning flight. After that, I was on the phone a short while to update our other sources, and when I turned back to the family, I saw Rushell and Jimmy's wife, Eva, crying, then laughing in one corner.

I was going over the next steps in my mind. Lady Ann and Quidato said there was still a chance the kidnappers would release the other two. I spoke with Secretary Puno, who told me he was mobilizing men and that there should be no other payments. He outlined his plans to me, and I held on to hope. Deep inside, I was afraid I wasn't being realistic. It was becoming harder to pull out and see the bigger picture, tossed and turned by every development and input. I was exhausted and somehow felt we were slowly losing control. They now had money, and I knew that changed everything.

Angel would give authorities an idea of the individual people involved in the kidnapping. If the police act according to the way they have in the past, once they get an idea of the people involved, they will look for their families. In these lawless areas, the only power you have is the gun and the relationships of the people who hold those guns.

The happiness over Angel's release was short-lived. It was quickly replaced by a sinking feeling. I looked down at my yellow pad scenarios, and I knew this was only the eye of the storm. It was about to get worse.

# Breakdown

9

A ngelo was gone. While Ces and Jimmy wanted to be happy for him, they began to worry about what would happen to them. After the sun set and the kidnappers left behind began to put up their hammocks and sleeping mats, Ces faced another dilemma. Commander Putol set his hammock up much closer to hers than before and although she complained about it, he only moved closer. The spectre of rape became more real — something she didn't want to confront. So far, the men had kept their distance. It helped that Jimmy and Angel constantly surrounded and protected her. The Abu Sayyaf members commented on it many times, asking Jimmy whether Ces was his wife. Jimmy boldly responded with pride that Ces was his reporter and his "Ma'am." "*Ma'am ko siya, Ma'am ko siya*," insisted Jimmy. In the twisted logic of the jungle, somehow that translated to respect for Ces.

As the days went by though, that respect began to gradually erode. This was a major factor in my determination to get our team out, the sooner the better — although I didn't know the details at that time. That evening, Ces asked Dinampo to speak to Putol to pull back, but Putol refused to move. Unknown to her, some of the men were speaking in Tausug about raping her. Dinampo overheard them but decided not to tell her because he was afraid she "would become hysterical."[1] Still she felt something had changed. When Putol fell asleep, she considered taking the bolo knife near her hammock and slitting his throat. She "let the thought pass" but resolved that's what she would do if he tried to lay a hand on her.

---

[1] Dinampo would later reveal this in court. When Ces heard it, she told me she got angry.

The men who brought Angelo returned shortly after midnight. Loud and boisterous, they seemed tired but happy. When they saw the placement of the hammocks, several of the men questioned Putol, who grudgingly moved his hammock away from Ces. (In the morning, he would tell her that the men were jealous of him). He joined the men for a short while, and the threat of rape receded — at least that night. Ces got little sleep. Around 1:30 a.m., Commander Putol gave her the cellphone and told her to call Jun Isnaji, who handed the phone to Angelo. She was relieved to hear his voice and asked whether journalists were aware he had been released. Somehow that seemed important to the kidnappers.

Quidato stayed with Angelo Thursday night. Around 3:30 Friday morning, they fled to a safehouse near the pier, where they hid and waited till the morning. When the navy plane arrived, Quidato walked Angelo across the tarmac into the plane to Zamboanga. Quidato stayed on in Jolo and remained undercover with the Isnajis. During the next few days as negotiations threatened to repeatedly break down, Quidato would play a crucial role — the point of trust in a process that could, at best, be described as chaotic. Because we agreed to Iglesia's proposal to cut contact with Ces, we were solely dependent on Quidato and Puno for information. Negotiations now shifted to Jolo, and Quidato became the focal point.

***

Can social network theory be used to fight terrorism? Yes, and there's one clear example from Indonesia, which expanded its counterterrorism forces and operations only after the Bali bombings in 2002. I remember when the Indonesian police's counterterrorism force, Densus 88 (also known as Detachment 88), was formed on June 30, 2003. I was outside the police station shooting videotape when the first computers were being lugged inside. I remember when intelligence authorities in Southeast Asia began using link analysis diagrams to track the terrorist network. I have a few of the early ones, programs given to them by their Western allies. Nearly a decade later, new technology allows a visualization of how the jihadi virus spreads from communities and societies to others through formative events and gatherings as well as through the power of weak ties, individuals who bridge groups. Given enough information, we can actually map the spread of the jihadi virus, identify hubs and weak ties bridging networks and do a more strategic approach to countering the violence by addressing it at its core. We can also see the broad picture of the tactics used by al-Qaeda and JI.

JI's strategy in every country in Southeast Asia has been simple: to foment chaos and violence. In Singapore, Hambali had a plot to attack the water pipelines bringing water from Malaysia to Singapore.[2] This is important because Singapore was kicked out of Malaysia in 1965, and its only source of water is the pipeline from Malaysia. Hambali wanted to revive the ethnic strife that caused race riots in the 1960s and fuel the conflict between "Chinese Singapore" and "Malay-Muslim Malaysia" in the hopes of triggering a jihad in Malaysia against Singapore. If Singapore thought it had been attacked, it might attack Malaysia, triggering a war. JI could then take advantage of the instability to overthrow the governments of both countries and establish an Islamic state. "It's the same doctrine the communists had," said Singapore's architect and first prime minister Lee Kuan Yew.[3] "In a chaotic situation, the organized minority will take over. So their objective is, it doesn't matter what it is, just cause strife within the country, strife between races and countries. In the chaos and the confusion that result, they will thrive and win power."

In the Philippines, al-Qaeda tried to create a Muslim brotherhood through the work of Mohammed Jamal Khalifa. The Abu Sayyaf raid of Ipil in 1995 was designed to trigger Muslim-Christian violence. Only the cohesiveness of the communities and the communication between religious leaders tempered reactions on both sides, and it became what it has always been — a law enforcement problem. Al-Qaeda and JI tried again, this time about a decade later through the Abu Sayyaf's spokesman, Abu Solaiman, who tried to foment conflict and divide Muslims and Christians through several of his radio broadcasts. Those attempts failed as well.

Still, JI succeeded in fuelling Muslim-Christian violence in Indonesia, specifically in Ambon and Poso beginning in 1998. I remember the breakdown of society and the difficulty of reporting in what effectively became a hamletted city with Muslim and Christian checkpoints, manned by angry young men who lost friends and family. By our count, about 10,000 people were killed in the violence. My CNN team of four, half-Muslim, half-Christian, split into two cars. I hired an off-duty Muslim soldier and Christian policeman to ride in each car. At a Muslim checkpoint, the Muslim

---

[2] Details available at http://www.mha.gov.sg/publication_details.aspx?pageid=35&cid=354. I also wrote extensively about how this fits into the activities of Jemaah Islamiyah and al-Qaeda in *Seeds of Terror: An Eyewitness Account of al-Qaeda's Newest Center of Operations in Southeast Asia* (New York: Free Press, 2003).

[3] Interview with Lee Kuan Yew, *Far Eastern Economic Review*, December 12, 2002.

car led the way and negotiated the entry of the Christian car (which included me); vice versa at a Christian checkpoint. It was anarchy and something I still remember vividly more than a decade later. There were two Malino accords from 2001 to 2002 designed to bring peace to the warring sides, but neither held completely. In 2005, three Christian schoolgirls were beheaded, and the government tapped Tito Karnavian, the head of the police anti-terrorism force, Densus 88, to lead a team to find the killers and help heal the communities. He led the Satgas Bareskrim Poso (Poso Criminal Investigation Task Force), which initially started with about 30 members drawn from Densus 88, the police bomb squad and Brimob (the police mobile brigade). His work there shows a modern day application of social network theory in intelligence and police actions.[4]

"I spent almost a year and a half to clear the JI networks over there," he told me. "JI wanted to create Poso as a *qaidah amina* — an Arabic term meaning safe base." It reminded me of al-Qaeda, which means "base." Both draw their meaning from the struggle of Islam's prophet Mohammed, explained Tito. Mohammed abandoned Mecca and retreated to Medina in order to create a *qaidah amina* — which became the foundation of Islam's spread to the rest of the world. Tito said Poso's communities were unhappy with the way the government asked them to sweep the deaths of their loved ones aside. "The grievances were exploited and tapped by the radical network to spread their ideology," said Tito, "to recruit people for JI and to convert the area into *qaidah amina*. JI is behind this. Local people were involved but they were driven by emotions, tapped and manipulated by JI."

Poso, the capital of Central Sulawesi province, is located about 1,600 kilometers north-east of Indonesia's capital, Jakarta. Although Indonesia is about 88% Muslim, Central Sulawesi is about equally divided between Muslims and Christians. In Poso, which experienced several waves of sectarian violence before Tito's arrival, the balance tilts slightly in favor of Muslims. Tito's team stepped into an ongoing war, and although he said they knew the men who actually carried out the beheadings, it was difficult to arrest them. He felt these men were supported by a majority of the community, and if the police arrested them, it would only bring up past unresolved violence of Christians against Muslims.

"One village was raided by the Christians, and almost 15 people were killed, including children," he continued. "They were beheaded. So it's

---

[4] Author interview with Brigadier General Tito Karnavian, Jakarta, Indonesia, March 23, 2011.

really hard for me, you know." Somehow Tito knew he needed to cut the ties to the JI network and, at the same time, build public support for the efforts of his team and the government — although delayed — for justice and order. "No counterterrorism effort is effective without public support. Popular support is really critical. My mission is to uncover the Islamist radical network and terrorist groups over there and to make Central Sulawesi and Poso peaceful. That is my mission. So I have to do it very, very carefully. If I make a wrong move like arresting someone I know who's involved in the bombing, but then I get public resistance, what happens? It can worsen the situation against the government. They're not satisfied with the government. They don't trust the government."

Tito is Muslim, and he described what the Muslims felt. "To the Muslims, we didn't do anything to prevent our Muslim brothers being killed by Christians, particularly in one boarding school raided by thousands of Christians. 300 to 400 people were killed, and until today this has not been fully uncovered yet. So you see the public does not support the government." He learned this lesson the hard way. When he first arrived, they tried to arrest one of the culprits. It ended in a shoot-out and a mob attack on the local police station which destroyed the post and vehicles. "Because of that incident," said Tito, "I said no more arrests. We need to get legitimacy first."

What he did next is a perfect example of law enforcement use of social network theory and mapping for operational purposes. He brought in a team of 60 intelligence agents who, over the course of six months, worked to map the society of Poso, identifying those who are pro-government, the ones against, and those who are neutral. In the process, they also mapped support for JI and the extremist networks. "The population of Muslims are around 80,000 over there. So we made a map of the local community: which one is really diehard for the Islamic network; which one is neutral; which one is really pro to the police and the government to do the investigation." After half a year of gathering information and identifying key leaders and influencers, Tito said it took him two months to create the actual map so they could use it for tactical purposes — to identify the leaders of each group. What they found after that work showed them that the pro-government group is "tiny." Anti-government is large, he added, but the neutral members of society were the largest. "So in intelligence operations," said Tito, "you need to identify and employ appropriate tactics for what you want to happen. You make the pro bigger." Then he focused on the group allied with JI: "You break the solidity of their relationship. Divide and conquer." Then they worked on gaining the support of the "neutrals" by trying to "co-opt them." Key to this work is identifying the patron-client relationships, the feudal structures in the society, and engaging leaders to win them over to the side of the police and government. By doing the map first, they could decide which tactic would work best with each community leader once they started engaging them. After gaining the support they felt they needed, they moved ahead with operations on January 22, 2007. "We did a really big operation in one day. We employed some 500 police officers, mobile brigade to capture more than 20 of them."

Tito and his men began the operations shortly after dawn on a quiet Poso street targeting the men who had been declared "wanted" since 2006. Despite their planning, they were still surprised. When they moved in, they confronted a much larger armed resistance group than they expected. "We got really strong resistance," said Tito, "really strong resistance even after all that work, even after most of the people agreed we should capture them. That gunfight lasted almost a whole day." By the end of the day, one police-man and 14 who fought them were dead. Many on both sides were wounded. The police arrested about two dozen people as they fled.

Tito spoke glowingly of their operations in Poso. He talked about his own personal sacrifices but asked I not write about them. He said that opera-tion — aside from the Bali bombings and other investigations he's led — was the most challenging and highlighted the key element of any counterterror-ism effort. "Any rule of law enforcement must be supported by public legiti-macy. It must have public support. That's number one. The war on terror, any insurgency, is actually a war about gaining the people's support, right? If one side can't get the public support, then it's unlikely it will win, but if you lose public support, you will lose."

Many of the problems Tito and his men faced in Poso appear in slightly different forms in the southern Philippines: among them, a lack of faith in governance; the abundance of firearms; the breakdown of law and order. They have dense social networks and communities that provide sanctuary for armed men who switch groups as easily as they change clothes: one day, they're MNLF, the next MILF and then Abu Sayyaf.

\*\*\*

On Friday, June 13 — Day 6 of their captivity — Ces woke up before sunrise and walked to Commander Putol. She asked him if they received the money. He said, "Yes, but some of the bills look old — like they didn't come from a bank." Ces was hoping negotiations would continue, but the day moved slowly. She realized that her family and ABS-CBN had cut contact. Whenever she called them, her call would be rejected. The only people she could speak to now were Lady Ann and Mayor Isnaji. She didn't want to lose faith nor did she want that to affect Jimmy. "There's a good reason why they're doing this," she told him. "We just don't know. Let's not try to figure it out and make things up. We might just get depressed." She said this like a mantra to try to keep their spirits high.

What she didn't know was that morning the chief of the national police told us the kidnappers "reverted back" to their original demand and wanted ₱15 million for their release. At our crisis center in Manila, we were in disarray. By now, I was in constant contact with Puno. He told me about the "backroom channeling" he was doing with key leaders in the area, including Nur Misuari. He also assured me they would be able to get Ces and Jimmy out without paying any additional money. He told me they would debrief Angelo, and he and his whole command team would go to Zamboanga on Saturday to personally handle an advance team to prepare a rescue operation. As expected, he also said that once they know who the kidnappers are, they would surround their families. This would be an additional pressure point. Glenda was getting a similar scenario from the military. Sabban and Quidato were in touch, but the friction points and inter-agency rivalry remained between the military and police.

Even though we weren't accepting her calls, Ces continued to text us. Every time the kidnappers gave her the cellphone, she would clandestinely send appeals and information. One of the texts told us to ask Mayor Isnaji to call the kidnappers and convince them Lady Ann is good. Ces also asked anyone from her family to call her. It was a strange day of inactivity, the eye of the storm.

The standoff began Friday for several reasons. At about 9:30 in the morning, Sulu Governor Sakur Tan called Mayor Isnaji to his office at the Provincial Capitol. Lady Ann, his vice governor, was also there. Although Puno told me he was working through Tan, who convened the provincial crisis committee Friday, I had my doubts, and events showed there were many competing interests which eventually caused the breakdown. Without letting us know, Tan called a press conference. Statements from that conference show how facts are distorted by fears and interests. When a reporter asked Isnaji whether a ₱5 million ransom was paid, Isnaji said, "the amount of ₱100,000 was paid for board and lodging." He was confused about whether to reveal that the money had been given to the kidnappers because he "was afraid" he was violating the government's no-ransom policy. In the same press conference, however, Lady Ann said that ₱2 million "was paid in advance to the kidnappers."[5]

Right after the press conference, Tan told Isnaji to back out of the negotiations[6] — something neither Tan nor Puno told me. During that time, Puno said Tan was working with us, but that didn't seem to be the case. Perhaps Tan wanted to exert his power over his territory. Regardless of the reason, based on Tan's command, Isnaji stopped negotiating with the kidnappers from Friday afternoon, through all of Saturday until Sunday morning, June 15.

There was a lot of distrust among those working to release the hostages. The police said Isnaji had taken a large chunk of the money that was given to him by Frank. To prove their case, they pointed to his bank records, which showed a large infusion of cash around this time.[7] Police said as much as ₱3 million may have gone to him.[8] Until today, Isnaji denies these claims.

Back in Manila, we were unaware of Isnaji's "withdrawal." I felt something was wrong, and there was a breakdown. There was some activity Friday, but nothing that moved negotiations forward.

Ces called Jun Isnaji and asked him to get Dinampo's wife for another call at 4 p.m. That was when Hainatul Dinampo spoke to her husband. Dinampo asked her "to raise money for his release." She was accompanied by another politician allegedly mired in numerous links to the Abu Sayyaf, Cocoy Tulawie. Ces' kidnapper, Sali Said, would later reveal the extent of Tulawie's involvement with the Abu Sayyaf: on at least two occasions, he allegedly hired members of the Abu Sayyaf to carry out political assassinations.[9] Although both attempts failed, this was a concrete example of how

---

[5] Mayor Alvarez Isnaji, *Joint Counter-Affidavit,* Quezon City, July 7, 2008, p. 10.

[6] Ibid., p. 10.

[7] Classified Philippine intelligence report: "Suspected Bank Accounts of Selected Members of the Isnaji Family," July 21, 2008.

[8] There were several instances this was mentioned in court, but it's clear in sworn statement of Winnie Quidato, *Court Affidavit,* Camp Crame, June 19, 2008, p. 3. He states, "On several instances after the release of Angelo, Mayor Isnaji has been telling me that they gave two million pesos (₱2,000,000) to the kidnappers instead of the five million pesos (₱5,000,000) which was the amount agreed upon as initial ransom money."

[9] Classified Phililppine intelligence report: "Custodial Debriefing Report of Sali Said@Abu Miqdad," Naval Intelligence and Security Group of Western Mindanao, March 1, 2011. Some details also in a classified U.S. intelligence document: "Task Force Sulu Significant Reporting," Joint Special Operations Task Force-Philippines, Joint Intelligence Support Element, INTSUM, May 1–8, 2011.

politicians nurtured the group for their own purposes. Tulawie has repeatedly denied any involvement with the Abu Sayyaf. Earlier, he had offered to help negotiate for us, but we opted to keep the team small. Tulawie asked Ces whether Biyaw (their "safe conduct pass") was one of the kidnappers. When she said yes, he told the military, which began an intensive manhunt. If all these charges are true, this is another example of how people change sides based on their vested interests and money.

Quidato was feeding the Isnajis and the kidnappers information he said was from local government officials who were in touch with the family. In reality, he was trying to manipulate them to release their hostages. He stayed with the Isnajis as much as he could and sent constant updates up his chain of command and to me. Not even he, though, knew Mayor Isnaji had stopped negotiating, probably because he was with Jun, who was still talking to the kidnappers. I marveled at how Quidato could keep all the different stories consistent. On Friday, he told them Ces' family was unreachable because they were at the hospital visiting their mother, who collapsed under the stress of the kidnapping.

A few hours later around 6 p.m., Ces sent another clandestine text: "We are on east slope Mt. Daho. Lots of men left. Now go delta."[10] Given all that was going on, that didn't hit us immediately. It took me a while to put together that many of the kidnappers left because they had already gotten money. After an hour or so, Richard yelled from the computer, "Maria, I think Ces wants a rescue." He had googled Delta force, a counterterrorism team that specialized in targeted missions like extraction and hostage rescue. I called Puno and relayed the message, which would soon reach President Arroyo. With Quidato, I discussed my fears about any rescue mission and brought up the case of the Burnhams. I knew how poorly prepared both the police and military were for a rescue attempt. Since nothing moved forward on Friday, I began to feel frustrated.

It was time to look for another option.

\*\*\*

The ringing was insistent, pulling her out of her dream. She shot out of bed and ran to the bathroom where her phone was charging. It was early Saturday morning, and the sun was just rising. 48-year-old Loren Legarda

---

[10] PACER transcript, Ces text, 6:00 p.m., June 13, 2008.

caught her image in the mirror. Slim, clear-complexioned, with long, black hair, she fits the stereotype of a Filipina beauty. A self-described "nerd," Legarda came from a middle-class family and worked her way up. Insecure as a child, she became an overachiever with a lot to prove. She said her secret is focus, describing herself as "more diligent than bright."[11] Except in her case, the hard work made her top of her class: valedictorian in grade school; cum laude at the University of the Philippines; valedictorian at the National Defense College for a masters degree in national security. The 5'3" beauty was a commercial model at 15 years old, and at 18 began hosting a Sunday television program on GMA7. She became a news anchor and reporter for RPN9 at 21. She left for the United States when she was 24 years old and worked as a television producer for a Los Angeles station. She returned to the Philippines in 1986 when ABS-CBN re-opened its doors 14 years after martial law shut it down. Legarda anchored its prime-time newscast.

Ambitious and driven, she quickly made a name for herself, forged in the euphoria of the days after People Power. She won more than 30 awards in the fledgling broadcast industry, but they weren't enough. After a little more than a decade, she decided she wanted to find solutions to the problems she was reporting. So she entered politics and ran for office in 1998. The years in broadcasting helped: she became the top vote-getter for the Senate during her first two wins. In 2004, she ran for Vice-President on the ticket of popular movie star, Fernando Poe, Jr. When they lost, they filed an electoral protest. Until today, Legarda maintains they were cheated of their win. In 2008, she was at the top of her political game. Popularity surveys showed she could have another shot at the top positions in the country, and she was gauging whether she could make it to the presidency. The latest survey showed her at the top of the presidential poll.

On Friday afternoon during the Senate session, she received a call from Charie asking for her help to bring Ces, Jimmy and Angelo home.[12] Legarda had a track record of negotiating releases, eight of them successfully. On Friday night, she called me to confirm we wanted her help. I had discussed it with Charie earlier, but this was a quandary. Puno asked me not to bring anyone else into the process, saying he would deal with the kidnappers and release our team safely. Legarda reminded me she was an honorary Muslim princess and had negotiated other hostage releases in the past. She asked me for a background of the armed groups in Jolo. She admitted she didn't know

---

[11] Author interview with Sen. Loren Legarda, Manila, Philippines, July 28, 2012.
[12] Author interview with Sen. Loren Legarda, Manila, Philippines, July 25, 2012.

this area nor the people as well as other parts of Mindanao. I didn't think she had the personal connections and would have to work through someone on the ground, but she is tenacious and has a broad social network powered by the clout of a senator.

I made a quick decision: given the uncertainty with the negotiators now, it made sense to have another plan. I outlined the process we were going through and asked her to update me on her actions. I told her about Lady Ann and Mayor Isnaji. She, however, was honest enough to say she would do all she could, but she would not disclose everything to me. She had a certainty that was comforting, different from Puno's calculated manner. While I was afraid the two groups might work at cross-purposes against each other, I realized in this situation, no one was in control.

Her phone rang again, and she picked it up. It was Day 7 of the kidnapping.

"Loren, this is Ces. I got your text message. They just gave me my phone now so I could call you. Loren, can you help us?"

"I'll do all I can, Ces. How are you?" she asked. Legarda started thinking about what she needed to do. She thought about the dangers for her. Her involvement would be political — and would be seen in that light. Her detractors would say she was publicity hungry. She had heard it so many times before. It was two and a half years before the elections, too far away to really help her, but no one would say that. Worse, if she tried and failed, it would be used against her. Why should she get involved and risk it? There would be more moments of ambivalence for her, but not now, not when she could hear the desperation in Ces' voice.

"I can't reach anyone else, Loren," said Ces, her voice choking. "No one from ABS is picking up my call." Her voice broke. "My family's rejecting my calls. You're my only hope." Legarda made up her mind. She asked Ces to give her more details, but the kidnappers didn't give them long to talk. "Loren, please tell my Mom and my sons I love them," said Ces, relieved to hear a familiar voice with authority and certainty. Her voice started to break again.

"I'll get you out, Ces. Don't worry. It will be an unconditional release." She gave her word. Now she'd have to kick into action. First step: get her network together. She started last night, but a lot more needed to get done. Once that was in place, she could get a suspension of offensive police and military operations, known as SOPO and SOMO. Shortly after her conversation with Ces ended, Legarda looked at her phone and saw a text from Ces: "I have faith in you. Please send my love to my Mom and my boys."

Back at the crisis center, I was trying to do a flow chart of action plans. It was hard to know whom to trust, and many times, I felt I couldn't trust anyone. I knew the simpler the variables, the better, the easier to control. Except there were too many vested interests. Puno and Razon had no love lost for ABS-CBN, and while I admired Puno's strategic view, I knew his priorities went beyond getting our team home. Legarda, on the other hand, was more closely aligned with us — both on a personal level and because she would need to maintain her reputation. The minute she got involved, she had only one priority, and I knew she would not take failure lightly. This is a woman I had seen bulldoze through roadblocks.

The danger, though, was that her very involvement would water down the strategy of attrition we were using through Puno — meaning the goal was to make the kidnappers desperate enough to give up their victims without additional ransom. They certainly wouldn't feel desperate if a senator was talking to them.

I decided to hedge and tell Puno I had spoken to Legarda. I wanted him to factor it into his equation in the same way I told Legarda about our efforts. Level the playing field and may the best strategy win. Later, Puno berated me: "Loren overestimated her clout. So you're an honorary princess, but that doesn't mean anything. The culture's different. She had some experience with the NPA. She was an emissary a couple of times, but it was with the Maranao, not the Tausugs. And then with this kidnapping, there's the smell of money. The minute you make the profile higher, it becomes more expensive, and then they feel more important. It just made life harder."[13]

At that point, I decided to keep a Chinese wall between the two efforts. Legarda was another card in play — for better or for worse.

***

On Saturday, Day 7 of the kidnapping, a few hours after Ces first spoke to Legarda, the military announced it arrested Biyaw. Puno and top leaders from the Department of Interior and Local Government as well as the Philippine National Police gathered in Zamboanga for a command conference led by their intelligence teams. By this time, Angel had identified at least 14 members of the Abu Sayyaf from pictures. After the meeting, Puno called me and told me their plans. Every time I had a question, he took the

---

[13] Author interview with former Interior and Local Government Secretary Ronaldo Puno, Manila, Philippines, March 12, 2011.

time to explain why he was making each decision. I could see he understood the personalities and the terrain. My only concern was that he didn't seem to put a priority on time. I wanted them out as soon as possible, but he took a longer view. I understood that since he'd dealt with these issues in the past, but I instinctively knew every day would count for Ces. When I told him that, he told me to be patient. This, he said, is a game of chicken or blind man's bluff. That did little to assuage my fears, and I had little reserves to shore up the confidence of the families with me in the crisis center.

It was becoming increasingly clear that Lady Ann was being marginalized by the kidnappers. We would have to deal with the Isnajis. The police told me they were beginning to suspect they were somehow involved. It was unclear whom we could trust because the whole affair was dominated by deception. Quidato was an undercover agent spinning a web of lies for the kidnappers. The elder Isnaji told a local news group that he would stop negotiating. Was it an indirect way of sending a message to the crisis center in Manila? At a certain point, only his son, Jun, was talking to the kidnappers. Quidato, who was now shadowing Jun closely, pretended to have a conversation with his superior in Manila to relay Jun's questions and concerns — except the person he called was Iglesia, and he was in our crisis center. It was elaborate play-acting on many fronts with our team's lives at stake.

On Saturday afternoon, Frank and Grech spoke with Jun. The goal, according to our police negotiators, was to get Jun emotionally involved. Jun's message was clear: he wanted the family to come to Jolo.

"It would be better if you come here so you can see the situation," said Jun.

"I understand, but my family is afraid. My mother's in the hospital. If she finds out that I'm planning to go there ... she'd think one child's already lost. Now I want to go there. It would be hard," said Frank. I had passed on to Frank what Quidato told the Isnajis earlier so we could keep our stories consistent.

"Okay."

"Can't they be released now?" Frank asked.

"They understand your situation, and we're looking for a way — but I can tell you, don't worry. Ces will be released. She'll be freed. You can tell your family. It's just the time that's the problem. Tomorrow or the next day, but I'm certain she'll be released," said Jun. Shortly after, Frank pulled the speakerphone closer to Grech, whose instructions from the police negotiators was to make Jun aware of the family's fears and to do her best to bind him to her emotionally.

It was easy to see the deep well of emotions she drew from. Once she let go, it was hard to stop. There wasn't a dry eye in the room among all of us listening, and by the end of the conversation, Jun promised he would do his best. The police told us it was necessary to get a personal commitment from him given the uncertainty of his father. It was important we maintain a direct line to him. Grech did that, but it was at great personal cost. After the call, she went to the room and didn't come out for at least an hour. It was difficult to touch the fear, the raw emotions then have to bottle them up again.

***

The second ultimatum came Saturday afternoon. Around 2:30 p.m. a series of conversations began between Quidato, pretending to be a local government official reporting to his boss, and Iglesia, the lead police negotiator who was pretending to be Quidato's boss. Again, the whole conversation took place on speakerphone with all of us gathered around the dining room table. Three things were conveyed: Jun was again in touch with the kidnappers. They gave a Monday 2 p.m. deadline for the rest of the money or they would kill the hostages. They were aware the hostages slowed them down and threatened to kill them if the military continued pursuit operations. So they demanded military operations stop.

About an hour and a half later, the kidnappers moved Ces and Jimmy to another site in barangay Bayog in Talipao, Sulu. Given the hours of trekking they had done, the two thought this was a short walk, particularly since it was downhill. It looked like a place that had been used by these men in the past. They quickly built a sturdier camp. Now Ces could sleep on a bamboo cot inside a "makeshift hut" — a structure made of nipa walls and a blue, plastic sheet tied above as a makeshift roof. Below her bed, they set up hammocks for Jimmy, Dinampo and Commander Putol. They had several of these structures around this one, and Ces noticed they now had a "makeshift kitchen." Dinampo told her they were on the west slope of Mt. Matanding.

By now it was clear our talks were headed for a breakdown: Puno was exerting pressure on local government, specifically Isnaji to resolve the problem and release the hostages. Isnaji and his son were beginning to realize they were in a difficult position: the police was beginning to suspect they may be involved in the kidnapping; neither had any love lost for the military. Lady Ann had effectively been marginalized: the kidnappers were saying she turned the ransom handover into a "photo-op" — referring to the photographer she took with her. Legarda's entry added another wild card that rekindled the Abu Sayyaf's demand for more money.

In one of the conversations, Jun told the family that he was afraid the military was considering him a suspect, particularly after it gave a press conference announcing its arrest of Biyaw, whom the marines presented to the media. Partly to calm Jun down and to reassure his father, Frank and Grech agreed to go to Zamboanga to meet with them on Sunday.

At 8:30 p.m. on Saturday, we received a startling proposition from Lady Ann. She said she wanted to do a "commando-style operation" to rescue Ces and Jimmy. According to her, Ces told her there were only ten men guarding the hostages, and she said if the family approves, she would launch a rescue. She said she had already informed General Sabban of her plans to lead the team. In retrospect, this may have been worth a try but at that time, I immediately said no. It seemed too ad-hoc, and again, I remembered Gracia Burnham describing their rescue, which killed two of three hostages. Frank told her the family preferred a more peaceful way of releasing Ces and Jimmy.

***

So where is the fight against terrorism in Southeast Asia a decade after the Bali attacks, 11 years after 9/11, which unmasked al-Qaeda's global networks? Osama bin Laden is dead. Al-Qaeda's core group has been degraded from about 4,000 at its peak to a few hundred. In Southeast Asia, law enforcement's successes chronicled in the preceding chapters have severely damaged the Darul Islam social network, which has had three regenerations since it first fought for independence in Indonesia. One goal has stayed constant: the yearning to create a state ruled by Islamic *sharia* law. That was the crude beginning of the jihadi virus. Social network theory gives us a new way of visualizing the spread of this virus. By mapping the network, like Tito Karnavian did in Poso, Indonesia, authorities can target hubs and weak links with specific action. This takes it into the realm of ideas, the ideological battle.

Malaysia was a key location for al-Qaeda: in 2000, it was a staging ground for the 9/11 hijackers. Malaysia's Special Branch worked closely with the CIA for surveillance operations of two of the men who would carry out the 9/11 attacks: Nawaf al-Hazmi and Marwan al-Shehhi. Zacarias Moussaoui, once dubbed the "20th hijacker" stayed in Malaysia and worked with Jemaah Islamiyah (JI). The interface between the two groups was JI's operations chief, Hambali, who was a leader of both JI and al-Qaeda.

It was only after the September 11 attacks that it became clear that there was an entrenched al-Qaeda network in Malaysia. There were two clear strands: an al-Qaeda cell using the country as a key transit point and staging area for attacks and a home-grown extremist movement that had been co-opted by JI — the Kumpulan Mujahidin Malaysia or KMM, founded by an Afghan war veteran. Two brothers exemplify its reach into Southeast Asia — Taufik Abdul Halim, who was arrested in Indonesia in 2001 after a bomb he was carrying exploded prematurely, and his brother, Zulkifli. Taufik trained in Pakistan and Afghanistan, fought in religious wars in Indonesia's Ambon fomented by al-Qaeda and JI and worked closely with the men who would later carry out the Bali bombings.[14] Taufik's brother, Zulkifli bin Abdul Hir, alias Marwan, is a leader of KMM and JI and was arrested in Malaysia and accused of killing a Christian member of Parliament, Dr. Joe Fernandez — the only al-Qaeda linked terrorist act in Malaysia. He escaped and fled to the southern Philippines, where he continued to work with Indonesians and Filipinos, spreading both ideology and technical skills. On February 2, 2012, the U.S. and Philippines launched the first smart bomb used to target terrorists in the Philippines against Marwan, now considered the most significant terrorist in Southeast Asia.[15] Although Filipino authorities claimed he and Singaporean Muawiyah were killed, they escaped the attack and are now in central Mindanao.

Singapore has taken the lead in defining and frontally fighting both the intelligence and ideological battles — although the country most vulnerable is Indonesia, which has the world's largest Muslim population. Around the world, religion and injustice have been twisted and used by jihadis to win new recruits. As I mentioned in an earlier chapter, when Singapore discovered the region's links to al-Qaeda shortly after 9/11, it supplied the information to neighboring countries, but only Malaysia acted on it. Within a few months, Singapore arrested the JI cell operating within its borders. It moved quickly to address how JI twisted Islam to win new recruits. Singapore addressed both the theory of religion and the spread of disinformation. It launched a nationwide dialogue, harnessing religious leaders and focusing on national resilience. The Muslim Religious Council of Singapore took a proactive approach, maintaining harmony by addressing problems before

---

[14] M. Ressa, *Seeds of Terror,* p. 70.
[15] M. Ressa, "US smart bombs used in Sulu attack," *Rappler,* March 22, 2012. Available at http://www.rappler.com/nation/2910-us-smart-bombs-used-in-sulu-attack

they arose. It did this by creating a register of religious teachers, who worked voluntarily with the government. Its Religious Rehabilitation Group (RRG) is devoted to correcting twisted propaganda and misperceptions of Islam. After the JI arrests, RRG worked in prison counseling sessions. Since 2005, RRG has worked on the rehabilitation of 26 former JI members and sympathizers who have been released.[16]

Beyond that, Singapore is spending resources on preventive measures, trying to predict how this threat will evolve. In the past decade, Singapore has become an intelligence hub, bringing together Western and Asian sources in regularly scheduled conferences and meetings as well as training scholars and officials like Tito Karnavian.

For Indonesia, the battle is more complex. One of its main concerns is how to clamp down on terrorists while retaining its hard-won democratic space after the end of the 32-year rule of former President Suharto. There's no doubt JI and other groups in the Darul Islam network took advantage of this new found freedom in 1998, much like bin Laden's brother-in-law and al-Qaeda operatives did in the Philippines a decade earlier after the people power revolt. That is one of President Yudhoyono's main concerns particularly in dealing with the emerging battle front in the virtual world. "If we control online media," he said, "it would be against the spirit of reform. It is against the prize of democracy. So we are now thinking about how to deal with these things correctly — how to maintain our national interest without sacrificing the spirit of our democracy." He outlines two main challenges: the prevention of more attacks by active intelligence and police work based on the more important goal—"promoting the awareness of the people." Fighting the ideological battle in each community and social network, like in Poso, is crucial to preventing the ideology from luring more recruits.

There's a growing awareness that "soft" power is now as important as police and military might in order to stop the spread of the ideology. The battle has moved — belatedly — to where it all began: the realm of ideas. The newest field of battle is the spread of the jihadi virus in the virtual world. This has been developing underneath the surface in the past decade. What our citizen journalism and social media campaigns have shown us is that the virtual world very nearly mirrors the behavior of physical social networks, except contagion happens at a faster rate. This means we can use the same social network theories to analyze potential spread online.

---

[16] D.M. Jones & M.L.R. Smith, "Organization vs. Ideology: The Lessons from Southeast Asia," *Current Trends in Islamist Ideology*, October 21, 2011.

Look at the growth of online sites in Indonesia alone: in 2007, there were 11; in 2011, there were more than 200.[17] These numbers are far less than the global influence online of al-Qaeda and its associate groups. We can break down the spread of the jihadi virus through the Internet into two phases: Web 1.0 ran from 2001 to about 2005, when the Internet was still largely another broadcast platform using one way publishing and distribution; and Web 2.0, when technological developments created a participatory culture, one that encouraged the creation of user-generated content and hit a tipping point in 2009 with social media sites like Facebook, Twitter and YouTube.

In 2001, there were fewer than 20 jihadi websites worldwide. By 2005, that number grew to more than 4,000. American officials acknowledged they took a beating online during this period: that al-Qaeda won Phase 1 because the government was too slow to react to the methodical online tactics of al-Qaeda's media arm. They used the Internet not just to spread their ideology but also to recruit, organize and even raise funds. "It was a source of frustration in the Bush administration that we were being outdone by terrorists by means of a technology that we had developed," said Juan Carlos Zarate, Bush's deputy national security advisor for combating terrorism, referring to how the Internet actually started as a defense program. "Putting out talking points to our ambassadors was not effective when dealing with viral messages emanating from al-Qaeda."[18]

There was, however, a dramatic seachange after Internet technology moved away from one way broadcasting towards a participatory culture created by blogs and social media. Like in Indonesia, this change began around 2007 but exploded in 2009 coinciding with the year social media overtook pornography as the number 1 activity on the Internet.[19] The viral spread of ideas and emotions on social media has amplified what started during Web 1.0. Individuals from Southeast Asia, Europe and the United States have become politically radicalized, learned operational details like how to make

---

[17] Data obtained from the International Centre for Political Violence and Terrorism Research (ICPVTR) Bahasa Indonesia Informatics Team.

[18] P. Buxbaum, "Public Diplomacy 2.0," *International Relations and Security Network,* April 22, 2010. Available at http://www.isn.ethz.ch/isn/Current-Affairs/Security-Watch-Archive/Detail/?lng=en&id=115247

[19] E. Qualman, "Statistics Show Social Media is Bigger Than You Think," *Socialnomics,* August 11, 2009. Available at http://www.socialnomics.net/2009/08/11/statistics-show-social-media-is-bigger-than-you-think/.

bombs and suicide vests, and connected with others who have acted as mentors in this radicalization.[20] The chat rooms and blogs act as echo chambers. They are harder for authorities to detect, and jihadists now no longer have to physically meet. They're free to read and ask questions in the privacy of their homes, lowering the risk of detection. The Internet also opens up a global world, increasing cross-border links, amplifying the strength of weak links. The pace of contagion increased exponentially with social media and can potentially increase more as the developing world gets more connected.

Still, U.S. officials say they believe al-Qaeda and its affiliated groups will lose the battle during Web 2.0. "I made the comment that al-Qaeda was eating our lunch on the Internet. I actually think that has changed," said former undersecretary of State for Public Diplomacy and Public Affairs James Glassman.[21] "The violent extremist groups that use the Internet are using it in the old-fashioned way. They're using it to instruct, to exhort, basically tell people what to do. We feel that around the world, young people are using the Internet to push back against violence in a new way, using social networking, convening large groups to have conversations, basically, to share information. And this is something that al-Qaeda and the violent extremist groups cannot stand. They cannot stand criticism. You know, sometime they'll post videos on YouTube until YouTube takes them down, and they get tremendous amounts of critical comments. They don't want that. Their whole philosophy is based on trying to isolate potential members and keep them away from critical comment, from discussion. So we want to take exactly the opposite tack, and we think that the technology that exists today is on our side; it's not on the extremists' side."

While that may be true at a philosophical level, there are many danger signals to keep track of. In Indonesia, the murky line between overt and covert terrorist groups allows large jihadi communities to converge on Facebook. For the first time in human history, Facebook connects more than a billion people globally, accelerating the potential spread of information and emotions. Many

---

[20] Nur Aslin Mohamed Yasin, "To What Extent Does Online Extremism Lead to Terrorism?" S. Rajaratnam School of International Studies, ICPVTR, AY 2010/2011, p. 18. One of the case studies looked at is Singaporean Abdul Basheer Abdul Kader. Other cases influenced by al-Qaeda are mentioned including UK case of Omar Farouq Abdul Mutallab, the 2003 Madrid bombings and 2009 Cairo Khan al-Khalili bombing (p. 23).

[21] U.S. State Department Briefing, Washington, DC, November 24, 2008. Transcript available at http://www.america.gov/st/texttrans-english/2008/November/20081124173327eai fas0.8017237.html

Facebook pages have been created to agitate against the arrests of terrorists like Abu Bakar Ba'asyir and other key figures. They've been used to rally support and raise money for the families they left behind. It's also interesting to note that the two most successful jihadi websites in Indonesia masquerade as news portals, meaning they're able to attract moderate Muslims and attempt to sway them to more radical perspectives. The websites have one other factor in common: they're run by the sons of JI leaders.

The most popular is http://www.arrahmah.com run by Muhammad Jibriel, the son of 1st generation JI leader Abu Jibril. Its tagline is "filter your mind, get the truth" and has a Facebook page and a Twitter account. 114,900 people like its Facebook page, meaning its posts appear on the walls of 114,900 people as of February 24, 2013.[22] At 3 p.m. on that day, 12,717 people were talking about its posts. The administrator of that Facebook page would see a demographic and geographic breakdown as well as other statistics that could allow it to expand its reach strategically. The friends of those 114,900 Facebook accounts can expand the reach of arrahmah.com's extremist views by a minimum of 33% and a maximum of 86%.[23] With that many followers, this account can have the potential to reach nearly 10 million other accounts, delivering its message directly to individual walls. This is clearly a much wider reach than JI was able to get at its peak through physical social networks. Add to that its 14,413 followers on Twitter[24] and Muhammad Jibriel and his supporters can reach a lot of people with their radical ideas without leaving the safety of their computers. Gone are the risks of detection in the earlier days. When he was arrested for his role in the 2009 Jakarta hotel bombings, another Facebook group pushed for his release — "Support for Mujahid Muhammad Jibriel Abdul Rahman."

The second website is http://www.muslimdaily.net — a website run by Abu Bakar Ba'asyir and his son with the tagline, "Inspiring The Truth." On the center of its frontpage is a banner saying "Free Our Ustadz" next to a picture of Abu Bakar Ba'asyir. When you click on the picture, you're brought to a page which you can easily share on Twitter and Facebook entitled "Free Abu Bakar Ba'asyir." The website has a Facebook page[25] and a Twitter

---

[22] Facebook page available at https://www.facebook.com/arrahmahcom.

[23] Mike Shaw, "The State of Social Media," *ComScore* presentation at the Online Marketing Institute, London, February, 2012.

[24] Twitter posts available at https://twitter.com/#!/arrahmah.

[25] Facebook page available at https://www.facebook.com/pages/muslimdailynet/1696539264-21830. Twitter posts available at https://twitter.com/#!/MuslimDaily

account, neither of which have large followers: as of February 24, 2013, Facebook likes are at 7,403 and Twitter followers number 5,475.

On-the-ground tactics used by JI and JAT for *dahwah* or preaching are now online — a streamlined attempt to turn more moderates into radicals. They're not alone. Many Abu Sayyaf members have Facebook pages. Facebook offers connectivity on a scale mankind has never achieved before so it's not just Southeast Asian jihadi groups using it — although they do have an advantage. On April 22, 2011, Abu Musab al-Dahik (most likely a pseudonym) posted a 23-page guide on a jihadi forum for how to "effectively" use Facebook. The greater danger posed for Indonesian and Filipino authorities, however, is in Facebook's and social media's power in these countries. U.S.-based *ComScore* said in 2010 that the Philippines is the social media capital of the world while Indonesia is the second largest Facebook nation globally.[26]

Now intelligence officials in the Philippines are tracking a Facebook account with extremist contacts in the Philippines, Indonesia, Thailand and other countries. They believe it's spreading the jihadi virus, and that Marwan and Muawiyah, who are both on the run, remain connected globally through their Facebook accounts.[27]

This is the battleground of the future.

\*\*\*

Every time Ces was alone now — bathing, changing in the bushes — she half expected someone to grab her and tell her she was being rescued. She wanted — no, prayed — to be rescued. Now, except for the deafening sounds of the jungle when she opened her eyes, it still seemed like she had them closed. The moon was behind clouds, and it was still too early for her to wake up. She thought about the young boys guarding her, switching from taunting rhymes about her own children and then becoming steely eyed in the last day or so. She'd been reporting on Mindanao a long time, and she thought to solve its problems, Mindanao really needed a leader who would look after its people. From what she saw, mayors seemed to want to keep their people illiterate. It was a way to keep their own hold on power. She cringed at her naivete in thinking the Abu Sayyaf would want to communicate its message. They had none. On Day 8 of their captivity,

---

[26] "State of the Internet with a Focus on Southeast Asia," *ComScore,* March 9, 2011.
[27] Interview with intelligence sources, Manila, June, 2012.

she realized the men holding them hostage were just after money. She'd tell me later, "I romanticized the struggle. You know, I wanted to see more. I said, 'Don't ask for money. Tell me about your story. Tell me, and I'll tell the people. They weren't interested in that." They just want money. Period.

At that exact moment before dawn Sunday morning, June 15, Ces' brother and sister, Frank and Grech were on their way to the airport. Cusi, from PACER, was assigned to stay with them every step of the way. Even though the arrangements were still unclear, we thought it best to keep doing what we could do. Frank and Grech would meet with Alvarez and Jun in Zamboanga. We wanted a greater emotional commitment; father and son wanted the money. When they boarded their 5 a.m. flight, I was coordinating with Quidato, trying to determine what message we wanted to send and the reality on the ground.

Ironically, Legarda was on the same flight from Manila to Zamboanga. Frank and Grech heard her talking on the plane about the hostage situation and what she was planning to do. She had asked to speak with Mayor Isnaji and was putting her own plans in motion. She told me Isnaji seemed reluctant to help in the negotiations, but she pushed him to do it. Since she had never met Ces' family, she didn't realize they were sitting just across the plane aisle from her. When the plane landed, Legarda was surrounded by people at the airport. Frank, Grech and Cusi quickly brushed by them and hoped no one would notice. Jun was supposed to give a time for the meeting by the time they landed in Zamboanga. Once he heard they weren't bringing any money, however, he decided to stay behind in Jolo. Quidato decided to stay with him, shadow him, and understand his motives better. Unknown to us, his father was coming to meet Legarda — and at some point, confirmed a meeting with Frank and Grech. During this time period, Quidato started discovering inconsistencies between what was happening and what Jun was telling him. Muddy waters were becoming even muddier.

*** 

Alvarez Isnaji listened to Loren Legarda when she called him. She said she got his cellphone number from Charie and me, and she began to outline her plan to him. Isnaji told her he didn't want to get involved and since the family was already talking to the kidnappers, they should continue dealing with each other directly. Legarda talked to him and gauged whether he knew the situation on the ground. She knew that if a mayor was good, he would know what's going on in his town. He knew the players, and he had an idea of how to get to them. She told him he was her "link to saving lives"[28] and convinced him to meet her at the Palmeras Hotel Sunday. His son also told him that Ces' sister and brother would come to see him in Zamboanga, but he didn't commit to the meeting.

At 10 a.m. on Sunday — Day 8 of the kidnapping — Isnaji's cellphone alerted him to an incoming text. It said: "Ces Drilon here, please call." He picked up the phone and dialed the number. Ces answered immediately.

"Mayor, they're giving another ultimatum for Monday at 12 noon," she said in Filipino.

"Ces, can I talk to them?" he asked. Ces handed the phone to the kidnappers, and he thought he was on speakerphone because he could hear several voices. He spoke to them in Tausug, the dialect of the area, and took the tone of a mayor admonishing young boys. "Why are you giving another ultimatum?" he asked.

"If you give us the money by the deadline, we'll release them."

"Listen to me. Release the hostages now. You can't give these deadlines because you have to give us time. Ces' family has given you all they have. They have no more money."

"But the family agreed to deliver the money!" yelled one of them. Isnaji was taken aback.

"Well, I don't know about that. Anyway, I've backed out as a negotiator. If they promised it to you then you should just continue talking to the family directly."[29]

***

Frank, Grech and Cusi headed to the Palmeras Hotel, where they checked in and got Room 212 under the name Ruel Rodolfo. Around 2 p.m., Alvarez Isnaji spoke on the phone to Grech and tried to pull out of the meeting. She convinced him to come although he said his time was limited because he wanted to catch a flight. Once he got there, he told them he spoke with the

---

[28] Composite picture of their first conversation pulled together from Isnaji's *Joint Counter-Affidavit*, IS No. 2008-617 and email interview with Loren Legarda on July 30, 2012.

[29] Conversation reconstructed from Isnaji's statements to Puno, Lady Ann, the media and court documents *Joint Counter-Affidavit*, IS No. 2008-617. Isnaji's actions are the subject of a pending legal case.

kidnappers, who were firm on their demand for ₱15 million. He asked for a week to produce it, but they countered and gave him only until Tuesday — extending their initial Monday deadline. Two key police officers joined the meeting: ARMM Police Regional Director Joel Goltiao and the intelligence operation's top officer, Police Senior Superintendent Reginald Villasanta. Goltiao passed the responsibility of getting the hostages out safely to Isnaji himself as an elected local government official. He pointed out that Isnaji was in the newspaper headlines that morning — a candidate for governor of the elections in about a month. Isnaji tried to distance himself from the kidnappers' demands, emphasizing he was only asked to help. It was a fore-shadowing of the problems we would have on Monday.

I was frustrated again. Although Puno told me about his team's plans, I couldn't see a quick resolution. In the meantime, Legarda had started mobilizing other people, and a lot more details were leaking to the media. This was the first time I could see from the other side, as the newsmaker, and gauge how slow, distorted and just plain wrong a lot of reports were. It's inevitable that the sources of information quoted tend to be the ones who know the least. Yet those statements also inevitably affect whatever operations are in motion.

On Sunday night with Frank and Grech back in Manila, we gathered in our crisis center and planned the next day's activities. Puno and I spoke about how we could publicly pressure the kidnappers. Ces' and Jimmy's families would broadcast public appeals for their release which would be targeted to the kidnappers, their families and friends. At our crisis center, I explained what we needed to do and why. I asked for volunteers. Grech would do the first one. Jimmy's daughter, Joy, would do a second one. We chose which stations would be transmitting in the area and made arrange-ments for the broadcasts.

In Jolo, Ces and Jimmy were just falling asleep in their makeshift hut when the kidnappers barged in. They accused them of trying to escape and brusquely tied their hands. Ces refused to give in to fear. She began to pray.

# Homecoming

# 10

The tension was palpable in the crisis center on Monday, June 16 — Day 9 of the kidnapping. We started holding masses in the living room so we could all take a breath and pray together. It seemed to help everyone. At 9 a.m., we held an assessment meeting with Iglesia's supervisor, Senior Superintendent Leonardo Espina.[1] We were getting constant updates from Quidato and Puno, including word that Isnaji had tried to back out of the negotiations. About half an hour earlier, Ces called him and asked him to stay. He agreed on one condition — that all contact pass through him. Aside from talking to the kidnappers, Isnaji was now also negotiating with Legarda. Lady Ann told us Legarda contacted her and asked if she could come to Jolo. On directions from the police, Lady Ann discouraged the trip.

Shortly after that, we heard Major Isnaji on Bombo Radyo, a Zamboanga City radio station whose broadcast was picked up by national television. Isnaji told the public Ces cried to him and appealed he stay to negotiate after he told her he was thinking of dropping out of the talks for the team's release. She said he was her only hope to live.[2] He said he repeatedly told the kidnappers Ces' parents have no more money, but they kept insisting on their demand. Ces also told him the kidnappers were clamping down on them and had tied her hands and Jimmy's. Isnaji said it was Manila who told him the demand was for ₱15 million. Then he challenged ABS-CBN: "Is ABS-CBN asleep? Has ABS-CBN shut down? I can't feel any effort from them. The kidnappers have given their deadline: 12 p.m. Tuesday."[3] It seemed suspicious to me and to Puno that Isnaji would bring ABS-CBN

---

[1] The equivalent rank of a senior superintendent in the military is colonel.
[2] Court transcript, *Counter-Affidavit*, IS No. 2008-617, July 7, 2008, p. 10.
[3] Translation of radio transcript, Bombo Radyo broadcast, June 16, 2008.

247

back into the equation. His radio broadcast was an appeal for money. Hearing him only made me doubt his motives even as I realized that now the battle had moved into the public arena.

Later that morning, the radio interviews of Ces and Jimmy's family began. The first interview was with DXMM Sulu. Before Grech and Joy went on the air, Iglesia reminded them of the purpose of the interviews. The goal is to appeal to the kidnappers — and more importantly — their families so they can push their relatives to release Ces and Jimmy.

"Thank you for giving me the chance to speak to your station," said Grech.[4] "I hope that this somehow reaches those who are worried about my sister, Ces, and her companion, Jimmy, that our families are doing all we can do to free the two, but we have limitations. Now we're praying to God to touch the hearts of those who are holding Ces and Jimmy. Please have mercy and let them go. Now my family's not just going through a hard time," at this point, Grech started crying, "our mother's sick and had a nervous breakdown because of what happened to Ces. That's why we're appealing to those who have Ces and Jimmy, please have mercy on us. Let them go." Grech could barely speak now, and she handed the phone to Joy.

"My name is Joy. I'm the daughter of Jimmy Encarnacion. I'm appealing to those who kidnapped my father to please let him and Miss Ces go. Please take pity on them," Joy said. She started to cry quietly, caught her breath then continued. "We need my father especially now that school is starting. We don't know where to get the money for our tuition. My mom doesn't know what to do without him. Please have mercy on my father and us and let him go." Then she broke down completely.

The word both Grech and Joy used repeatedly was "*maawa*," which has no direct English translation. It encapsulates pity, mercy, empathy and is an emotionally loaded word. Shortly after this, we got word from Isnaji that the kidnappers gave us a reprieve. The deadline was moved to Tuesday.

As this was happening in Manila, Ces and Jimmy began to feel a shift in the way the kidnappers were treating them. They tied Jimmy's hands behind his back. Ces' hands were tied in front of her. Their hands were freed only when it was time to eat. Both noticed Dinampo wasn't subjected to the same treatment.[5] Ces thought constantly about her sons and the life she had

---

[4] Transcripts from radio broadcasts, June 16, 2008.
[5] These statements appeared in court documents: *Ces Drilon*, PNP-CIDG Sworn Statement, June 25, 2008 and *Jimmy Encarnacion*, Sworn Statement, June 30, 2008.

cavalierly led. Although she told herself the men would do nothing to harm them because they wanted the ransom, she was ambivalent. She didn't want them to get more money to continue this cycle. She wanted a rescue, but each passing hour of uncertainty eroded her confidence as she tried to control her growing fear.

\*\*\*

To get a better idea of the social networks at work, let's look again at the kidnapping through the eyes of a lower-ranking member of the Abu Sayyaf. 5'4" Aljebir Adzhar, better known as Embel,[6] was 20 years old at the time Ces, Jimmy and Angelo were kidnapped. He was a trusted messenger and errand boy of another Abu Sayyaf leader, Gumbahala Jumdail, better known as Doc Abu. The group which kidnapped the ABS-CBN journalists was led by Radullan Sahiron, who worked closely with Doc Abu and Albader Parad. During the initial stages of the kidnapping, authorities thought Parad was behind the kidnapping while some of the kidnappers were part of Doc Abu's group.

Doc Abu gave virtually permanent sanctuary for years to the leaders of Jemaah Islamiyah, Marwan and Muawiyah. This was part of the reason, Sahiron told his people, that Doc Abu was killed on February 2, 2012 after the Philippines and the United States targeted the JI leaders who were considered HVTs or High Value Targets. "Marwan is the most important Malaysian terrorist," said Rohan Gunaratna, the head of the International Centre for Political Violence and Terrorism Research in Singapore and the author of *Inside Al-Qaeda*. He has worked very closely with al-Qaeda, Jemaah Islamiyah, the Rajah Solaiman Revolutionary Movement, the Abu Sayyaf and the MNLF factions. He's on the radar of many organizations. Muawiyah's "the only Singaporean active in terrorism," said Gunaratna. "They are the two most important international terrorists currently operating in Southeast Asia."

Embel's life shows the power of social networks — magnified in Jolo because opportunities are rare. He knew Marwan and Muawiyah well. His father worked for Doc Abu, who often hid in their family's home. Soon, he

---

[6] Information about Embel came from interviews with intelligence officials and classified Philippine military intelligence report: "Debriefing Report on ASG member Aljebir Adzhar @Embel," December, 2010.

and his brother began working for the Abu Sayyaf as well. Embel became part of the Abu Sayyaf's support network: he informed Doc Abu of government troop movements and alerted the group to any possible dangers. He ran personal errands for Marwan, including bringing Marwan's wife to a designated safehouse for conjugal visits. Embel said Marwan specifically asked for chicken *siopao* when Embel went to market. There's another interesting family connection: Embel's sister is married to a member of the MNLF.

Embel was arrested by authorities on December 7, 2010. He told them what he knew about the kidnapping of the ABS-CBN team and of the three ICRC members which happened six months later. He said the kidnapping of the Red Cross volunteers was "orchestrated" by the jail guard at the provincial capitol, Raden Abu, the son of a police officer working with the Intelligence group.[7] Embel's revelations again show the complex links tying law enforcement to the criminals and terrorist. Abu, a police officer has an aunt married to another Abu Sayyaf leader, Albader Parad — the man who hostaged the ICRC workers and negotiated with authorities. The local government official he negotiated with was his cousin, Vice Governor Lady Ann Sahidulla.

Embel told authorities the groups of Doc Abu and Radullan Sahiron had a fierce falling out over the ransom money from Ces' kidnapping. That was part of the reason Parad kidnapped the ICRC workers — to get more money. This was verified by another key member of the group which kidnapped Ces, Jimmy and Angelo: Sali Said. Interconnected by kinship ties and friendship which earned him the trust of Sahiron, Said did the actual kidnapping — picking up the ABS-CBN team for their supposed interview with Sahiron and bringing them into the jungle. By his account, he became a close friend of Jimmy, whom he was assigned to guard.

By the ninth day, Said was starting to feel sorry for Jimmy. He said he even gave Jimmy his drawstring pants. What he didn't tell me though was that he took Jimmy's brand new jeans instead. Said knew the drill. He had been through this a few times in past kidnappings, but he didn't want to see Jimmy hurt. He knew that part of the plan was to scare them, but you never know how far this could go. In the past, some kidnap victims would have been physically harmed at this stage — blows, mutilations, even a finger cut off.

At this point, though, both the police and military began to prepare rescue operations. It was coming from the top leaders: Armed Forces Chief

---

[7] Ibid., p. 3.

General Allaga gave the go-ahead. General Sabban, in charge of the marines in Jolo, had already put intelligence agents in place. The police had Operation Island Deep under Villasanta's team. They had what they felt was a secret weapon, a man I introduced earlier as Mohammed, one of the founders of the Abu Sayyaf. Except now he was a double agent working for the police. It was the first time the police was carrying out operations like this in Jolo. The intelligence team felt that Mohammed's inside knowledge would give them that edge. For Mohammed, it was the first time he would return to Jolo after he had been captured. Also for the first time in a major kidnapping, the military — through General Sabban — began integrating operations and intelligence with the police.

I was concerned about Isnaji's statements dragging ABS-CBN back to the forefront of the negotiations. I wanted to clarify what exactly Isnaji had told reporters and why. There was a lot of confusion, and it seemed like no one was in control. Three groups were now moving simultaneously from Manila, and among them, there was little trust. There was our crisis committee, working through the negotiators, Lady Ann and the Isnajis, along with the acting intelligence chief, Winnie Quidato, on the ground. The second group was led by Secretary Puno, who headed the local government and the police, and by the ninth day, I was working closely with him. Still, I know we didn't really trust each other. Neither of us knew exactly what the third group was doing. It was the wild card: Loren Legarda and her men.

When Grech called Isnaji, he told her the kidnappers were informed money was coming from Manila. The same message reached me through Quidato, who remained with Jun Isnaji: someone told the kidnappers ₱15 million was coming. I began to wonder whether this was real or another case of miscommunication. If so, where was it coming from? I called Puno on the other line and asked him about it. Although officially, the govern-ment can't give ransom, sometimes individuals did. Puno said he would look into it. By eight o'clock Monday evening, I couldn't see a clear line of attack. I knew I was working only on the peripherals and not directly on the problem.

That evening, Charie and I visited Legarda in her Makati home. In the time we were with her, I realized she was running her own, maverick operations. She had a former armed forces officer as her aide, and she had created an ad-hoc team that was moving on the ground. She wouldn't tell me the details, but she said not to worry. I told her about the command team led by Puno, and she said, "You can't just rely on that." Unlike Puno, she was optimistic. We would get them out safely, she said, not later but now.

Again, I worried these uncoordinated efforts would, at some point, collide, but it was comforting to see her tenacity and single-minded focus on getting them home safely.

As we were speaking, Ces was in Jolo coming to terms with what she wanted. She cried thinking about her four sons, but she wiped her tears away. She was preparing to accept the worst possible situation: that she would be killed. She didn't want to beg these young boys for her life. She thought even if she did, if they meant to kill her, they would. She prayed and asked for the ability and grace to accept her death. She didn't want to fight it. She wanted to dictate her terms in a situation where she had no control. She could control herself and accept her death with dignity.

She woke up early on Tuesday, June 17, Day 10. It was the day of the ultimatum. Once there was light, she got up and asked if she could call Loren Legarda. She felt so relieved when Legarda picked up the phone.

"Ces, how are you?" Legarda asked.

"I'm okay. Loren, is it true that Mayor Isnaji backed out as a negotiator?"

"He was threatening to pull out, but I convinced him to stay. Don't worry." It was the first of several calls that day. Ces started to cry. At one point, Jimmy, who was sitting nearby, heard Legarda's voice warning the kidnappers that they shouldn't hurt the hostages. He again noticed that although he and Ces had been tied up, Dinampo remained free. As the sun rose and the deadline drew nearer, the kidnappers seemed to be making a point that they would be happy to kill their hostages.

The kidnappers told Ces to call her family around noon, two hours before the deadline. She called Legarda instead. The panic was rising in her voice.

"Loren, aren't you going to help me. They're putting a bolo knife to Jimmy's neck. They're going to behead him." Ces started crying. "Loren, why aren't you helping me? Aren't you going to do anything?"

"Let me talk to them. Let me talk to them," Legarda demanded. There was a rustling sound as the phone changed hands. "Don't you dare touch Ces," she commanded in Filipino. "We're going to go there. I'll go." No one was talking.

"We know you," a young-sounding voice said in Filipino. "We carried your bag ... with Maas" — referring to MNLF leader Nur Misuari. Then Legarda began to think the young men's fathers were members of the MNLF. They talked a while longer, and Legarda realized how young the kidnappers were. Ces came back on the phone.

"Loren, please, aren't you going to do anything to save us?" Ces asked plaintively. "They've given up on us. They're going to behead Jimmy."

"What do they want?"

"They want ₱15 million."

"*Putang inang mga mukhang perang iyan!*"[8] Legarda cursed crisply in Filipino.

"Loren, you're on speakerphone!" Ces admonished.

Legarda backtracked. "*Hindi, ibig sabihin, ano ba 'yan! Ang mahal mahal.*"[9] Then she added, "Stay put. Stay strong. Don't worry, Ces. I'm going to go there. I'm going to pick you up. I'm going to save you. You'll be okay."

"Please tell me if there's money. Otherwise, I'll prepare for my fate." Ces was afraid now. Legarda tried to reassure her, but it was about to get worse. The kidnappers had a script they followed. They knew this was the time to pressure their hostages, who would communicate their panic to the other end of the line. Behind Ces, the men were threatening to behead Jimmy. Someone hit him, and he doubled over. As he did that, another one tied a rope from his arms to a cloth they wrapped around his neck. Another waved a bolo. One of the men slapped Ces while she was talking to Legarda. Ces screamed and began to cry. Legarda was momentarily stunned; she was alone and panicked. Ces slumped over the cot and, hugging Jimmy, cried on his shoulder. Legarda found her voice and cursed loudly again. She again warned the kidnappers not to harm their hostages.

At that point, money was arriving in Zamboanga on a plane. Puno and his team had been monitoring all the conversations, and he was upset. He didn't know who brought in the money, just that he hadn't been informed. He asked his men to stop the cash from leaving the airport. "I held the money because you didn't learn your lesson," Puno told me much later. "You give it that way, and they take it. You're not going to get Ces back. You're gonna get the other guy back. It's the second time they're going to do it to you. That's where I was angry. Didn't you all learn the first time it happened? You paid and got the most junior guy. Now there's another payment. What makes you think Ces is going to be released? We were

---

[8] It's hard to find a translation for this Filipino curse. Directly translated, *Putang Ina* means "your mother's a whore." The sentence directly translated is "Your mother's a whore, their faces look like money." In meaning, however, it more closely resembles this phrase: "The greedy sons of bitches."

[9] Directly translated, this sentence is "No, I mean, what the hell! That is so expensive."

monitoring all the conversations. When I held the money, Isnaji was already going crazy, right? He's starting to panic. Okay. If you're going to give the money to him, then you have to make sure you have one of his sons."

Puno decided to teach everyone a lesson. He told his officials to hold the bag of money. Half an hour earlier, I had moved to Legarda's house because she called to tell me the release was going to happen. A few minutes after I arrived, I received two calls. The first was from Quidato, who asked me if we had sent any money in. I said, "No, we didn't." The second call was from Puno's aide, Brian Yamsuan. His voice was adamant when he accused me of doing something without letting them know. I told him we hadn't done anything.

I walked outside Legarda's dining room into her Balinese-styled patio, but through the glass partition, I could see Legarda was juggling calls from three telephones, sometimes handing one to her aide. There was obviously a problem. At one point, she asked me whether I knew Quidato. I said, "Yes, I do. He's working with us." Shortly after, Quidato called to say he got a frantic call from Isnaji telling him the money he expected had been held by local officials. He asked Quidato, whom he believed to be a local government official, to release the bag so it could be brought to the kidnappers. At this point, my head was reeling trying to put the different pieces of the puzzle together.

In Jolo, Commander Putol handed the cellphone to Ces and asked her to call her family. She called Legarda again. Jimmy strained against the rope tying his hands, and he started to cry. The cloth around his neck felt like it was choking him. He was hogtied, and one man was holding his arm while another was holding his head. He felt the blood drain from his body and rush to his head. His hands felt cold. Sali Said pulled out a bolo with a blue handle, grabbed Jimmy's head, pulled it back and put the sharp blade against his neck. He said, "Pray now because in a short while, you're going to die. This bolo has beheaded two men. You'll be the third."

As the men moved to pick up Jimmy, he started to plead for mercy. Ces couldn't stand to see Jimmy threatened like this. She stumbled in front of him and said, "Behead me instead." That stopped the men momentarily until one of them slammed his rifle butt against Jimmy. Another hit him with the bamboo bed. Ces pleaded, "Please, please, one last call, one last call to my family!"

Then the phone rang. Ces saw Said pick up the call. Then he laughed and spit on the ground. When the call ended, he turned to them and said, "It's over. You're free."

\* \* \*

A look at Filipino jihadists in the virtual world today show much activity, fund-raising and numerous attempts to integrate into a global jihad. The strand I followed began on November 6, 2011 when a 3 minute, 20 second video was uploaded on YouTube, the world's second largest search engine. It was on an account created by a man familiar to Filipino authorities, the man who took over the leadership of the Rajah Solaiman Movement (RSM). The video showed a masked Filipino jihadist it identifies as a commander, Abu Jihad Khalil al-Rahman al-Luzoni, speaking in Arabic and asking Muslims around the world to support and contribute to their jihad in the Philippines. He called on Muslims to unite and help their brethren, saying there was "no way to restore the Islamic Caliphate and the glory of the religion but through jihad."[10]

Intelligence sources from three different countries say Abu Jihad is 31-year-old Khalil Pareja, a Christian convert to Islam — also known as *balik Islam*[11] — tied to the leadership of the Rajah Solaiman Movement or RSM. When RSM's leader, Ahmad Santos, was arrested, Pareja took his place. There's a family link: Pareja's sister is married to Santos. There are other ties: Pareja was trained in explosives and bomb-making by JI leaders Umar Patek and Dulmatin.[12] Pareja says Patek chose him because he was *balik Islam*: Patek felt that Christian converts understand the teachings of Islam better. "Patek was even aware that Muslims in Mindanao are unruly, not united and even fighting each other because of *rido*,"[13]or clan war, he added. Patek may have had a personal bias: his wife, according to Pareja, is a *balik Islam* from General Santos City who fought with the MILF.[14]

Pareja, as Abu Jihad, not only posted jihadi materials on YouTube, he was also active on Facebook — a case study of how one man can connect jihadists and terrorists from multiple countries through social media. Intelligence sources from two countries say he created the Facebook page *Jaysh at Tawheed* in May 2011. It had more than 300 friends from all over

---

[10] English translation of Arabic message of Abu Jihad Khalil al-Rahman al-Luzoni. Video uploaded on YouTube, November 6, 2011.

[11] The phrase literally means "return to Islam."

[12] Details from classified Philippine intelligence document: *Dinno-Amor Rosalejos Pareja @Abu Jihad/Khalia/Ur Rahman/Muhammad/Rash/Ahmad/Arlan/Al-Luzoni/Jake Fajardo*, CTD-DRP-03052012-014, March 5, 2012.

[13] Ibid., p. 10.

[14] Ibid., p. 10.

the world, giving extremists from Indonesia, Bangladesh, Saudi Arabia and other countries a safe place to connect. Six months after he created the page, Pareja said he received a private message (PM) from a man who introduced himself as Gerald.[15] They became friends and started chatting regularly.

Over time, Gerald told Pareja he was a member of al-Shabaab, Islamist militants who control much of southern Somalia.[16] It seems Osama bin Laden's death in 2011 helped pave the way for closer ties between al-Shabaab and al-Qaeda. In February 2012, al-Shabaab's leadership pledged allegiance to the man who replaced Osama bin Laden as al-Qaeda's new leader — Egpytian engineer Ayman al-Zawahiri.[17] This was announced on a video uploaded on the Internet by al-Qaeda's media arm. This agreement showed that despite severe degradation and the death of bin Laden, al-Qaeda continues to grow, with Somalia now becoming a hub for operations in Africa.

Pareja told Gerald he was Abu Jihad. Gerald invited him to go to Yemen to join the jihad led by al-Qaeda's Yemeni affiliate, al-Qaeda in the Arabian Peninsula or AQAP. Counterterrorism analysts characterize AQAP as the "most active and lethal Qaeda affiliate, intent on striking at both the U.S. homeland and regional targets."[18] In mid-2012, U.S. authorities used a CIA sting operation to foil an AQAP plot to bomb U.S.-bound airplanes with explosives hidden in the bodies of terrorists. Experts said AQAP's master bomb-maker, Ibrahim al-Asiri, had been working on body bombs, surgically implanted explosives in the stomach or rectal cavity. AQAP was also involved in other foiled plots against U.S. targets: the "underwear bomb" used in an attempt to take down North-west Flight 253 in 2009 and the "printer bombs" in the failed cargo bomb plot in 2010.[19]

---

[15] Gerald may or may not be his real name. Terrorists use pseudonyms frequently, and the Internet allows anonymity to reach new levels. What's clear, though, is that the private messages between Pareja and Gerald continued to the point that Pareja was convinced of Gerald's identity and started to make plans based on his offers.

[16] Al-Shabaab's formal name is al-Shabaab al-Mujahideen. It's waged an insurgency against Somalia's government and its Ethiopian supporters since 2006. The relationship between Al-Shabaab and Al-Qaeda date back to the 1990's, when al-Qaeda set up a base of operations in the Somali state similar to what it had in Afghanistan.

[17] "Al-Shabaab joining al-Qaeda, monitor group says," *CNN*, February 9, 2012. Available at http://articles.cnn.com/2012-02-09/africa/world_africa_somalia-shabaab-qaeda_1_al-zawahiri-qaeda-somali-americans?_s=PM:AFRICA

[18] Jonathan Masters, "Al-Qaeda in the Arabian Peninsula (AQAP), *Council on Foreign Relations*, May 24, 2012. Available at http://www.cfr.org/yemen/al-qaeda-arabian-peninsula-aqap/p9369.

[19] M. Ressa, "Al-Qaeda and Afghanistan: 1 year after bin Laden's death," *Rappler*, May 2, 2012. Available at http://www.rappler.com/world/4663-al-qaeda-afghanistan-1-year-after-bin-laden-s-death

One of its leaders, American Anwar al-Awlaki was a "master in the use of the Internet,"[20] and although he was killed by the U.S. in 2011, his messages continue to resonate and win recruits online. Awlaki was prolific on YouTube — among those he influenced: the London attackers who carried out Britain's 9/11 on July 7, 2005 (commonly referred to in the intelligence community as 7/7). He had his own website (now taken down by authorities) which attracted extremists and the head of AQAP, bin Laden's secretary, Nasir al-Wuhaishi. He consulted bin Laden and appointed Awlaki the head of AQAP's external operations, in charge of terrorist attacks outside Yemen and Saudi Arabia — his position when he died. Awlaki was a cyberworld superstar because he was an eloquent speaker and understood the virtual world. His ideas remained with AQAP, which continues his online recruitment efforts.

Pareja said Gerald told him AQAP "had established an Islamic state in the province of Abian in Yemen"[21] and had already recruited "Filipinos studying from the Islamic schools in Saudi Arabia, Egypt and Sudan."[22] He asked Pareja to join the jihad in Yemen and help lead the Filipinos. He said they would stay in Yemen for 10 years. After five years, they could choose to return to the Philippines at which point AQAP "would provide them funds to continue jihad to establish an Islamic Caliphate."[23] He offered to pay Pareja's travel expenses to Yemen. Pareja accepted the offer and was scheduled to travel between April to June of 2012. He never made it because Filipino authorities arrested him on March 1.

However, the story doesn't end there. When Pareja uploaded his video exhorting support for jihad in the southern Philippines in 2011, it showed him speaking in front of a black flag. Other websites and video messages around the world prominently display the black flag including in the Middle East, Afghanistan, Somalia and Yemen. In the Philippines, authorities are monitoring a website called "Islamic Emirate of the Philippines: The Black Flag Movement."[24] One post titled "The True Islamic Hero" shows a picture of Anwar al-Awlaki as well as other al-Qaeda operatives with Arabic titles and

---

[20] R. Gunaratna, "Al-Qaeda after Awlaki," *The National Interest*, October 19, 2011. Available at http://nationalinterest.org/commentary/al-qaeda-after-awlaki-6026

[21] Details from classified Philippine intelligence document: *Dinno-Amor Rosalejos Pareja @Abu Jihad/Khalia/Ur Rahman/Muhammad/Rash/Ahmad/Arlan/Al-Luzoni/Jake Fajardo*, CTD-DRP-03052012-014, March 5, 2012, p. 12.

[22] Ibid., p. 12.

[23] Ibid., p. 12.

[24] Available at http://islamicemirateofthephilippines.webs.com/

translations, including "The Martyr of Dawaah." It includes links to other extremist websites, including those run by al-Qaeda and its proxies. Another entry says: "This is the Truth!" and asks the reader to "open your eyes and know the TRUTH that the commercial media hides." It includes news updates, audio and video lectures as well as photos of an MILF breakaway faction led by Ameril Umra Kato and his Bangsamoro Islamic Freedom Movement. While all public accounts show activity on the site isn't alarming, it provides a gateway for radicals: there is a "Contact us" portion, an online poll and a donation portal. Although it's unclear whether there is any real world link to al-Qaeda, it's clearly inspired by al-Qaeda's lore and subculture.

The black flag taps into a secret motivation of al-Qaeda: a "narrative that convinces them that they're part of a divine plan,"[25] writes former FBI agent Ali Soufan. Al-Qaeda believes its black banners herald the apocalypse that would bring about the triumph of Islam.[26] It's based on what they believe is a hadith, or a saying, of the prophet Muhammad: "If you see the black banners coming from Khurusan, join that army, even if you have to crawl over ice; no power will be able to stop them, and they will finally reach Baitul Maqdis [Jerusalem], where they will erect their flags." Khurusan is a name for a historical region covering north-eastern and eastern Iran and parts of Turkmenistan, Uzbekistan, Tajikistan, Afghanistan and north-western Pakistan. This is where al-Qaeda believes the Islamic version of Armaggedon will emerge. Bin Laden's 1996 declaration of war against the United States ends with the dateline, "Friday, August 23, 1996, in the Hindu Kush, Khurusan, Afghanistan."

In the Philippines, authorities recovered video explaining the black flag inside the laptop of a Malaysian jihadist during an attack targeting Marwan and Muawiyah in August, 2012. The video verifies what CIA sources and former FBI agent Ali Soufan wrote in his book that the black flag is a powerful symbol for al-Qaeda. All this brings us back to Pareja. Before he left the Philippines, Gerald asked him to do one more thing: "to establish the link between the group of Marwan and the AQAP."[27] Although he was arrested before he could do that, it seems someone else may have had the same

[25] A. H. Soufan, "The Black Banners: The Inside Story of 9/11 and the War Against al-Qaeda," (New York: W. W. Norton & Company, 2011), loc 196 of 10851 on Kindle.

[26] Ibid., loc. 148 of 10851.Soufan explains the meaning of the black flag and the narrative connecting religion and jihad it created for al-Qaeda.

[27] Details from classified Philippine intelligence document: *Dinno-Amor Rosalejos Pareja @Abu Jihad/Khalia/Ur Rahman/Muhammad/Rash/Ahmad/Arlan/al-Luzoni/Jake Fajardo*, CTD-DRP-03052012-014, March 5, 2012, p. 12.

intent. The Malaysian who owned the laptop with the black flag video, Fikrie, arrived in the Philippines on April, 2012 Malaysian intelligence sources said Fikrie was in touch with Marwan on Facebook, and that is partly how he found his way to the central Mindanao location of Marwan and Muawiyah. Among the weapons and rocket launchers recovered by authorities, they also found a hardcover book written in English. Its title is *Islami Emirate Afghanistan*. Below that is the logo of the Islamic Emirate of the Philippines.

Let me end with the Facebook page created by Pareja. Filipino authorities say one of its "friends" is a Facebook pseudonym used by Marwan, who — even while on the run — updates it from his cellphone. Another "friend" is a Facebook page from Australia with a picture of the black flag prominently displayed on its banner. It has 1,789 friends[28] from countries like the U.S., Indonesia, Canada, Lebanon, Kenya, South Africa, Saudi Arabia, Malaysia, Indonesia and Nigeria. Australia's intelligence services say several of the people formerly identified with Jemaah Islamiyah's Mantiqi IV, its fund-raising arm in Australia, may now be linking together again in the virtual world.

One of the Australian Facebook account's "friend" is Abu Ameenah Bilal Philips, a Canadian national who lives in Qatar and appears on Peace TV, a 24-hour satellite Islamic television channel.[29] A confidential document provided by U.S. intelligence says in 2004, Philips headed the Islamic Information Center (IIC) in Dubai, United Arab Emirates (now known as Discover Islam).[30] It provided funds to the Rajah Solaiman Movement (RSM) in the Philippines, the group of Christian converts Pareja headed at his arrest, responsible for the worst maritime terrorist attack in Southeast Asia.

There's one last connection that brings us back to where we began: the groups which funded RSM in the Philippines as well as the Islamic Information Center were all created by Osama bin Laden's brother-in-law, Mohammed Jamal Khalifa. Although Bilal has long denied any terrorist connections, he was secretly indicted in the 1993 bombing of the World Trade Center and deported from the United States in 1994.[31] Since then, he

---

[28] Friend count of 1,789 is as of June 29, 2012.
[29] You can find Bilal Philip's biography on Peace TV's site available here http://www.peacetv.tv/en-gb/speakers/drbilal-philips
[30] Classified U.S. report on Abu Ameenah Philips, July 2, 2004, p. 1.
[31] "Interview with Bilal Philips," *Intelwire*, Tuesday, April 19, 2011. Available at http://news.intelwire.com/2011/04/interview-with-bilal-philips-about.html

was expelled from a number of Western countries: denied entry to Australia in 2007[32] and deported from the UK and Germany in 2010.

During the time Khalifa was in the Philippines, Bilal visited Cotabato City and planned to build an Islamic center in Sultan Kudarat, Maguindanao. Khalifa and Bilal may well have worked together in the Philippines. In 1993, Bilal was in Manila with Clement Rodney Hampton-el, also known as Dr. Rashid, shortly before he was arrested in the U.S. for the World Trade Center bombing.[33]

Now Bilal is on Facebook, linked to Pareja's page (which has since been taken down). His journey, like many others here, shows how the jihadi virus spread through the years from bin Laden to Facebook.

\*\*\*

When Ces heard the kidnappers say they were going to be released, she was relieved for a moment. Then anger surged through her. She looked at Jimmy as they began to untie him and wanted to make the kidnappers pay for what they did to him. The men left them, and she could hear the jubilance in the camp.

Ces was convinced her kidnappers did not believe in anything but money. Her hands were shaking as she picked up her bag which she had used as a pillow the past 10 days. Inside, she felt her pen and notebook and breathed a sigh of relief. She and Jimmy were going home. She thought of her family — her mother and sisters and brother as well as her four sons. She thought about the time they were in Disneyland, and her boys wanted her to go inside the haunted house. She refused because she was scared, but now she thought how silly to be afraid of a hall of mirrors. She resolved to take them back there. Nothing could scare her anymore; nothing could be worse than what she had gone through. She knew it was still too soon, but she began praying again — thanking God they had made it this far.

They began their journey back to civilization around 4 p.m. on Tuesday, June 17. Just two hours earlier, Ces had been ready to die. She and Jimmy were still riding an emotional rollercoaster. They walked for hours, watching as the sun set over the jungles. While they were walking, Ces asked one of her guards how Commander Putol lost his arm. Her head was swirling with half-formed

---

[32] "Fed: Radical Sheik Barred from Australia," *Australian Associated Press*, April 4, 2007.

[33] Classified Australian report on Abu Ameenah Philips, July 2, 2004, p. 1.

ideas and questions. When they stopped to rest, she took out her journal and wrote a few of them down: "What kind of life will I go back to? What about these people? What is life to them? What is their purpose? What is mine?"

Jimmy had his camera stuffed in the sack. He and Ces argued with the kidnappers because some of them wanted to keep the camera. They won the argument, and as they trudged through the jungle, Jimmy again began to shoot. He had also been transformed by this experience. He didn't know how it had changed him, but for now, it was strangely comforting to do what he knew best. So he clandestinely shot video which would later be used by the police to identify the kidnappers.

The group finally reached their meeting point seven minutes before midnight. Ces, Jimmy and Dinampo were released at Barangay Sinumaan, Talipao, Sulu to Jun Isnaji and four policemen. During the handover, Ces had enough presence of mind to check whether any of the police or military would follow her kidnappers. They didn't, making her think perhaps the authorities were afraid or unable to follow them deeper into the jungle. They drove to the Isnaji home where they ate, showered and dressed. The two were bewildered, surrounded by a flurry of activity. That was when I finally got to speak to Jimmy and then Ces on Quidato's cellphone.

"Ces, are you okay?" I asked.

"Oh, Maria, I'm so sorry."

"Don't worry, Ces. We'll deal with all that later. We're all just so thrilled you're safe. I need to know — are you okay? Did they touch you?"

"No, no, I'm okay. I was starting to get worried, and it would've been different if we stayed longer I think."

"Thank God! But as soon as you get back, we'll do a medical check-up, and you just have to let me know if you want me to make any special arrangements." I was afraid she had been raped so instead of speaking in code, I jumped in and asked her about it directly. She told me she had been worried they would try, but she and Jimmy got out in time. I asked if she wanted to have a private room and have her doctor examine her away from the boys. She said there was no need for any arrangements at the hospital.

"No, Maria, that's okay. I'm okay."

"Oh my God, that's such a relief to hear."

"Maria, I'm so sorry about what I did."

"It's okay, Ces. Your family's here, and they want to talk to you." I handed my cellphone to Grech and walked away. I took deep breaths: joy, relief and exhaustion mixing together. I walked outside the room and leaned over the balcony. Libby followed me, and we hugged each other. I asked her for the key to her room, which was just down the hall. I wanted to be alone to think about the next steps of getting them home. I texted Gin to think about what messages would need to be publicly communicated. I started scribbling on my pad, trying to anticipate potential pitfalls ahead. I called Gabby to tell him the good news. I asked if we could use the plane one last time to pick up our team.

I called Malacanang Palace to thank President Arroyo for her support. I called Puno, and he told me how upset he was about the chain of events. He scolded me for several minutes but was already thinking many steps ahead saying they had evidence the Isnajis were working with the kidnappers. He said he wanted to put a stop to these instances of collusion and was thinking of arresting them and filing cases. He asked if we would help since so many kidnap victims choose never to confront reality. I said we would support it if the evidence was clear.

While we were speaking, I saw the number of Loren Legarda flash on my phone. Puno was wrapping up, and I was able to pick up her call on the fifth ring. I thanked her for all she had done to help. She said she was arranging a small private plane to go to Zamboanga and asked if I wanted to ride with her. While I admired her single-minded focus, I wondered whether we would become part of a publicity campaign. I dismissed it as an uncharitable thought. For tonight, I would thank God and everyone involved in our team's safe release. Legarda played a critical role. Ces and Jimmy were safe, and they were coming home. I had nothing but profuse thanks and good feelings for the woman who barreled through all the roadblocks. I said yes, we would pick up Ces and Jimmy together. Legarda said she would take care of food, and I said I would talk to their families and bring clothes for the two of them.

As we were wrapping up, another number popped up — Winnie Quidato. It seemed a subtle tug of war was going on inside the Isnaji residence with the rivalry between the police and military back in full force. General Sabban and the military wanted custody of the team, but Quidato had been tasked by the police and local government hierarchy to bring them to Zamboanga. He asked me to let Ces and Jimmy know the role he played. I laughed when he told me why and told him about our plans to meet them in Zamboanga City in the morning. Regardless, I told him I would let both Ces and Jimmy know the crucial role he played in their release. I thanked him profusely for his courage and quick thinking.

I walked back to the crisis center, where a small celebration going on as we all heaved a collective sigh of relief. Someone had brought wine and was passing glasses around. I called for one final meeting where I outlined what would happen next: Legarda and I would pick up the team from Zamboanga and take them back to Manila. Once here, Libby suggested we first bring them to the hospital for a check-up. That was where they would be reunited with their familes. A team was assigned to take care of the logistics.

This was going to be our last night at Discovery, and the realization made us stop, hug each other and laugh. Someone took out a camera, and we posed for a picture. Every time I look at it now, I remember the pain, anguish and uncertainty of those 10 days. Then I look at the brilliant smiles on our faces, and I remember that glorious moment of relief. I don't remember who gave a copy of our "family picture" to everyone in that room, but whoever did wrote two lines at the top: "June 9–18, 2008 *Napalaya namin si Ces, Jimmy at Angelo (We Freed Ces, Jimmy & Angelo)*" — literally the 10 pressure-cooker days we lived together in that room and the task we had to accomplish. The 10 days were a taut, emotional rollercoaster thriller which could have so easily turned into our worst collective nightmare.

Picture of Discovery Suites Team.

\*\*\*

Some analysts say the kidnapping of Ces Drilon, Jimmy Encarnacion and Angelo Valderrama triggered a rash of others — that the money paid encouraged the Abu Sayyaf to grow kidnap-for-ransom as an industry even more. That may be true, but it's not just this one; it's every single one that happened before and after it. The way this kidnapping played out had two direct effects: one is the greater involvement in Mindanao of the police's Special Action Force and counter-terrorism group; the other is in solidifying Radullan Sahiron's control and power of the kidnap-for-ransom groups.

Nearly five years later, Sahiron and his men are still at it. Some say they're even stronger because different groups are working together under their protection, merging crime and terrorism. At the end of February, 2013, authorities said Sahiron was involved with or provided protection to the kidnappers of "a United Nations" of victims in Jolo, including two European birdwatchers, Swiss Lorenzo Vinciguerra and Dutch Ewold Horn; a Jordanian journalist who interviewed Osama bin Laden, Baker Atyani; Japanese Toshio Ito, who has been held hostage since July 21, 2010; and three Malaysians.[34]

Sahiron did turn away the kidnappers of one high-profile kidnapping: a 54-year-old Australian, Warren Richard Rodwell, kidnapped from his home in the southern Philippine town of Ipil, Zamboanga del Sur on December 5, 2011.[35] A former Army soldier, Rodwell came to the Philippines to marry the girlfriend he met online. He was alone in their home in a residential subdivision when "at least six armed men" burst in and kidnapped him. Neighbors heard a gunshot, and police found blood on the scene when they arrived. Rodwell was wounded. As of this writing, he has been held hostage for one year, three months and one day.

His case shows how the Abu Sayyaf along with suspected and former members of the MNLF[36] are experimenting with Facebook as a public distribution platform. It accomplishes two things: it exerts pressure on government

---

[34] On March 14, 2010, the Philippine police in the Autonomous Region in Muslim Mindanao (ARMM) took Ito off the list of kidnap victims. They said he developed "Stockholm Syndrome" and is now a cook for the Abu Sayyaf. Others, however, dispute this. More details available here http://newsinfo.inquirer.net/165123/japanese-still-a-hostage-not-abu-sayyaf-cook-academics-say

[35] D. Santos, "Search for Abducted Aussie Continues," *Rappler*, December 6, 2011. Available at http://www.rappler.com/nation/223-search-for-abducted-aussie-continues

[36] Intelligence sources say they believe suspected and former members of the MNLF may be involved.

Screengrab of Abu Sayyaf's page on Facebook.

authorities, and it allows the kidnappers to break an impasse in negotiations by going directly to the public. There have even been attempts — although feeble — at crowdsourcing ransom. This is how it evolved.

A month after he was kidnapped, the kidnappers sent a package to his Filipina wife, Miraflor Gutang. It was sent from "Tagum City" and contained a "memory card" with Rodwell's "proof of life," according to PNP's Directorate for Integrated Police Operations Chief Director Felicisimo Khu. The card held a photo of Rodwell with a date stamp of "12/12/2011."[37] On December 30, 2011, Khu told reporters the kidnappers were "initially demanding ₱1 million ransom" or about US$23,000.

"We are also getting reports that it is the group of Puruji Indama of the Abu Sayyaf group that's holding Rodwell captive," Khu added, "That's the same group that kidnapped the U.S. citizens Gerfa and Kevin Lunsmann in July this year." Filipino-American Gerfa Yeatts Lunsmann was freed in October, 2011. Her son escaped two months later and walked for two days before he was found.[38] The Abu Sayyaf demanded ransom from their family in the United States.

---

[37] D. Santos, "Kidnappers 'initially demanded P1-M,' *Rappler*, January 6, 2012. Available at http://www.rappler.com/nation/736-kidnappers-initially-demanded-p1-m

[38] "First pictures of boy, 14, who escaped barefoot after five months being held hostage by Muslim militants in the southern Philippines," *Mail Online*, December 12, 2011. Available at http://www.dailymail.co.uk/news/article-2072591/Kevin-Lunsmann-released-months-hands-Phillippines-kidnappers.html

On January 5, 2012, a government official handed me Rodwell's first proof-of-life video[39] which had been delivered to his wife. On the video, Rodwell said his captors are demanding US$2 million in ransom, double the initial demand: "To my family, please do whatever to raise the two million U.S. dollars they are asking for my release as soon as possible." He looked gaunt, his eyes tired and unfocused. Reading his message, he spoke haltingly, occasionally choking on his words, overcome with emotion. "I was former army of my country but it is different here, particularly the terrain. The only solution to ensure my safety is to go with whatever they need ... To the Australian Embassy here in the Philippines, this is your constituency appealing for his life," said Rodwell.

A second video leaked to Australian media four months later. In the video, Rodwell was holding a newspaper dated March 26, 2012.[40] Again, he reiterated the call for ransom. Little was revealed publicly in succeeding months. In Australia, his cousin, wanting only to be identified as Susan, asked the public for help to raise money.[41] The Australian government maintained its no-ransom policy. It was still unclear exactly where he was being held and by exactly whom, but on August 15, 2012, a Philippine intelligence document pinpointed his location: Al-Barka, Basilan, the site of a controversial killing of special forces soldiers in November, 2010. [42] It's a unique place where armed men from the Abu Sayyaf, the MILF and the MNLF are embedded and interrelated in communities. There is no better place in the southern Philippines to illustrate how armed men change identities: one day, they're MNLF, the next the Abu Sayyaf.

Shortly before midnight of Wednesday, December 26, 2012, a YouTube account identifying itself as the "official channel of the Al-Harakatul Islamia [sic]" — the formal name of the Abu Sayyaf — uploaded a third "proof-of-life" video: in it, Rodwell looks noticeably thinner. Looking weary, Rodwell, with sunken cheeks, short cropped hair and wearing a black t-shirt, holds up

---

[39] "Kidnapped Australian appeals for help," *Rappler,* January 5, 2012. Text and video available at http://www.rappler.com/nation/703-kidnapped-australian-appeals-for-help
[40] "New video of Australian kidnapped in the Philippines," *Rappler,* May 7, 2012. Available at http://www.rappler.com/nation/4915-new-video-of-australian-kidnapped-in-ph
[41] J. van Aanholt, "Kidnap victim Warren Rodwell gone, but not forgotten," *The Northern Daily Leader,* October 14, 2012. Available at http://www.northerndailyleader.com.au/story/396343/kidnap-victim-warren-rodwell-gone-but-not-forgotten/
[42] M. Ressa, "Fiasco in Basilan," *Rappler,* October 25, 2011. First posted on Facebook and available at http://www.rappler.com/thought-leaders/159-fiasco-in-basilan

a local paper dated December 15, 2012.[43] "This video clip today is to say that I am alive," Rodwell tells the camera. He is in front of a light, patterned sheet with light-blue flowers – an attempt to hide his location. "I am waiting to be released. I have no idea what's going on outside. I am just being held in isolation."

A few hours later, a Facebook account shared the video with this message: "Attention!!!! ... Warren Rodwell Australian kidnapped victim." It gives a mobile number saying, "He is in need of help." Authorities began investigating the mobile number, which also appeared on the YouTube account. Western and Filipino intelligence sources told me they were certain the YouTube account belonged to the Abu Sayyaf because of its past activity — it was created May 11, 2010 with video seen more than 25,000 times — and because of the accounts it connected and the network it created. The Facebook account which shared the video incorporates the black flag.

The owner of the mobile number wanted to bargain, said a source in touch with him. The asking price was US$2 million, but if half was delivered, the kidnappers would hand Rodwell over. The cellphone owner said whoever paid that US$1 million to them could still demand the full ransom from the family and turn a quick profit. This is the way they think and the way things work. Except this is the first time kidnappers have turned to social media for ransom — seemingly looking for anyone who will pay a price.

Frustrated Australians reacted on social media. On Twitter, Aurpar25 picked up the idea, saying "if we all put in 1 dollar..." Gary Cannell disagreed: "unfortunately, pay one lot of idiots, it encourages others." BS2502 tweeted: "the unfortunate thing is governments do pay ransoms [sic] when it's in their best interest. It's bad luck if your [sic] just a peaceful Mr. Nobody who nobody has heard of and this happens because the chances are the government just closes up and pulls its policy rhetoric."

A group of Australians who started a Facebook page for Rodwell[44] began an online petition on a site called *communityrun*, a project of GetUp Australia. The petition, which has been shared on Facebook and other social media sites, is addressed to the Australian government and says "Warren

---

[43] M. Ressa, "Seen on Facebook: Kidnapped Australian," *Rappler*, December 26, 2012. Available at http://www.rappler.com/nation/18620-seen-on-facebook-kidnapped-australian
[44] Facebook page available here https://www.facebook.com/groups/320782604609489/?sid=0.6010830542072654

Screengrab of a Facebook post on Rodwell's kidnapping.

Rodwell has been held captive by the Abu Sayyaf Group, a Muslim terrorist group for over one year. Enough is enough. Get him out now."[45]

Australia's Foreign Minister Bob Carr said "confirmation of Mr. Rodwell's welfare is welcome," but "his prolonged captivity is a major concern."[46] Negotiations for Rodwell's release have been going on since January, but transcripts of conversations I've seen show a confusing process, particularly when it came to details about ransom. Both the Australian and Philippine governments say they will not pay ransom, but the reality as you've seen in this book is that negotiations revolve around an exchange of

---

[45] Online petition available here http://www.communityrun.org/petitions/free-warren-rodwell

[46] Full statement of Australian Minister for Foreign Affairs Bob Carr available here http://foreignminister.gov.au/releases/2012/bc_mr_121227.html

**Roddykay** 12 hours ago
somali pirates get paid - obviously cargo is more important than human life
Reply · 👍 👎

**aurpar25** 13 hours ago
if we all put in 1 dollar ........
Reply · 👍 👎

Top Comments

**Gary Cannell** 1 day ago
Sad situation. Unfortunately pay one lot of idiots it encourages others.
Reply · 3 👍 👎

**bs2502** 17 hours ago
The unfortunate thing is governments do pay ransoms when it's in their best interest, it's bad luck if your just a peaceful mr nobody who no body has heard of and this happens because the chances are the government just closes up and pulls it policy rhetoric. For fucks sake Ms Gillard pay the ransom, use my tax money, Warren is an Aussie and served in the Australian Defence Force protecting our country, the country you run. It's time he came home. PAY UP.
Reply · 2 👍 👎

Reactions of Australians on Rodwell's kidnapping on social media.

money.[47] Sources familiar with the negotiations say they lack a clear leader, and there seem to be differing tactics among Australian agencies like the Australian Federal Police and the Australian Secret Intelligence Service. That was denied by Andrew Byrne, the Deputy Head of Mission at the Australian Embassy in Manila. "I'd point out that the Philippine government is leading the response to Mr. Rodwell's kidnapping, assisted by Australian Government agencies as appropriate," said Byrne. "The Australian agencies are working to the same objective and their efforts are tightly coordinated. Any suggestion that they are taking different or separate approaches simply has no basis in fact."

---

[47] J. Craven & M. Johnston, "PM says no to ransom as Aussie pleads for life," *news.com.au*, January 5, 2012. Available here http://www.news.com.au/world-old/kidnapped-aussie-pleads-for-his-life/story-e6frfkyi-1226236989968. For Philippine government reaction, see L. Murdoch & A. Jacinto, "Philippines rules out ransom talks over held Australian," January 6, 2012. Available here http://www.smh.com.au/national/philippines-rules-out-ransom-talks-over-held-australian-20120105-1pmyo.html

Photo of Warren Rodwell surrounded by his kidnappers posted on Facebook on
January 29, 2013.

On Tuesday, January 29, 2013, the kidnappers used Facebook again —
this time posting a picture of a shirtless, kneeling or sitting Rodwell. Visibly
thinner, he is surrounded — for the first time — by three armed, masked
men who tower over him, one of them wearing army camouflage fatigues.
The black flag is hanging on a blue backdrop behind them. The Facebook
post, claiming to be from the Abu Sayyaf, threatened to kill Rodwell, telling
the Australian government "we will give you a chance to save his life before
it's too late ... otherwise, he will suffer unusual way of Death." Filipino intelligence sources verified the authenticity of the photo and traced the location
of the cellphone number listed on the post. The picture and the post were
deleted less than 24 hours later.

Social media is changing what was once a closed dialogue between kidnappers, their victims and governments. It's now engaging the public.
51-year-old Australian Fiona Sholly is a key driver of both the Facebook page
and the online petition trying to keep Rodwell in the public eye. Although
she didn't know Rodwell personally, she wrote me, "I was so worried about
this person being left with his kidnappers in a jungle that I started a Facebook
account. My group and I started a petition. When I saw the December, 2012
video, I was devastated. He looks to have lost all hope ... I feel like I have let
him down, and I just want to free him."

Rodwell's message in that video reverberates for me as well. He minces
no words about how he feels. "I personally hold no hope at all for being
released," he says in the video.

Then he captured the way I felt in the 10 days I led our crisis team: "I do not trust the Abu Sayyaf. I do not trust the Australian government. I just don't trust anyone."

\*\*\*

While we were celebrating, the police and military were making travel arrangements. At nearly 3 a.m., Ces, Jimmy and Dinampo boarded a military helicopter to Zamboanga along with the head of the police and military as well as the Isnajis. They landed at Edwin Andrews Air Base in Zamboanga City and were met by the top brass: National Police Chief Avelino Razon; Lieutenant General Nelson Allaga, the Commander of the Western Mindanao Command; Admiral Emilio Marayag, Commander of the Naval Forces in Western Mindanao; Police Director Jaime Caringal and other senior police officers. The three were then brought to the Special Action Forces Seaborne office for processing and a medical check-up. Soon after, intelligence records show Sabban authorized pursuit operations — a joint police and military force led by Task Force Comet, Sabban's unit in Jolo.

It was still dark when Legarda and I arrived at the airport hangar. We were quickly shuttled onto the tarmac where we boarded the small plane. Although neither of us had slept, we talked about what we had lived through. Legarda told me how angry and frustrated she was when she heard the kidnappers slap Ces. I could only compare that with the moment when the kidnappers gave their first ultimatum with Angel, but I was surrounded by the crisis team. I could only imagine what the slap must have been like for Ces and for Legarda, who absorbed its psychological impact alone in her home. She said going through that galvanized her resolve to get Ces and Jimmy out safely.

The flight took less than an hour. It was just daybreak when we landed in Zamboanga. Legarda's team was efficient. We were whisked from the airport to the La Vista Del Mar Beach Resort, where Ces, Jimmy and Angel spent the night. Angelo had stayed with the police all this time to try to identify the kidnappers, and he was here now. I asked to see the three of them immediately and was taken to Ces' room. There were separate "huts" in the beach resort. Each nipa hut had a hammock, a bamboo table and benches outside. I knocked on the door. When Ces opened it, I walked in, and we hugged each other tight. She started crying. I looked at her closely. Her eyes were bloodshot, and her face, arms and legs were peppered with insect bites. We spoke for a while, and then a female officer came to bring us coffee and to tell me the commanders wanted to talk to me. I told Ces to shower and get dressed. We were going home.

Before the press conference at La Vista del Mar Beach Resort in
Zamboanga City. From left: Angelo Valderrama, Ces Drilon, Jimmy Encarnacion.

When I got to the hall, I asked to see Jimmy and Angel. I hugged
them both, thrilled that they were safe. Jimmy handed me the tapes he
shot while they were held hostage, and I thought of his incredible courage.
Quidato, who was with the two men, asked if his office could dub the
tapes so they could begin to identify the kidnappers. I agreed and saw
some officers off to the side with video equipment ready to do that.
Someone told me there would be a press conference and then the team
would formally be handed over to me. They asked if I wanted to speak. I
said no. I had nothing to say. While they were setting up, I found Angelo
and Jimmy, and we went back to get Ces. Their rooms were in an area of
the resort cordoned-off from the journalists, who were beginning to
arrive. When Ces finally came out, we had at least half an hour together
before they called us in.

We were sitting outside, looking out over the ocean. It was a time to
breathe for all of us: for me to hear their stories and for them to exult in their
new-found lives. Quidato took a picture of the three of them I still have. Ces
was wearing a long white shirt and jeans. In her hands, she was holding the
pen and notebook where she had written everything. She showed me parts
of her journal and told me how slowly time passed in captivity.

We walked into the press conference together. I saw how — despite their joy at their release — Ces, Jimmy and Angelo's nerves were frayed. Ces spoke candidly about the interview she went after, the mistakes she made, their kidnappers and the man she believed double-crossed them, Mameng Biyaw. Her eyes started to tear when she talked about her family and looked at me when she said she expected to be held accountable for her mistakes. At the end of the questions, the three of them walked towards me, and I hugged them all. I thought of their families waiting in Manila.

It was time to bring them home.

# Epilogue

Landing in Manila

On Wednesday, June 18, 2008, as we were getting ready to board the private plane from Zamboanga to Manila, Alvarez Isnaji and his son Jun were taken to the airport in an unmarked car. The Isnajis said they thought they were going to a nearby hotel so they could sleep. Instead, they were handed boarding passes by Senior Superintendent Jose Pante.[1] They said they were surrounded by plainclothes policemen who bundled them onto the flight and shadowed their every move. When they landed in Manila, they were met by more plainclothes officers who took them to the police's

---

[1] Alvarez and Jun Isnaji, *Joint Counter-Affidavit*, IS No. 2008-617, July 7, 2008, p. 2.

Criminal Investigation and Detection Group (CIDG) in Camp Crame, the national police headquarters. There they were questioned and arrested. Charges were quickly filed against them.

Father and son would be detained from that day in June 2008 until April 12, 2010, when the Taguig Regional Trial Court (RTC) Branch 271 cleared them of the charges and set them free. But their freedom was short-lived. In November 2011, the RTC decision was overturned by the Court of Appeals, which said the trial court had used "grave abuse of discretion" in handing down its ruling. Instead of returning to prison, the Isnajis fled, and the case remains unresolved.

Sali Said said the kidnappers were paid 10 days later. Radullan Sahiron called the men together and told them much of the money needed to be used for weapons purchases and to keep their operations going. He distributed different amounts to each participant, but the key, most trusted group, including Said received only ₱200,000 each. Commander Putol, whose real name is Sulaiman Pattah, was angry and he fought with Sahiron. It was bad, said Said. At one point, Sahiron drew his gun and looked like he was going to shoot his Sub-Lieutenant. Soon after, Commander Putol left Sahiron's group and joined the MNLF. In fact, all of the Abu Sayyaf members who actually kidnapped Ces, Jimmy and Angel have since left Sahiron's group. Sali Said left, was arrested and imprisoned for nearly two years. He was released in February, 2013.

Loren Legarda would go on to run for Vice President in the 2010 election. She lost but returned to the Senate, and near the end of 2012 ranks as one of the top candidates for the Senate in the 2013 election.

Winnie Quidato's role would be announced publicly by then Interior and Local Government Secretary Ronaldo Puno. His pictures, displayed on television and the front pages of national newspapers, effectively put an end to his days as an undercover field operative.

Ces Drilon, Jimmy Encarnacion, and Angelo Valderrama went back to their families, greatly changed by their 10 days in the jungle. On July 5, 2008, ABS-CBN suspended Ces for three months "for disobeying orders not to go to Indanan, Sulu." In an internal memo to me, she wrote: "I respectfully accept the sanctions you deem proper in my disregard of your order. I cannot put into words how deeply I regret having put my team in danger." In an internal announcement addressed to our reporters and employees, I stressed the need to hold Ces accountable for "the grave consequences of her error in judgment." At the same time, I commended her courage, her presence of mind in sending out coded messages, and her willingness to sacrifice her own life in order to save her team.

# Index